The North...

Cambr
Unit 4
Teacher's Manual

Revision Editor
Ed Phinney
Chair, Department of Classics & Faculty Director, University Foreign Language Resource Center, University of Massachusetts at Amherst, U.S.A.

Consulting Editor
Patricia E. Bell
Teacher of Latin & Assistant Head of Languages
Centennial Collegiate and Vocational Institute, Guelph, Ontario, Canada

Editorial Assistant
Barbara Romaine
Brattleboro, Vermont, U.S.A.

CAMBRIDGE UNIVERSITY PRESS

Published by the Press Syndicate of the University of Cambridge
40 West 20th Street, New York, NY 10011-4211, U.S.A.

The Cambridge Latin Course was funded and developed by the University of Cambridge School Classics Project and S.C.D.C. Publications, London, and is published with the sponsorship of the School Curriculum Development Committee in London and the North American Cambridge Classics Project. The work of the School Curriculum Development Committee has now been assumed by the National Curriculum Council.

© NCC Enterprises Limited 1992

This edition first published 1992.
Reprinted 1997

Printed in the United States of America

ISBN 0 521 34859 5

Contents

Introduction	page	5
The Roman Setting of Stages 35–40 in Unit 4		5
The Public and Private Life of Domitian		5
List of Events in the Reign of Domitian		6
Transition from Facsimile to Original Latin, Stages 41–48, Unit 4		7
Presentation of Grammar		8
Time Allocation for Unit 4 in High School		9
Time Allocation for Unit 4 in College/University		9
Correlation of Unit 4 with American National Examinations		10
Concessions to the Limitation of Time		10
Filmstrips		11
Teaching Methods		13
First Reading, or Initial Comprehension		13
Second Reading, or Exploration and Discussion		14
Historical and Cultural Topics		17
Consolidation of Grammatical Points		19
STAGE COMMENTARIES		20
The Language Information Section		199
PART ONE: Review Grammar		201
PART TWO: Reference Grammar		209
PART THREE: Supplementary Reading		210
PART FOUR: Complete Vocabulary		211
Diagnostic Tests		212
Appendix A: Cumulated List of Checklist Words (Stages 1–48)		219
Appendix B: Cumulated List of Word-Search Words (Stages 1–40)		235
Appendix C: Cumulated List of Synonym-Search Words (Stages 41–48)		241

Contents

Appendix D: Classified Examples of Some Grammatical Points	242
Appendix E: Time Chart of Events in the *C.L.C.*, Stages 1–48	245
Appendix F: Summary of Changes from the North American Second Edition	248
Bibliography	250

Introduction

The Roman Setting of Stages 35–40 in Unit 4

Stages 35–40 in Unit 4 bring to a close the episodic, Latin historical novel which began with Stage 1 in Unit 1. Quintus, Caecilius' young son who survived the eruption of Vesuvius (A.D. 79), has traveled and matured enough by Stage 40, some eight years later (A.D. 87), to testify for the prosecution against Salvius in a senatorial trial in Rome. When the prosecution is successful and Salvius exiled, the Emperor Domitian promises Quintus his support *ad honōrēs petendōs* (Stage 40, "*damnātiō*," lines 16–17, p. 103). The career of Quintus in Rome is thus successfully launched as Salvius sails away to his miserable exile, Myropnous the dwarf – avenged at last – plays a triumphant tune on his pipes, and the long story comes to a satisfying close.

Stages 41–48 in Unit 4 contain original and adapted original passages from several Roman authors, two of whom (Martial and Ovid) were introduced in Stages 36 and 39 respectively. Other authors included are Pliny the Younger, Phaedrus, Catullus, Vergil, and Tacitus. The settings vary from historical Baiae (Campania) in A.D. 59, Misenum (near Mt. Vesuvius) in A.D. 79, and Bithynia (Asia Minor) in circa A.D. 110, to mythical Crete and Sicily.

The Public and Private Life of Domitian

The Emperor Domitian was an absolutist, who held all the political power in the Roman empire (see Unit 3 Teacher's Manual, pp. 5–6). Although some noblemen complained among themselves about the constraints his power imposed on their ambition, they publicly went along for better or worse with his policies. Others disagreed with him publicly and brought on themselves political and economic ruin, deportation, or even execution. Students should consider, therefore, some of the moral choices which faced Romans in public life during Domitian's dictatorship.

Domitian was not so successfully dominant in his private life. In A.D. 70, he married Domitia, the daughter of the Emperor Nero's most famous general, Gnaeus Domitius Corbulo; thus her name was the feminine form of her father's *nōmen*. When Domitian divorced Domitia in A.D. 83, because of adultery (see Unit 3, Stages 33–34), he took his niece Julia into the palace as his mistress. The next year, A.D. 84,

Introduction

although he accepted his wife back, there is no indication that he banished his mistress-niece, and the three perhaps lived together in an uneasy *ménage à trois*. Eventually Julia died because of an abortion which Domitian is said to have forced on her (Suetonius, *Life of Domitian* 22), but later when Domitian had been assassinated and cremated (Suet. *Dom.* 16–17 (=Unit 4 students' textbook, Supplementary Reading, p. 352, lines 32–56)), his ashes were secretly mixed with hers in a tomb inside the Temple of the Flavians (Suet. *Dom.* 17 (=Supplementary Reading, p. 352, lines 54–56)), a temple perhaps identical with the Temple of Vespasian and Titus in the Forum of Rome (see photograph and map of Forum in Unit 3, pp. 167 and 168). Domitia survived him, but although she bore him a daughter and son (Suet. *Dom.* 3), the son had died early and Domitian had been forced in A.D. 90 to adopt two distantly related boys to insure that a family member would succeed him (Suet. *Dom.* 15 (=Supplementary Reading, pp. 348–50, lines 9–13)). The two boys, with the fictional *praenōmina* of Titus and Publius, appear in Unit 4, Stage 39, as students of the rhetor Quintilian in the imperial palace. But these adoptive sons, whose official names were Vespasianus and Domitianus (Suet. *Dom.* 15 (=Supplementary Reading, p. 350, lines 10–11)) are not heard of after Domitian's death in A.D. 96. Domitian's successor Nerva, appointed emperor by the senate, was not a member of the Flavian family, and so this dynasty came to an end.

List of Events in the Reign of Domitian

Listed below are various events in the reign of Domitian. They are correlated with the dates we have imagined for the stories in the latter part of Unit 3 (Stages 29–34) and the initial part of Unit 4 (Stages 35–40).

A.D.

81 *Stages 29 and 30:* Domitian ascends throne; dedicates arch to his deified brother Titus

82 *Stages 31 and 32:* Domitian accepts first of seven successive consulships; Flavius Sabinus is consul

83 *Stages 33 and 34:* Usipi (a Germanic tribespeople) rebel against Romans; Paris dies and the Empress Domitia is divorced
Stages 35 and 36: Domitian has Flavius Sabinus executed; takes Sabinus' widow Julia (daughter of Emperor Titus and thus Domitian's niece) as mistress; celebrates triumph over Chatti (a Germanic tribespeople); has three Vestal Virgins executed; Martial has been living in Rome since A.D. 64

84 *Stage 37:* Agricola and Romans win battle over Caledonii (a Scottish tribespeople) at mons Graupius; Domitian recalls Agricola; assumes title "Germanicus"; takes back Domitia as wife
85 Domitian becomes censor for life; begins military campaign against Dacians (a Rumanian tribespeople)
86 Salvius is consul (?); campaign against Dacians ends in disaster; Martial publishes Book I of his epigrams
87 *Stage 40:* Salvius is put on trial (?)
88 Domitian holds secular games; Saturninus, Roman governor of Upper Germany, rebels; Domitian becomes increasingly dictatorial and cruel; political spies and trials proliferate
89 Domitian has philosophers deported
90 *Stages 38 and 39:* Domitian declares Flavius Clemens' two young sons as heirs; appoints Quintilian as their tutor; has Chief Vestal Virgin buried alive
91 Glabrio and Trajan (future emperor) are consuls; Domitian forces Glabrio to fight in arena, then has him deported
92
93 Agricola dies; Domitian begins "reign of terror"; has younger Helvidius Priscus executed
94
95 Domitian has philosophers deported second time; Flavius Clemens is consul; Domitian has Clemens tried and executed; has Glabrio executed in exile; has Epaphroditus executed
96 Supplementary Reading, pp. 348–53: Domitian is assassinated; Nerva (an elderly senator) ascends throne; senate declares *damnātiō memoriae* of Domitian

Note: Some earlier Stages were also set in the reign of Domitian: Unit 2, Stages 13–16, in A.D. 82; Unit 3, Stages 21–28, in A.D. 83. Unit 1 was set in A.D. 79 (with one flashback to A.D. 59 in Stage 8); Unit 2, Stages 17–18, in the winter of A.D. 80–81, and Stages 19–20, in the spring of A.D. 81 while Titus was still emperor. Titus died on September 13, A.D. 81 (s.v. Year 81 in "Time Chart" in Appendix E below, pp. 246–9).

Transition from Facsimile to Original Latin, Stages 41–48, Unit 4

From Unit 1, we have aimed in the Course to prepare students, in both language and social background, to read Roman authors. This goal is especially important in Unit 4, as it contains the last passages of facsimile Latin which students will read before concluding with Stages 41–48, where the readings are adapted or taken wholly from original Latin texts.

Introduction

Stages 35–40 introduce themes and literary conventions which students are likely to meet in original Roman authors, such as praise of country life, the conflict of *amor* and *pietās*, and the characteristic form of a Latin letter or epigram. Although Stages 35–40, like previous Stages, consist mainly of facsimile Latin, they also include a sampling of original Latin verses by Martial and Ovid. Because these verses are presented, in Stages 36 and 39, in prose contexts which are designed to illuminate them, encourage students to examine some of the ways by which poets like Martial and Ovid achieved their effects.

The reading material in Stages 41–48 consists of selections from several Roman authors, Catullus, Ovid, Phaedrus, Vergil, Petronius, Pliny the Younger and the Emperor Trajan, and Tacitus. The reading material in the Supplementary Reading (= Part Three of the Language Information Section (pp. 334–53)) consists of selections from Pliny the Elder, Pliny the Younger, Petronius, Tacitus, and Suetonius. The selections in Stages 41–48 are supplemented, as in previous Stages, by language notes, drills, background material, Words and Phrases Checklists, Word- and Synonym-Searches, and the Review and the Reference Grammars in the Language Information Section. The subject matter of the reading and background material includes the myth of Daedalus and Icarus and its treatment in art, Roman provincial government exemplified by Pliny's Bithynia correspondence, the love affair of Catullus and Lesbia, the folktale of the Widow of Ephesus, the eulogy of the good wife Turia, the eruption of Vesuvius, the murder of the Empress Agrippina, and the boat race in Vergil's *Aeneid* with a translation of Homer's Iliadic chariot race (Vergil's literary model for the boat race) added for comparison. The subject matter of the Supplementary Reading includes an original Latin story about a werewolf, the life and death of Pliny the Elder with some animal stories from his encyclopedic *Natural History*, Agricola's defeat of the Caledonian tribespeople at Mt. Graupius, and the life and death of the Emperor Domitian. Grammatical and historical notes face the Latin selections in the Supplementary Reading.

The reading material in Stages 41–48 and the Supplementary Reading have been selected, arranged in a sequence, occasionally abridged and (in the case of prose texts) adapted in accordance with a grammatical outline which continues and develops the grammatical outline of the earlier Units.

Presentation of Grammar

In addition to practicing grammatical points learned in earlier Units, the reading material in Stages 35–40 introduces several important points

Introduction

which occur frequently in Roman authors, such as the various forms of indirect statement, the historical present tense, the gerund with *ad*, and some of the typical noun + adjective patterns of word order found in Latin verse. It also completes the introduction of indicative passive and subjunctive active forms into the grammatical outline.

With the introduction, in Stages 40–48, of the subjunctive passive forms into the reading material, the presentation of the main morphological features of the language is completed. The reading material in Stages 40–48 also introduces most of the major syntactic points not already met and discussed in the Course, such as conditional clauses, the main uses of the gerund, and jussive and deliberative subjunctives; also practiced are a number of other features such as the historical present tense and infinitive, *fīō*, "poetic" plurals, the use of *-ēre* as a 3rd person plural perfect form, and the interlacing of pairs of noun + adjective phrases in poetry.

Time Allocation for Unit 4 in High School

As we suggested in the Unit 1 Teacher's Manual, p. 14, Unit 4 should normally constitute, in a four-year sequence, the third year's work, or Latin, Level III. In a three-year sequence, students should finish Stages 35–40 toward the end of their second year and thus have more time in their third year to finish Stages 41–48 and read selections from the Cambridge Latin Texts – particularly *Libellus* (selections from Catullus, Horace, Martial, and Ovid); Pliny's *Letters*; Tacitus' *Agricola*, *Annals* or *Histories*; or Vergil's *Aeneid*, Books II, IV, VI, or VIII – or the "Themes in Latin Literature" series: *amor et amicitia* (theme: interpersonal relations), *imperium et civitas* (theme: politics and diplomacy), *multas per gentes* (theme: travel), or *urbs antiqua* (theme: urban life and problems) – published in Canada by Irwin Publishing and in the United States by the Cambridge University Press.

Time Allocation for Unit 4 in College/University

At the college or university level, Stages 35–40 should be started at the end of the third semester of a non-intensive four-semester course, and completed, with all of Stages 41–48, in the fourth semester. In colleges or universities where only three semesters are allotted to the elementary and intermediate sequences, Stages 35–40 should be studied, with selections from Stages 41–48, in the last two-thirds of the third semester. Where only two intensive semesters are allotted to elementary and intermediate Latin, Stages 35–40, with selections from Stages 41–48, should be studied towards the end of the second semester. In colleges or

Introduction

universities with quarter-terms instead of semesters, Stages 35–40 should be divided between the fifth and sixth quarters, leaving the rest of the sixth quarter for Stages 41–48.

Correlation of Unit 4 with American National Examinations

Because the majority of American high school students taking the A.T.P. "College Board" Achievement Test in Latin are likely to take it in June of the Latin III year, encourage them, if at all feasible, to complete as much of Unit 4 as possible before the testing date, as Unit 4 will be their first introduction to Latin poetry (Stages 36, 39, 42, 44–45, and 47) and mildly adapted original Latin texts (Stages 41, 43, 46, and 48). If a student completes Unit 4 well ahead of the June testing date, he or she may read original Latin texts in the Cambridge Latin Texts (C.L.T.) or the Themes in Latin Literature series (see above, p. 9). These books, all published or distributed in the United States by Cambridge University Press and in Canada by Irwin Publishing, are particularly recommended because they draw on the sentence patterns, vocabulary, and grammatical features emphasized in the *Cambridge Latin Course*.

Many high school students take the Level III–IV National Latin Exam (sponsored by the American Classical League and the National Junior Classical League) in early March of their Latin III year. If so, they may take the Prose Level III–IV Exam if they have completed Stages 35–40 but not Stages 41, 43, 46, or 48; or the Verse Level III–IV Exam if they have completed most of Stages 36, 39, 42, 44–45, or 47 with the selections from Catullus, Phaedrus' *Fables*, Vergil's *Aeneid*, Ovid's *Ars Amatoria* and *Metamorphoses*, and Martial's *Epigrams*.

Concessions to the Limitation of Time

If you discover that either the limitation of time or the learning disabilities of students will not allow them to read all the stories and poems within the Stages planned, omit a selection here and there rather than omit groups of consecutive stories or poems or, worse, entire Stages. If necessary, omit some or all of the exercises or selections listed below, providing for the stories or poems a brief English summary to insure continuity. If the selection to be omitted contains difficult new sentence patterns, vocabulary, or grammar, summarize the plot and ask students to translate the sentences containing the new sentence patterns, grammatical features, or examples of vocabulary which will be listed later in the checklists.

Introduction

Stage 35　"ex urbe," lines 12–21; "vīta rūstica," lines 12–17; exercise 2
Stage 36　"Marcus Valerius Mārtiālis" II, lines 1–20 *or* "epigrammata Mārtiālia" IV-VI; exercise 4
Stage 37　"amīcī prīncipis"; "cōnsilium Domitiānī" I, lines 14–32
Stage 38　"Pōlla"; "prīdiē nūptiārum," lines 1–22; "cōnfarreātiō" II
Stage 39　"hērēdēs prīncipis" II, lines 1–24; exercise 2
Stage 40　"cognitiō," lines 28–35; "dēspērātiō" I
Stage 41　"carcer" I and II
Stage 42　"Mārtiālis" II and III; "Ovidius"; exercise 2
Stage 43　"Tūria" II and III
Stage 44　Sections II and III; exercise 2
Stage 45　Poems III and V
Stage 46　"tremōrēs" II, lines 15–21; "tenebrae," lines 12–16; exercise 3
Stage 47　"Gyās et Cloanthus" II; "victor" I; exercise 3
Stage 48　"īnsidiae" II; "naufragium" II

One way of covering a passage quickly when time is short is a variation of a consolidation method suggested on p. 19 below: first the students study the glossary, then you translate the whole passage aloud for them, pausing at regular intervals to ask them to supply the translation of a particular word or phrase. Follow this by as much consolidation work as time allows – consolidation of grammar, vocabulary, or content, or all three.

Filmstrips

Cambridge Classical Filmstrip 3, "Rome," contains visual material suitable for use with Stages 35–40. It includes the following topics:

1–11　Forum, arch of Titus, and other monuments
12–16　Entertainment
17–26　Trade and grain supply
27–28　Insulae
29–31　Water supply
32–35　Death and burial

Cambridge Classical Filmstrip 4, "Additional Material," contains visual material suitable for use with Stages 41–48. It includes the following topics:

6–16　Pompeii and Herculaneum (for Stage 46)
35–37　Hunting (for Stage 35)

In this Manual, reference to particular frames is given by filmstrip frame number, and also (where appropriate) by slide number for the

11

Introduction

benefit of those teachers who are using the slides which accompanied the first edition of the Course. Unless otherwise stated, references are to Filmstrips 3 or 4 and to the Unit III or IV slides.

Teaching Methods

First Reading, or Initial Comprehension

Continue using the basic lesson plan suggested in the Unit 1 Manual, pp. 9–12 (introduction; comprehension (= "first reading"); exploration and discussion (= "second reading"); consolidation; testing; and review), but also vary it frequently. Your students will be grateful. For example, if the text is fairly easy, read it aloud, pause after each word, phrase, or clause, and ask volunteers to supply a translation. Or ask the class to study the next sentence and when someone knows the translation, ask him or her to put up a hand. If the text is rather hard, read the text to the class once or twice, give students a few minutes to study it further on their own, and then ask comprehension questions to be answered in writing and graded in class by the students themselves. (For examples, see the Unit 4 students' textbook, "Vergilius," p. 150, and p. 106 below.)

Reading aloud by the teacher becomes especially important in Stages 41–48. Your initial reading can help students to group the words correctly into phrases and clauses, and thus steer them away from trying to translate mechanically word by word. Reading poetry aloud is especially important, since the word order may be unfamiliar, and students troubled by a phrase or clause which overruns the line. For example, in the students' textbook, "Phaedrus," lines 3–4, p. 140:

> ...longēque īnferior agnus. tunc fauce improbā
> latrō incitātus iūrgiī causam intulit...

a pause after *incitātus* and an absence of pause after *improbā* will help the class to relate the participle correctly to *fauce improbā*. Students can sometimes comprehend a good deal by ear alone while listening to your initial reading, even with their books shut, if you list the meanings of new or crucial words on the blackboard ahead of time.

The questions printed in the students' textbook are deliberately varied. Some are straightforward comprehension questions; others explore the content more deeply, in the way described on pp. 15–16 below. Where both types of question are appended to a particular text, they are indicated by a division into "A" and "B" questions respectively. There is a similar variety in the questions suggested in the Stage Commentaries of this Manual (see pp. 20–198 below). Your inclinations, the needs of your students, and the time available will all affect your decision about whether and how to make use of each set of

Teaching Methods

questions, and when to supplement or replace them with your own. Notice one point in particular: very simple comprehension questions can often help students through texts of considerable difficulty. (For examples, see pp. 100–03 below, "Catullus" I and II.) But make sure that students can support their answer to a comprehension question by quoting the relevant Latin words.

In Stages 41–48, the quantity of vocabulary in some passages may cause problems, especially in poetry; for students may continually interrupt their initial exploration of the text by searches through the facing vocabulary to find the meanings of new words, as these are frequently unguessable from the context because they are juxtaposed with other equally unfamiliar words. In such cases, reverse the usual principle – faithfully followed in Units 1–3 – that new words should be met by students in a continuous context, and, instead, preface the reading of the passage with a study of the facing vocabulary, reinforcing the students' grasp of the new words by encouraging them to recall related Latin words or synonyms which they have met previously, to compose simple Latin sentences into which the new word would fit, or to suggest English derivatives.

The reading material in Stages 42, 44–45, and 47, original Latin poetry, is designed to present the students with a gradual progression of difficulty, but this aim cannot always be consistently realized. For example, it may happen that an otherwise easy poetic passage, suitable for one of these Stages because of its intrinsic interest, may contain an exceptionally difficult couplet, which cannot be simplified (like a difficulty in a prose text) by adaptation nor eliminated by simple omission. If so, maintain momentum during the first reading so that students do not lose sight of the text's content by over-concentrating on the linguistic difficulties. Sometimes you can help by quickly giving them a simpler or more familiar example of the feature which is bothering them; for example, *necesse est nōbīs fugere* might be used to explain an impersonal use of the gerundive like *nōbīs fugiendum est*. Otherwise, if there is no alternative, simply translate the troublesome phrase or line. Later, when the general sense of the whole poem or passage is understood, return to the difficulty and explain it properly without having disrupted the continuity of the first reading.

Second Reading, or Exploration and Discussion

A cardinal principle throughout the Course has been that students should not only study the reading material from a linguistic point of view but also explore and discuss its content. In Stages 41–48, where original Latin texts take the place of facsimile Latin, allow ample time for full exploration and discussion. A good discussion, moreover, can develop naturally out of your straightforward comprehension questions. Proceed, for example, from questions like "What did X do at this point and what was Y's response?" to more searching questions about the characters' motives and behavior and, where appropriate, to further questions like "Who do you think was right, X or Y?"

Do not be shy about making up your own comprehension questions. You have several sources available to you. Scholars' articles and commentaries which consider the text from a literary point of view often suggest ideas for the teacher to explore with students. Balme and Warman's *Aestimanda* blazed a trail in extending this approach to work done at the collegiate level. Textbooks which continue this development include those of Balme and Greenstock, Stace and Jones, Tingay, and Verity. (See Bibliography, pp. 252–58, for these and other citations.) The journal *Didaskalos*, a discontinued publication of the Joint Association of Classical Teachers of Great Britain (J.A.C.T.), contained numerous articles relevant to the teaching of classical literature, especially in its 1966 issue (Volume 2, Number 1). Sharwood Smith, 48–61, 87–89, is perceptive and helpful, covers an astonishing amount of ground in a few pages, and has a valuable bibliography. Consider also the format and questioning techniques suggested by textbooks, anthologies, and editions of literary works used by English or French teachers at the high-school and college levels.

The question "How would you read this aloud?" can often lead to a useful discussion. To read aloud with correct expression, a student must first consider the tone of a passage and decide, for example, whether a Catullus poem is intense or casual, or whether a chapter of Tacitus contains any variations in mood. Equally useful is the interpretative question "What does the writer mean?" For example, ask the class "Study Vergil's phrase *inhorruit unda tenebrīs* and explain what was happening to the sea," or "Explain the comment attributed by Tacitus to Nero, *illō diē sibi tandem darī imperium*." Other ways of sharpening the students' appreciation of a writer's words include exploring the points of correspondence in a simile or examining the literal meaning of a word used metaphorically, through such questions as "What does Catullus mean when he uses the word *ūror* for his reaction to Lesbia's infidelity? What does *ūror* mean literally? How is 'being on fire' an appropriate way to describe his feelings?"

Explore also the effect which a writer achieves by such figures of speech as alliteration, repetition, assonance, variation of word order, and antithesis. For example, Vergil raises the tension of his story at one point by placing the verb's subject at the end of a long sentence, thus telling the reader (or listener) that one boat is in the lead and describing the scene before revealing which boat it is; Ovid sometimes uses alliteration to point the climax of his narrative; Catullus often exploits antithesis to convey the conflict of contradictory emotions; Tacitus, at a key moment, uses a long sentence to build up a picture of calm serenity, then shatters the picture with violent action, described in a few terse words. Ask students "What is the effect of the alliteration, antithesis, etc.?", or put the question the other way around by asking "How does Ovid show that this is a crucial moment in the story?" or "How does Catullus make it plain that his feelings for Lesbia are now very mixed?", thus eliciting "alliteration," "pairs of contrasted words," etc. as part of the answer.

While students are still feeling their way with a new text, use "leading" questions such as "What words does Tacitus use to emphasize Nero's terror?" "Where in the poem does the angry tone give way to sadness?" When the students are more confident and experienced, ask them more "open-ended" questions such as "What impression does Tacitus give of Agrippina in this chapter?" or "Is there a change of mood at any point of the poem?" Some of these questions may have more than one possible answer; if so, do not try to impose your own interpretation or that of an "authority," but encourage your students to offer and defend their own opinions. Also, allow your students to express their preference for one poem or passage over another, even if it is unfavorable. If students honestly dislike a particular poem or text, let them say so, but also ask them to say why.

Many students, especially those who have read very little literature in any language, often respond more fully to a literary text if it has some point of contact with their own experiences. They enjoy recognizing elements of a familiar situation and can instinctively sympathize with the writer or characters in the text. Help your students spot analogies with their own experiences, often with incidental comments such as "The Nicomedians gathered around and watched the fire, just like people who run out of their houses to stare at an accident," etc. Avoid direct questions about students' personal experiences; the question, "Have you ever been in Catullus' situation, Joe?" is too personal to generate anything except embarrassment. But give the students an opportunity to draw upon their own experience without explicitly referring to it, through such questions as "Do you think that what is really bothering Catullus is the feeling that he's been taken for a fool?".

Translation is normally regarded as a means of testing comprehension, but it can also be a valuable tool in sharpening students' appreciation of the text. Select a short portion of text (e.g. a passage of Vergil from Stage 47) for intensive study, and work with the class to produce the best possible shared translation, but written, as students make their contributions, on the overhead projector or up on the blackboard. Or let the class look at one or more published translations (see p. 152 of the Unit 4 students' textbook for an example), not because a translation can faithfully represent an original but because the teacher can often throw light on the characteristics of the Latin text by asking such questions as "Which of these translations would give a more accurate idea of Vergil to a reader who did not know Latin?" This might lead to an attempt by students individually to produce their own polished translations.

Classroom exploration of a text should reflect the fact that Latin literature was written for reading aloud. As suggested above, the teacher's own reading should play an important part in the students' first encounter with the text, and the question "How would you read this aloud?" should introduce literary considerations like tone and mood, in both poetry and prose. Work on any of the Stages, furthermore, should conclude with a reading of all or part of the text, either by the teacher (in which case, students might have their books closed) or by members of the class who have each studied and rehearsed their assigned section. This reading might then be tape-recorded and played back so that students can hear and judge themselves.

After the students have had enough time to listen to verse, introduce them to the idea of syllable length and practice reading lines aloud. For suggestions, see pp. 64–5 below; hexameters are probably the most suitable lines for this purpose. In due course, students can proceed to the principles of scansion, and practice analyzing hexameters into feet. Use this exercise solely as a reinforcement, not a substitute, for reading aloud and listening. Awareness of meter comes more through the ear than the eye.

Historical and Cultural Topics

The exploration of historical and cultural topics which has featured prominently in earlier Units should continue here. Such questions as "From whom did the emperor get advice on state matters?" "How were the provinces governed?" "How did Roman emperors carry out their work?" and "How did the Romans get divorced and what was their attitude to remarriage?" arise naturally from some of the texts in Unit 4 and are pursued further in the background material. Other texts contain incidental references which can be followed up and explored; for example, Catullus' poem about Egnatius mentions the noisy and emotional scene around the defendant in a court trial; the "laudātiō Tūriae" refers to the proscriptions of the second triumvirate; and Vergil's account of the boat race illustrates the practice of promising the gods a *vōtum* in return for the fulfillment of a prayer. A simple chronological framework for events and authors is provided by two time charts in the students' textbook, pp. 157 and 232.

When possible, link a historical or cultural reference in the reading material with what the students already know, or use it as a starting point for further investigation. Invite students to make deductions ("What is the emperor's main concern, judging from his reply to Pliny?") or ask for explanations ("Why didn't the emperor himself testify against Salvius?" "Why was the freedman readier than the commander of the praetorian guard to take on the job of killing Agrippina?"). At other times, ask broader questions, encouraging students to draw upon outside evidence ("What seems to you to have been the Romans' attitude to the people they conquered?"). In other questions, focus on particular Roman concepts or values ("What do you think the writer means by *fortūna* or *imperium*?" "Why is Tacitus so scornful of Nero?"), and draw comparisons with the modern world; contrast Turia's attitude to her marriage, for example, with modern attitudes.

Adolescents, like many adults, are likely to be interested in personality and prepared to discuss the historical characters who appear in the text. Elicit a character sketch by asking "What sort of person does Pliny's mother seem to have been?" You can raise such questions equally well, of course, about fictitious characters, but when you ask them about historical people, they acquire an extra dimension. Invite students to comment on the characters' behavior as well. Tacitus, with his penetrating and sometimes cynical insight into human psychology, and his habit of supplying two alternative explanations for an action, offers a particularly good opportunity for discussing such questions as "What was Nero's reason for acting like this?" This can lead in turn to the discussion of value judgments ("Did Rufilla have good reason for abandoning Salvius?" "Was 'Vespillo' [his actual name is unknown] right to reject his wife's suggestion?" "Were Pliny and his mother justified in lingering so long at Misenum?"). Encourage students to put themselves in the shoes (sandals?) of a historical character and imagine what it would have been like to be in his or her situation; for example, at various points in Stage 41, ask the class "What would you have done if you had been Pliny? How would you have solved his problem?"

Several of the texts, especially those which narrate historical events, provide opportunities for considering them critically as source material. Tacitus, for example, often offers scope for the question "How much of this narrative is statement of fact, and how much is opinion?" You could ask about any historian or orator "Where do you think he got his information from?" or "How fair are his comments on this character?"

Students, accustomed as they are to political advertisements on TV, are often good at detecting "spin" or bias. Ask students to write an account of an incident from a standpoint different from that of the writer; for example, "How would the friend of Pliny's uncle have described the ruckus which he had with Pliny and his mother?"

Consolidation of Grammatical Points

Consolidation continues to be essential. Regularly review the grammar previously learned so that students can refresh their memory and you can identify the points which students have forgotten or misunderstood. After the students have read, explored, and discussed a poem or passage, return briefly to one or two grammatical points and make sure they have been understood. If not, practice them further; for by now the students will be sufficiently familiar with the passage and its vocabulary, meaning, and background to be able to concentrate profitably on grammatical details. Select nouns and adjectives from the text for testing the students' ability to recognize case, gender, and number. Drill verbs by asking students to substitute for a verb form in the text another in a different tense or person (see Unit 1 Manual, p. 11). You will find outlines of the various grammatical points introduced Stage by Stage at the head of each of the Stage Commentaries below, or in the "Scope and Sequence" chart available without cost from the N.A.C.C.P. Resource Center (see Bibliography, p. 252 below); and in many of the Stage Commentaries themselves, additional suggestions for consolidation. The language notes, drills, and Checklists in the students' textbook provide still more opportunities for consolidation.

Following are several useful ways of consolidating a poem or passage after students have read (and sometimes reread) it:

1 (Useful if time is short): translate the passage aloud, but in order to keep the class alert and involved, sometimes read a particular word or phrase in Latin and ask the class to supply the translation.
2 After the students have closed their books, read the passage aloud, pausing sometimes to check (by comprehension questions or requests for translation of the phrase or sentence which you have just read) that they are following the story. With an able class or one with older students (or with any class if the story is easy), sometimes omit a key word while you are reading and ask the class to supply either the missing word or its English translation.
3 Give a written quiz on the grammar and/or content of the passage.

Stage Commentaries

The chief grammatical and cultural features introduced in each Stage are listed at the beginning of each Stage Commentary, followed in the Commentaries for Stages 35–40 by summaries of the narrative, and in those for Stages 41–48 by digests of the literary works, and both summaries and digests, in turn, by fuller listings of the chief grammatical points and sentence patterns.

The comments on the reading passages normally include some of the following types of material:

1 brief explanations of historical or cultural points referred to in the text;
2 comments and suggestions about possible linguistic difficulties (especially in poetry);
3 suggestions for exploring the historical and/or literary content of the text;
4 and, in the Commentaries for Stages 41–48, suggestions for consolidating and reviewing grammatical points and vocabulary (see next paragraph).

The scale and scope of this Manual preclude extended comments on the language and content of the stories, poems, and adapted texts. For such comments, and for scholarly discussion, especially of the material in Stages 41–48, refer to the standard commentaries. You are not expected to work through methodically the various suggestions for questions and approaches to the text; these are to be treated as a "bank" from which you can make a selection, supplementing and replacing the Manual's suggestions with questions and approaches of your own.

The notes on most reading passages in Stages 41–48 include a "Vocabulary Check," in which a variable number of words are selected from the text and listed in the Manual for you to practice (if you wish) with your students after they have read it. Your students could have their books shut while practicing these words, or could have them open so that the context might remind them of each word's meaning. If your students are reading poetry, ask them to practice the words immediately *before* the relevant poem or passage is read (see "Teaching Methods," p. 13 above). The words in the "Vocabulary Checks" are almost always words which occur in the Course's Checklists (occasionally others are included, such as words which happen to occur frequently within a particular Stage); a few fairly easy words are included, but the "Vocabulary Checks" are designed to practice words which, though common, are easily forgotten or confused. Sometimes an important but troublesome word which occurs in a number of consecutive reading passages is included in the "Vocabulary Check" for each passage so that repetition may assist in memorization. Feel free to substitute other words of your own choice.

References to slides are to the *Cambridge Latin Course* slide sets which were published with the first, British edition of the Course and were sold in North America. Unit and slide number are indicated; e.g. "IV.42" refers to slide 42 of the set which accompanied Unit IV in the first edition.

Books and articles are normally referred to by the name of their author(s). For details of title, publisher, etc., see Bibliography, pp. 252–58 below.

STAGE 35: RŪS

BRIEF OUTLINE

Reading passages	City news and country news
Background material	Country villas
Chief grammatical points	1st and 2nd persons singular: present, future, and imperfect passive (including deponent)
	indirect statement with present active infinitive after present verb of speaking, etc.

NARRATIVE POINTS

A.D. Date	Setting	Characters Introduced	Story Line
83	(in letters): Italy	Manius Acilius Glabrio, Gaius Helvidius Lupus, Helvidius (son of Lupus)	Glabrio writes from Rome about Domitian's triumph over the Germans and procession with Spanish slaves in German clothing; discusses Domitian's council and private life; praises Martial's poetry, but says he flatters emperor too much. Lupus replies, tells about country life, warns Glabrio against writing his opinion of those in power: Lupus' father was exiled and killed for criticizing Vespasian (Domitian's father); Lupus used to like Ovid, now prefers Martial; Lupus' son Helvidius apparently has a girlfriend in Rome.

Stage Commentaries

GRAMMATICAL POINTS

1st and 2nd persons singular: present, future, and imperfect passive (including deponent)
  e.g. *dum ego strepitū urbis vexor, tū carmine avium dēlectāris.*
indirect statement with present active infinitive after present verb of speaking, etc.
  e.g. *in epistulā tuā dīcis tē valdē occupātum esse.*
further examples of predicative dative
  e.g. *salūs enim tua mihi magnae cūrae est.*
fruor, dignus + ablative
  e.g. *nunc tamen vītā rūsticā fruor.*
    en splendidus Imperātor quī, paucīs homunculīs victīs, sē dignum triumphō putat!

SENTENCE PATTERN
verb of speaking, etc. + ACC & INF
  e.g. *amīcus meus Silānus, quī cum Agricolā in Britanniā nūper mīlitābat, dīcit Calēdoniōs in ultimīs partibus Britanniae habitāre.*

Title Picture

This is a composite picture of countryside activities similar to several Roman mosaics. Use it to illustrate either "vīta rūstica" or the background material. Ask students to list and describe the various activities; several will be familiar to them from earlier Units.

ex urbe

Glabrio writes a letter to his friend Lupus, who is at his country estate. He envies Lupus his leisure, as things have been busy in Rome. Domitian has just celebrated a triumph for his "conquest" of the Germans. Many Romans, however, are secretly cynical about this so-called "victory," since the alleged prisoners of war in the triumphal procession appear to have been Spanish slaves dressed as Germans. In Britain, Agricola is about to advance against the Scots (*Calēdoniī*). Glabrio is a member of the emperor's advisory council, and is often at a loss when asked his opinion, because he feels it is ignoble to lie, but hazardous to speak the truth. Glabrio concludes his letter with a critique of the poet Martial. He likes him very much, but with one reservation: his verses are elegant, but he praises the emperor too much. Glabrio begs for a letter from Lupus, and asks his friend to visit him as soon as he returns to the city. Lupus' reply ("vīta rūstica") follows. The imagined date of the correspondence is A.D. 83, shortly after the events of Stages 33 and 34 (see above, p. 6).

Stage 35

Glabrio's letter and Lupus' reply introduce several topics and characters that will reappear in later Stages: the personality of Domitian and the nature of his principate (a general theme of Stages 35–40); the emperor's *cōnsilium* (Stage 37); Agricola's campaigns in Britain (Stage 37, also connected to earlier material in Unit 3, Stage 26); the literary work of Martial (Stage 36) and Ovid (Stage 39); the girlfriend of Lupus' son (Stage 38). There is a passing reference to Domitian's German triumph (mentioned again in Stage 37), and some disparaging comments about Roman doctors (subject of two epigrams by Martial in Stage 36). Both the correspondents, Glabrio and Lupus, compare city with country life.

Although M'. Acilius Glabrio became consul in A.D. 91, he eventually brought down on himself the full fury of Domitian, was forced to fight in the public arena, and when he survived, was deported and eventually executed in A.D. 95 on a charge of "atheism" (perhaps he sympathized with the beliefs of Jews or Christians). Glabrio appears in Juvenal, *Satire* IV.94ff., as a member of Domitian's council (further details in Juvenal, ed. Duff 183–84). Ask students for their impressions of Glabrio's character, and thus prepare the way for his later appearances in Stages 36 (where he walks out of Martial's *recitātiō*, protesting a poem which shamelessly flatters the emperor), 37 (where he loses control of himself during the emperor's council meeting) and 40 (where he leads the prosecution at the trial of Salvius).

Domitian's reign was notable for two trials of Vestal Virgins who were charged with unchastity. In the earlier trial (mentioned by Glabrio in lines 29–33 of the students' textbook), two or three Vestals were found guilty but were allowed to choose the manner of their deaths rather than be buried alive as required by law. Cornelia, the chief Vestal, was acquitted. On the second occasion, some years later, Cornelia was retried, found guilty, and buried alive. These trials are mentioned in Suetonius, *Domitian* 8; the execution of Cornelia is described by Pliny, *Letter* IV.11. Plutarch, *Numa* 10, has a dramatic account of the live burial of a Vestal (Sherwin-White 283 notes that Plutarch could have witnessed the execution of Cornelia). Although the ancient sources tend to treat the trials as an example of Domitian's cruelty, there seems to have been no real doubt about the guilt of the accused, and in the earlier cases Domitian in fact tempered the full severity of the law (see above). Accordingly, Glabrio's comment, in lines 32–33, stresses Domitian's hypocrisy rather than his cruelty.

Domitian's campaign in Germany against the Chatti in A.D. 83 is belittled by his ancient critics, such as Suetonius, *Domitian* 6, and Tacitus, *Agricola* 39.1 (both were writing after Domitian's assassination and following a tradition hostile to him); it is Tacitus who mentions the allegation attributed to Glabrio in lines 17–19, that the triumphal

Stage Commentaries

procession was a sham. Archaeological evidence, however, supports the view that the campaign was in fact very successful, but, as Ogilvie and Richmond in their edition (285) point out, many citizens would have been disgusted by Domitian's ludicrous exploitation of his success: he appeared regularly in the senate wearing the crimson toga of a victorious commander, and he renamed the month of September *mēnsis Germānicus*.

1st and 2nd person singular forms of the present and future tenses of the passive are now introduced. During initial exploration, guide the students to the meaning of the sentences in which these forms first occur, *prīmā ... salūtor* (line 6) and *aliquandō ... vīsitor* (lines 7–8), using contextual clues like *ā clientibus meīs, ab eīs* etc., and if necessary, comprehension questions like "What does Glabrio say happens to him at the first hour?"

For the third example, *dum ego ... avium dēlectāris* (lines 9–10), refer students to the captioned picture at the bottom of p. 2 of their textbook. This is the first of a series of captioned pictures used in Stages 35, 36, 38, and 39 to highlight and illustrate new grammatical points; a sentence from the text containing a new form or rule is illustrated by a detailed drawing, with the sentence repeated in bold face as a caption. This device is intended to help students in two ways: while they are exploring the passage, the picture will help them understand the sentence, and when they have read the passage, you can refer them to the captioned picture and focus their attention on the new grammatical point. Here, for example, have the caption translated by a student, write the translation on the blackboard, and then have students find further Latin examples of the new point and translate them.

In the left-hand picture, Glabrio is shown in the forum in front of the curia (see Filmstrip 8); in the right-hand picture Helvidius is relaxing by the river, his reading abandoned.

First Language Note (*1st and 2nd Persons Singular, Present, Future and Imperfect Passive*)

Students met the present and future tenses of these forms in the first reading passage. The note adds the imperfect tense, since it is an easy extension of the same principle (it will appear in the next passage, "vīta rūstica").

Elicit from the class that the endings *-or* and *-ar* indicate "I," while *-ris* indicates "you (sg.)." When drilling further, concentrate on one point at a time; compare the endings of the three tenses while keeping the same person, e.g. *salūtor, salūtābor, salūtābar*, or contrast the 1st and 2nd person endings within the same tense, e.g. *vexābar* and *vexābāris*. Unless the students are exceptionally able, only use examples in which both the person and the tense are varied (e.g. *moneor* contrasted with *monēbāris*) in the context of complete sentences where temporal adverbs serve as clues, as they do in the examples in paragraph 4 of the students' textbook.

The note deliberately focuses on the basic point and avoids complications for the moment. The exposition in paragraphs 2 and 3 concentrates on the paradigm of the first conjugation, while the future tense of third and fourth conjugation verbs is excluded (one example appears in "vīta rūstica," line 41, in an easy context). Later, when reviewing these forms, make use of the material in the Language Information Section (hereafter called LI Section), pp. 283–397, for study and practice of these three tenses in all four conjugations. You may use additional material later in the second half of Unit 4 (i.e. Stages 41–48).

Invite comment on *cōnor*. In particular, elicit that:

1 the 1st and 2nd person endings of *cōnor* are identical to those of the passive of *portō*, e.g. *-or, -āris, -ābor, -āberis* etc.;
2 the meanings of the forms of *cōnor* are active, e.g. "I try," "you (sg.) try," "I will try" etc.;
3 the 1st and 2nd person endings of *cōnor* thus conform exactly to the normal pattern of deponent verbs, i.e. passive form but active meaning.

vīta rūstica

Lupus sends a reply to Glabrio in which he indicates that the pleasant life in the country has its unpleasant distractions, such as frequent harassment from his tenant farmers. He adds, moreover, that he has recovered from a recent illness only by ignoring the advice of a country doctor. Regarding the campaign of Agricola, Lupus has recently heard from his friend Silanus, a legionary commander whose assessment of the situation is that the Scots are indeed ferocious warriors, but no match for the Roman troops. Lupus remarks that he shares his friend's enthusiasm for the poet Martial, preferring his work now over Ovid's. The letter then takes a serious turn: Lupus warns Glabrio to be more circumspect in his criticism of "a very powerful person" (i.e. Domitian), pointing out that his – Lupus' – own father was exiled and later killed for criticizing Vespasian, father of the present emperor, too openly. Lupus urges Glabrio, therefore, to watch his step.

Glabrio's correspondent Lupus is a fictitious member of a historical Roman family, with a tradition of hostility to the principate. Helvidius Priscus senior was the leader of a group of senators who, partly under the influence of Stoic beliefs (see Unit 3, pp. 221–22), openly opposed the emperor and advocated the restoration of the old republican form of government. Helvidius himself made a point of

Stage Commentaries

always being disrespectful to the Emperor Vespasian at meetings of the senate; he was deported and eventually put to death.

His son, Helvidius Priscus the younger, was a victim of the reign of terror which began in A.D. 93 (see above, p. 7), in which one after another of Domitian's victims were charged with *maiestās* (treason) or atheism. He had earlier held the consulship, but was now living quietly out of public view. He wrote a play, however, which could be interpreted as a satire on the emperor's private life, and this was enough to make Domitian furious with him. He was accused before the senate on some unknown charge, condemned, and executed. For further details about both Helvidii, see Tacitus (ed. Ogilvie and Richmond) 133 and 308, and Sherwin-White 242–43 and 748.

Lupus, the supposed author of the letter in the students' textbook, is an imaginary brother of Helvidius Priscus the younger. He shares his family's anti-monarchic feelings, but his father's fate has taught him to be cautious in expressing them. Accordingly, in the final paragraph of his letter, he warns Glabrio to be careful. Lupus' teenage son, mentioned in lines 28–33, is the lover of Polla in Stage 38; Lupus himself does not reappear in the reading material, but is a character in diagnostic test 12 on pp. 212–13 below.

Illustrate the description of country life in lines 7–11 with this Stage's title picture. After students have read the letter, ask them, as you did with the previous story, for their impression of the writer's personality. Elicit comments on Lupus' tolerance of young people, his scant respect for professional advice, the warmth of his concern for his friend Glabrio, and his anxiety about possible consequences of Glabrio's outspokenness.

Indirect statement now appears for the first time in the course. We introduce it gradually during the first half of Unit 4 (Stages 35–40), one type of infinitive at a time, beginning with the present active infinitive in this Stage. The verb of speaking, thinking, etc. which introduces the indirect statement is normally expressed and placed in front of the accusative noun, and is restricted almost entirely to the present tense. Sentences with a past verb of speaking, like *dīxī servum labōrāre*, in which the present infinitive *labōrāre* has to be translated as "*was* working," do not appear until Stage 40. As usual in this course, the text is designed so that students grasp right away the meaning of the new sentence pattern from its context and analyze it later. For example, introduce the first example in the story, *vīcīnī ... latēre* (lines 8–9), by inviting the class to translate *vīcīnī enim crēdunt*, then asking "What do Lupus' neighbors believe about the woods?" or (if the students are capable) "Put your hand up when you see what the rest of the sentence means."

The story contains opportunities for further practice of the 1st and 2nd person passive forms. As in "ex urbe," a captioned drawing is

Stage 35

provided, but this time it shows both 1st and 2nd person forms. Put the translation of the caption on the blackboard, and then have students find and translate additional examples. (The left-hand picture shows Glabrio at his morning *salūtātiō*, while in the right-hand picture Helvidius is being pestered by his tenant-farmers while riding around his estate.)

"ex urbe" and "vīta rūstica" contain several examples of expressions of time, involving both the accusative and ablative cases. If time allows, review these expressions.

Drills

Exercise 1   Type: vocabulary
            Grammatical point being practiced: antonyms

Exercise 2   Type: completion
            Missing item: verb
            Test of accuracy: sense and personal endings
            Grammatical point being practiced: 3rd person singular and plural, future tense, introduced in Stage 33

Exercise 3   Type: substitution
            Grammatical point being practiced: relative pronoun

Second Language Note (*Indirect Statement*)

Consolidate the new pattern of indirect statement in the following manner:

1 Before the class period, make an overhead projection transparency of the text of "vīta rūstica" down to ... *meliōrem habēre* (line 24).
2 With a felt-tipped pen, underline the indirect statements in the text. Take a transparency and two or three different colored felt-tipped pens (preferably with water-soluble ink) to class.
3 In class, have students read "vīta rūstica" up to ... *meliōrem habēre* (line 24) in their textbooks.
4 Project the prepared transparency. Ask students to translate the underlined indirect statements.
5 Have students read language note, paragraphs 1 and 2. Then ask students to identify infinitives in the sentences underlined on the transparency. Circle infinitives with another color. Ask students to identify subject accusatives, e.g. after a student has found the infinitive *habitāre* in line 20, ask him or her, "Find an accusative noun indicating who does the inhabiting." Circle accusative subjects with a third color.

Stage Commentaries

6 Read language note, paragraph 3. If time allows, circle the introductory verbs *dīcis* (line 5), *crēdit* (line 22) etc. with a fourth color, and point out that the introductory verb is usually followed by "that" in English.
7 Ask volunteers to translate sentences in language note, paragraph 4. Ask which sentences are direct or indirect statements. Make up additional examples if necessary.
8 Finally, ask students to retranslate the examples of indirect statement on the transparency.

Students are sometimes bothered by indirect statements which contain two accusatives, e.g. *crēdō servōs dominum timēre*, and ask "How can I tell who is doing the action if both words are in the accusative?" Tell them that in sentences like these Latin uses word order (as English always does) to differentiate: the doer of the action is normally mentioned first. But show also, with examples like *crēdō puerum vīnum bibere*, that in practice ambiguity seldom arises, since the correct meaning is usually obvious from the context.

The Background Material

Balsdon *Life* 188 and 194–222 is valuable and entertaining too. Paoli 70–77, 243–48 also provides much useful material.

Observe that the practice of leaving the city during the hot summer months is still very much a feature of present-day life among wealthier Romans; the Pope, for example, leaves the Vatican every summer for his residence in Castelgandolfo. Use maps of Italy, including the bay of Naples and environs of Rome, to establish the location of some of the places mentioned in the text. Explain that places like Laurentum and Tibur were not early versions of modern-day bedroom towns. A man like Pliny might well, as indicated in the text, have done a full day's work in the city but still have reached his country villa by nightfall; after arriving, however, he would have stayed there for several days.

Quote or have students study relevant material in the ancient sources, and then discuss it with them: Pliny, *Letters* I.6 (hunting; note the photograph on p. 8 of the students' textbook which shows part of the Piazza Armerina mosaic of a hunt (see also slides IV.23–6)); II.17 (the Laurentine villa; see photograph of model in the students' textbook, p. 13, and below, under "Suggestions for Further Work"); III.19 (contemplated purchase of adjacent property); IX.15 and IX.36 (life on estates); IX.37 (tenants in debt); X.8 (to Trajan, asking for leave of absence), and many other letters; Martial, *Epigrams* IV.64 (villa of Julius, high above Rome); X.30 (fishing from bed) and I.62 (the lady visitor to Baiae who *vēnit Pēnelopē abiit Helena*). Lewis and Reinhold I, 440–50 collect material on land management from Cicero, Cato, and Varro, with material from Columella in II, 167–75.

Have students explore further the point that land was virtually the only means of investment for an upper-class Roman; students may be able to think of modern sources of income, such as interest from savings, mutual funds, stocks or bonds, whose equivalents were almost or entirely non-existent in antiquity. Note the ban on senatorial participation in trade and Roman prejudices about "gentlemanly and ungentlemanly occupations": Cicero, *De officiis* I.42 and (quoting Cato) II.25 (translation in Lewis and Reinhold I, 439–40 and C.S.C.P. *Roman World* items 33 and 86). Compare the figure of 400,000 HS, which Pliny received from one of his villas each year (quoted on p. 15, last line, of the students' textbook) with other figures, such as those given on p. 131 of the Unit 3 Teacher's Manual.

Suggestions for Discussion

1 If the class had lived in first-century Rome, would they have shared Glabrio's preference for country rather than city life? Would city life have had any compensating advantages?
2 What picture of himself does Pliny present in (for example) *Letters* I.6 and IX.15? Is it a credible picture? Does he really consider his hunting exploit as a mere joke? Is he presenting himself in IX.15 simply as an amateur landowner, or is the reader meant to be impressed by Pliny's skill at estate management? Is there any way we can tell whether Pliny is giving a true picture of himself? For example, when he published his letters, would he have included details his readers knew to be untrue? For a study of Pliny's character, as revealed (unconsciously) in his description of his villas, see *Omnibus* 4, pp. 31–32.

Words and Phrases Checklist

cūrae esse in the Checklist provides a convenient opportunity to study and practice the examples of the predicative dative in the LI Section, p. 311, paragraph 4c.

Supplement study of the Checklist with a vocabulary review. For example, spend a few minutes testing the class orally on recent Checklist vocabulary. You might translate a review story rapidly to the class, asking them to supply the translation of particular words and phrases. Because they have the context to help them, use this method to practice relatively unfamiliar or troublesome words. If the words are familiar, ask students to provide a contextual sentence, preferably in English unless they are capable of generating sentences in Latin, e.g. "I don't know *utrum* I should go *an* stay." Vary this last drill by giving declined or conjugated forms of the Checklist word, e.g. *cavē* from *caveō*.

Suggestions for Further Work

1 Ask students to compare the account of Pliny's Laurentine villa in their textbook, pp. 12–13, with the plan and the model in the photograph. (The model is in the Ashmolean Museum, Oxford, England.) Or give students the fuller plan, from Pliny, trans. Radice 305, in which almost every room is alphabetically keyed to the translation of Pliny, *Letter* II.17 in 75ff. If you read the translation aloud to students, let them use the alphabetical key to follow Pliny's description both on the plan and (in the case of some rooms) in the photograph of the model.
2 Students might investigate additional visual material illustrating villas and country life. McKay and Masson both have excellent photographs, including several of Hadrian's villa at Tivoli. Some of the slides also contain useful material, e.g. 35–36 and IV.64–77. Examples of wall paintings of country life can be found in Dilke 33, Balsdon *Life* 80, C.S.C.P. *Roman World* items 15a and 19a, slides IV.17 and V.39–40. Although the paintings themselves are seldom in good condition, they still convey an impression of the scale and splendor of the villas.

STAGE 36: RECITĀTIŌ

BRIEF OUTLINE

Reading passages	epigrams of Martial (introduced in a recitatio)
Background material	recitationes
Chief grammatical points	present subjunctive
	verse word order: separation of noun and adjective

Stage 36

NARRATIVE POINTS

A.D. Date	Setting	Characters Introduced	Story Line
83	Rome	Marcus Valerius Martialis (the epigrammatist, known in English as Martial); assorted characters mentioned in his epigrams	Martial reads his epigrams aloud; some are extemporaneous about people in the audience. Glabrio walks out following Martial's shameless flattery of the emperor.

GRAMMATICAL POINTS

present subjunctive (including *sum*, *possum*, *volō*)
  e.g. *hem! audītōrēs nōbīs imperant ut taceāmus.*
3rd person plural perfect in *-ēre*
  e.g. *"centum mē tetigēre manūs Aquilōne gelātae."* (Martial)
ablative of comparison
  e.g. *"haec, Auguste, tamen, quae vertice sīdera pulsat,*
       pār domus est caelō sed minor est dominō." (Martial)

SENTENCE PATTERNS

increased complexity of elements governed by an omitted verb
  e.g. *ego hūc invītātus sum ut recitem, tū ut audiās.*
verse word order: separation of noun and adjective
  e.g. *"cūr nōn mittō meōs tibi, Pontiliāne, libellōs?"* (Martial)
verse word order: N+ADJ phrase inside another
  e.g. *"aether contingit nova nostrī prīncipis aula."* (Martial)

Title Picture

This shows the poet Martial giving a *recitātiō*. Students may be intrigued by the different expressions on the faces of the spectators. Use this picture to introduce the theme of this Stage.

Marcus Valerius Mārtiālis

The poet Martial gives a reading of some of his poems, contending with whispering and interruptions. Most of his selections are short, derisive epigrams aimed at Martial's acquaintances, or his exaggerated caricatures of them. A few unfortunate members of the audience who call attention to themselves during the recitation are repaid with Martial's ridicule in epigrammatic form. One member of the audience, Manius Acilius Glabrio, abruptly and indignantly gets up and leaves the auditorium when, toward the end of his reading, Martial recites a verse extravagantly praising the emperor.

Stage Commentaries

The epigrams of Martial included in this passage are I.32 (*nōn amō tē, Sabidī*); V.43 (*Thāis habet nigrōs*); VII.3 (*cūr nōn mittō*); I.38 (*quem recitās*); VIII.36 (on Domitian's palace, adapted); and I.47 (*nūper erat medicus*). Use comprehension questions to make sure that students understand the stage directions and dialogue which introduce each epigram; they often contain clues to the epigram's content. Next, lead the class through the relevant part of the appended vocabulary list, then read the epigram aloud and establish the meaning through either comprehension questions, translation, or a mixture of both. On occasion, take the class through to the punchline, making sure they have understood the epigram that far, and then say, "Look now at the last line / half-line, and put up your hand when you've got the point / can translate it." In this way, give the students a chance to see the point for themselves.

Discuss with the class which of the alternative reasons they prefer for Martial's not being able to say why he doesn't like Sabidius (I, lines 13–16).

The epigram about Thais and Laecania (I, lines 21–23) may prompt some students to inquire about forms of Roman dental care. For false teeth, see *Omnibus* 3, p. 21. For methods of cleaning teeth, see Martial, *Epigram* XIV. 56 and Pliny the Elder, *Natural History* XXX.8 (ashes of dogs' teeth mixed with honey) and XXXVI.42 (pumice); the bizarre habit supposedly practiced by Spaniards, Catullus XXXIX.17ff. The Empress Messalina's favorite toothpaste was ashes of stags' horns, mastic gum from the Greek island of Chios, and salt from the Hammonian desert of Egypt (Scribonius Largus, *Compositiones* 60).

Domitian's great palace (*Palātium*) on the Palatine hill from which it took its name (described in II, lines 8–14, and illustrated in the students' textbook, p. 21, stood on the site of the old *domus Augustana*. It was previously mentioned in Unit 3, Stages 31, 33, and 34, and in particular was the setting for Paris' private performance of "Venus and Mars" for the empress (see also Filmstrip 9, 10, and 13; slides IV.28, 29, and 32). The first two verses of the epigram (lines 11–12 of the students' textbook) are in fact a simplified version of Martial's original (VIII.36). When students have read the whole epigram, they may enjoy, with some help from you, reading Martial's actual couplet:

clārius in tōtō nīl videt orbe diēs.
septēnōs pariter crēdās adsurgere montēs;

The class may be able, in the first half of the couplet where Diaulus' past and present occupations are stated, to anticipate the drift of the joke (II, lines 29–30). Encourage such anticipation, as it is part of intelligent reading. You might tell the students, for example, after the first line: "Ask yourself what comment Martial is likely to make about

Stage 36

Diaulus, and when we've read the next line, see whether you were right."

Many of Martial's effects depend on antithesis. Ask students, for example, "Which word in the first line of the Pontilianus epigram corresponds to *tuōs* in the second line?", then go on to note similar contrasting pairs in other epigrams. The epigrams about Thais and Laecania, and about Diaulus, are particularly rich in antithesis.

The entire passage contains numerous examples of the accusative plural of *versus*; the ablative singular *plausū* also occurs, II, line 17. If time allows, have students turn to the LI Section, p. 284, and review the models there of fourth-declension nouns. For other fourth-declension nouns from previous Checklists, see Unit 3 Teacher's Manual, p. 51, and to those lists add words from the Checklists in Stages 25–36:

Fourth declension, m. or f.: *aditus*, m. (27); *adventus*, m. (27); *cāsus*, m. (32); *cōnsulātus*, m. (34); *cursus*, m. (29); *gemitus*, m. (28); *manus* "band (of men)," f. (27); *metus*, m. (28); *strepitus*, m. (30); *vultus*, m. (31).

Students may need help with the relative clause in II, line 5, where the antecedent is postponed, and in II, line 30, where the antecedent is omitted.

First Language Note (*Present Subjunctive*)

Encourage students to comment on the forms of the second, third, and fourth conjugations, as set out in paragraph 4. They should also be able (with a little prompting if necessary) to suggest a reason why the present subjunctive of the first conjugation developed in a way different from the others.

For further practice, ask students to spot the many examples of the present subjunctive in "Marcus Valerius Mārtiālis," starting with I, lines 24–25, which are repeated as the caption under the picture on p. 19. Review the syntax of some of these examples by asking why the subjunctive is being used. If students hesitate, have them study the LI Section, pp. 316–17, paragraphs 1–5.

epigrammata Mārtiālia

This is another series of epigrams inveighing against various characters either known to or invented by Martial. Tucca (I) wants to make a profit off Martial's writing. Sextus (II) is a "fish-face." Symmachus (III) is a doctor who exploits his patients and aggravates their illnesses by subjecting them to the treatment of his apprentices. Catullus (IV) curries favor with Martial by claiming to have named him as an heir in

Stage Commentaries

his will. Quintus (V) must be blind himself, to be in love with one-eyed Thais. (This is one interpretation of a poem which can also be seen from a nearly opposite point of view.) Vacerra (VI) is a literary snob, who only appreciates books of a certain vintage, and regards contemporary literature as, ipso facto, inferior.

The six epigrams are VII.77 (*exigis ut nostrōs*); II.87 (*dīcis amōre tuī*); V.9 (*languēbam; sed tū*); XII.73 (*hērēdem tibi mē*); III.8 (*Thāida Quīntus amat*); and VIII.69 (*mīrāris veterēs*).

I *dē Tuccā* Tucca's implied occupation of bookseller is confirmed from other of Martial's epigrams.

II *dē Sextō* Students should see fairly quickly that Sextus, according to Martial, has walleyes or generally bloated features. Ask them to look in the first line of the couplet for a word which contrasts with *aquā*, and they should be able to find *ardēre* without difficulty and catch the implication that Sextus' oozing face would quickly dampen any passionate flames.

III *dē Symmachō* Use the illustration on p. 24 to help students with the split phrase *centum ... manūs ... gelātae* in line 3 of the epigram.

IV *dē Catullō* The students are likely to grasp the point that a written promise is more reliable and has more legal authority than an oral one. Ask the class, "Where will this information be written? When will Martial be in a position to read it?" Students should realize that Martial will not believe Catullus until he sees his will, by which time Catullus will be dead and unable to renege on his promise.

V *dē Quīntō* The sentence pattern ACCUSATIVE + NOMINATIVE + VERB is now becoming increasingly common in the students' textbook, and this epigram contains two examples. If it causes difficulty, have students review additional examples in the Unit 2 LI Section, p. 185, paragraph 4.

VI *dē Vacerrā* The question in the textbook, p. 25, should encourage the class to suggest several contexts in which a modern Vacerra praises the past at the expense of the present: sports, the writing of novels, architecture, painting, the younger generation, restaurants, etc. Ask students, "Is Vacerra's praise worth having? What is Vacerra's opinion of himself?" They should realize that Martial enjoys ridiculing people who pride themselves on the very characteristic in which they are defective. Vacerra has no critical sense, but sets himself up as an authoritative critic. Compare Sextus in Poem II. The article by Levens is helpful.

If the genre of satirical epigram seems unfamiliar or pointless to some students, invite them to suggest modern parallels ("If Martial were

Stage 36

writing today, for which TV program or magazine would he be writing?") Encourage students to express their preferences (and dislikes) from among the epigrams they have read. Ask them to memorize their favorite two-line epigram, but first recite each choice to them metrically so that they can memorize it with a poetic beat. Poems I, II, III, and V contain elegiac couplets; epigrams IV and VI, hendecasyllabic lines. Memorization of an epigram will reinforce students' comprehension of its meaning and make them more aware of the rhythm.

Students have now met many instances where a word used in one part of a sentence has to be "supplied" in another part, e.g. *vīlicus medicum quaerēbat, astrologus mūrem* (Unit 2, Stage 20, p. 142, line 30); some easy examples are collected in the Unit 2 LI Section, p. 189. This linguistic feature, called ellipsis, is particularly common in poetry. Draw students' attention to it here by writing some examples on the blackboard (e.g. Epigram III.4: *nōn habuī febrem, Symmache: nunc habeō...*), and ask the class to reconstruct the sentence as it would be with the omitted words included. If necessary, start with an English example and move to progressively more difficult examples in Latin, including some where the word has to be supplied in a different person:

Mr. Smith traveled by train, Mr. Jones by car.
centuriō gladium ferēbat, optiō hastam....
senex in hortō..., servus in vīllā dormiēbat.
ego gemmās habeō, tū pecūniam....
ego in urbe..., tū rūrī habitās.
ūnum oculum Thāis nōn habet, ille duōs..........

Thāis nigrōs ... habet, Laecānia dentēs niveōs ....
  quae ratiō est? haec ... ēmptōs habet, illa ... suōs ....

If supplying ellipses is too difficult for the class, postpone this exercise until they have read more verses. Ellipsis is illustrated and discussed in a language note in Unit 4, Stage 47.

Second Language Note (*Verse Word Order: Separation of Noun and Adjective*)

The students' textbook has already included several examples of noun and adjective separation; the relevant words have usually been underlined. Now this language note provides further practice.

Amuse the class with the verse of Ennius in which the noun itself, rather than a NOUN + ADJECTIVE phrase, is divided:

saxō cere- comminuit -brum.
With a stone he split his he- -ad.

Stage Commentaries

Invite suggestions about Ennius' reason for dividing the word in this way. If students are baffled, ask if they think the *meaning* has anything to do with it.

Discuss the reason why *validā* (paragraph 5, sentence 4) agrees with *manū*, not *arma*. Remind them of the different pronunciation between the nominative and ablative singular of the first declension (e.g. *validă* vs. *validā*), and the identical nominative and accusative plural forms of neuter nouns (*armă* and *armă* etc.).

Drills

Exercise 1 Type: vocabulary
Grammatical point being practiced; adjectives in *-ōsus*

Exercise 2 Type: completion
Missing item: verb
Test of accuracy: sense
Grammatical point being practiced: deponent verbs, introduced in Stage 32

Exercise 3 Type: transformation
Grammatical point being practiced: singular and plural of nouns, adjectives and pronouns (all cases)
Since this is a fairly difficult exercise, you may need to help some students with it.

Exercise 4 Type: completion
Missing item: verb
Test of accuracy: sense and personal endings
Grammatical point being practiced: 3rd person singular and plural, perfect active and passive, introduced in Stages 6 and 30
Follow this exercise with further practice of the perfect and pluperfect passive.

The Background Material

For information on recitationes, see Paoli 171–72, Balsdon *Life* 44–45, and the lively but exaggerated description in Carcopino, chapter VII. 4. Ogilvie 12–13 and Hammond and Scullard s.v. "recitatio," have brief but helpful summaries. On the related topic of books in the Roman world, there are numerous sources of information, e.g. Kenney and Clausen 3ff., Hammond and Scullard s.v. "books," Paoli 174–85, Cowell 163–69, Dilke 136–40, Tingay and Badcock 95–96, Reynolds and Wilson 30–32, and *Omnibus* 1, pp. 1–4, and 7, pp. 21–23.

Stage 36

The quotation on p. 31 of the students' textbook is from Pliny, *Letter* I.13; read the whole letter in translation to the class. Have students study and discuss other ancient sources: Martial, *Epigrams* III.44 and 50 (the pest Ligurinus described on p. 28 of the students' textbook); Juvenal, *Satire* VII.36–47, 82–87 (arrangements for a recitatio); Pliny, *Letters* II.19; V.12; VI.17; VII.17; and IX.34. The difficulties of handling an ancient book are well illustrated by Pliny's story (II.1) of Verginius Rufus, who died from a hip broken when he slipped on a polished floor while trying to retrieve a scroll which was coming unwound. To help students visualize this mishap, refer them to the photographs on p. 29 of their textbook or to slide 35 of Unit IV.

Slides IV. 35 and 36 are from a collection from a child's grave at Colchester, England. They date from the second half of the first century A.D. and were imported from abroad. The relief on p. 29 is from a fourth-century casket for Christian relics. It supposedly depicts Jesus teaching the apostles.

The story of the historian who canceled his recitatio (p. 30 of the students' textbook) is in Pliny, *Letter* IX.27. Some scholars have suggested that the historian was Tacitus. If some students suggest that the historian was acting in a cowardly manner, point out to them that under Domitian's successors the general policy was to let bygones be bygones and not rake up memories of past crimes from Domitian's reign. Illustrate this policy with the anecdote in Pliny, *Letter* IV.22, about the informer Veiento. He will appear as a character in Stage 37.

Suggestion for Discussion

"What modern equivalents can you suggest for recitationes?" Students will probably begin by suggesting works of literature which are written for, or lend themselves to, performance, such as plays, radio dramatizations, and poems read to an audience by the author or an actor (increasingly common in recent years in bookstores or coffee houses). But encourage them to widen the field to include non-literary events which, like recitationes, are staged chiefly for publicity, such as a film première or a new car show, complete with press conferences, invited guests, and searchlights scanning the sky.

Suggestion for Further Work

The class might read more examples of Martial's epigrams, either in the original (with help from you) or in translation. Poems like I.109 (the puppy-dog Issa) and V.34 (epitaph on the little slave-girl Erotion

Stage Commentaries

"Lovey") show Martial in a mood very different from that of the epigrams in Stage 36.

STAGE 37: CŌNSILIUM

BRIEF OUTLINE
Reading passages — the emperor's council
Background material — { the emperor's council
{ the senatorial career
Chief grammatical points — indirect statement with perfect active and passive infinitives after present verb of speaking, etc.

NARRATIVE POINTS

A.D. Date	Setting	Characters Introduced	Story Line
84	Rome: palace of Domitian on Palatine Hill	Domitian's council: Lucius Catullus Messalinus, Quintus Vibius Crispus (senator and ex-consul), Aulus Fabricius Veiento, Publius Cornelius Fuscus (commander of praetorian guard).	Agricola sends a letter to Domitian, telling of his victory at Mt. Graupius, describing his method of acculturating Britain, and requesting permission to invade Ireland. Domitian asks opinions of council members, including Glabrio and Epaphroditus; this scene shows political maneuvering and characteristic behavior of the various council members.

GRAMMATICAL POINTS
indirect statement with perfect active and passive infinitives after present verb of speaking, etc.
   e.g. *Agricola dīcit exercitum Rōmānum Calēdoniōs superāvisse.*
perfect subjunctive
   e.g. *nōn satis cōnstat quot hostēs perierint.*
fear clauses
   e.g. *timeō nē inquiēta sit Britannia, dum Hibernia īnsula in lībertāte manet.*
ūtor + ablative
   e.g. *veritus tamen nē Domitiānum offenderet, verbīs cōnsīderātīs ūsus est.*
future perfect passive
   e.g. *sī Hibernia quoque ab Agricolā victa erit, tōtam Britanniam in potestāte nostrā habēbimus.*

SENTENCE PATTERN
NOM + *est* + gerundive of obligation
   e.g. *tua tamen sententia amplius est explicanda.*

Title Picture

This shows Domitian surrounded by leading members of his council (*cōnsilium prīncipis*) who take part in the stories of this Stage. Except for Domitian, the portraits are imaginary but the characters are all historical. Some notes on their careers appear in the commentary below.

Model Sentences

The setting for the model sentences is the immediate aftermath of the battle of mons Graupius, A.D. 84, in which Agricola crushed the last major effort at resistance by the Caledonii (ancestors of the modern Scots). Here he dictates a dispatch informing the emperor of the Romans' victory.

Indirect statement, which has so far been restricted to examples involving the present active infinitive, is now extended to include the perfect infinitives. The perfect active infinitive is introduced here, the perfect passive infinitive in "cōnsilium Domitiānī I" on p. 40 of the students' textbook. The verb of speaking etc. continues to be restricted to the present tense.

The model sentences contrast Agricola's original *ōrātiō recta* with the report of his words in *ōrātiō oblīqua*. One student might read and/or translate the *ōrātiō recta*, then another the *ōrātiō oblīqua*. Elicit comments from the class, either now or after they have read the next story "epistula," on the following points:

1 the change of case of *exercitus Rōmānus* etc., to *exercitum Rōmānum* etc., as in previous examples of indirect statement;
2 the new form *superāvisse* etc., for *superāvērunt* etc.

epistula

Agricola writes from Britain to announce a great victory over the Scots. In an effort to discourage insurrection and win loyalty from the conquered people, he has been somewhat lenient in collecting taxes, and has had success in encouraging native leaders to adopt Roman customs. Agricola now asks the emperor's permission to invade Ireland. He believes that this will be an easy victory, and will ensure the permanence of the Roman conquest of Britain.

This is a fictitious reconstruction of the dispatch from Agricola mentioned by Tacitus, *Agricola* 39, and summarized in the model sentences. While the contents of the letter, as given in the students' textbook, are wholly imaginary, the three main topics are consistent with Tacitus' account: the defeat of the Scots (*Agricola* 36–37); the

Stage Commentaries

pacifying and Romanizing of the tribes of Britain (21); and Agricola's belief that an invasion of Hibernia (Ireland) was necessary to complete the conquest (24). Students may recall some details of Agricola's career from earlier stages of the course, e.g. Unit 2, p. 39, and Unit 3, pp. 101–103.

Introduce or follow this passage with a reading of the translation of *Agricola* 38, in which Tacitus describes the grim scenes which followed the battle of mons Graupius. Comment on and discuss Agricola's carrot-and-stick policy of humanity to those who surrender and brutality to those who resist. Note also Agricola's tact in phrases like *victōriam nōmine tuō dignam* (line 11). Ask students, "Why might Agricola's victory be a touchy subject for Domitian?", and recall from Stage 35 the emperor's much-ridiculed triumph over the Germanic Chatti.

From time to time, as a variation from the usual procedure, ask students, on their first reading of a paragraph, to search the text for answers to a series of comprehension questions. Ask these questions orally and have students answer them in writing. For example, ask on the final paragraph of "epistula":

What is Agricola afraid of, while Ireland remains free?
What two things does he say the Romans will achieve if they overcome the Irish?
What information has he received about Ireland? From whom?
What personal belief does Agricola have about Ireland?
What mood are the soldiers in?
What is being waited for?

Since the questions themselves contain many clues to the meaning of the text, most students should be able to produce without difficulty a translation of the complete paragraph after they have answered the questions.

After students have read the entire passage, point out *redigī* (line 5) and *obtinērī* (line 27) as examples of the present passive infinitive. Review these types of infinitive further by asking students to transform present *active* infinitives of verbs from previous Checklists into present *passive* infinitives, e.g. *appellāre* to *appellārī*. For non-deponent verbs (in their perfect active indicative forms) from the Checklists of Stages 1–30, consult Unit 2 Teacher's Manual, pp. 70–71, and Unit 3 Teacher's Manual, pp. 42 and 111. Below are listed verbs from the Checklists of Stages 31–37, grouped according to conjugations:

First conjugation: *appellāre* (32); *certāre* (intr., 33); *culpāre* (37); *damnāre* (34); *dōnāre* (36); *dubitāre* (37); *ōrāre* (31); *perturbāre* (37); *putāre* (35); *recitāre* (36); *relēgāre* (35); *revocāre* (37); *secāre* (31); *spērāre* (31).
Second conjugation: *cavēre* (intr., 35); *imminēre* (intr., 34); *invidēre* (intr., 37); *movēre* (33); *pendēre* (intr., 34).

Third conjugation: *addere* (32); *animadvertere* (36); *compōnere* (32); *condūcere* (32); *convertere* (32); *discere* (37); *effundere* (32); *exstinguere* (34); *ignōscere* (intr., 32); *impōnere* (34); *neglegere* (31); *offendere* (36); *opprimere* (32); *scindere* (32); *tangere* (36); *vehere* (31); *volvere* (31).
Third "-iō" conjugation: *conicere* (33); *ēicere* (33); *excipere* (33); *obstupefacere* (33); *reficere* (31).
Fourth conjugation: *subvenīre* (intr., 32); *vincīre* (31).
Irregular conjugations: *inesse* (intr., 35); *praeterīre* (31).
Note: intransitive verbs rarely have passive forms.

There is one example of a perfect subjunctive (*perierint*, line 12). Do not comment at this point, since the required sense is clear from the context. A language note on the perfect subjunctive will appear in Stage 38, by which time students will have encountered additional examples.

The line drawing in the students' textbook is based on a sestertius of Domitian, A.D. 84, of which a photograph appears in Tacitus (ed. Ogilvie and Richmond), plate IV. Students should observe Domitian's wreath, and the "victory" motif on the reverse of the coin, showing a triumphant horseman and his fallen enemy. (Cf. Filmstrip 2, frame 33; slide II.60). The legend reads:

IMP(ERATOR) CAES(AR) DIVI VESP(ASIANI) F(ILIVS)
DOMIT(IANVS) AVG(VSTVS) GERM(ANICVS) CO(N)S(VL) X
P(ONTIFEX) M(AXIMVS) TRIB(VNICIA) P(OTESTATE) III
IMP(ERATOR) VII P(ATER) P(ATRIAE) S(ENATVS)
C(ONSVLTO)

(Imperator Caesar, son of the divine Vespasian, Domitianus Augustus Germanicus, consul for the tenth time, chief priest, holder of tribunician power for the third time, imperator for the seventh time, father of his country: by decree of the senate.)

amīcī prīncipis

In Rome, the emperor's council (consisting of several statesmen, and the emperor's freedman Epaphroditus) has been summoned to the palace at dawn. In a corner, the elderly senator Crispus, who will be called on first in any discussion, is trying to find out from Messalinus why the emperor has summoned them. Messalinus, however, does not know, and when Crispus asks him to support whatever opinion he expresses, the wily Messalinus replies that he will offer no opinion until he hears what Epaphroditus has to say.

The first speaker in the dialogue, Lucius Valerius Catullus Messalinus (on right of picture), is much criticized in the ancient sources as a lackey

Stage Commentaries

of Domitian and an enthusiastic advocate of the death penalty for "crimes" of *maiestās*. His blindness, says Pliny, *Letter* IV.22, made him all the more inscrutable. Like several characters in this Stage, Messalinus appears in Juvenal, *Satire* IV, a witty description of a meeting of the council, parodying an almost completely lost poem by Statius. Messalinus is described there in lines 133ff.; see Duff's edition 185–86 for commentary.

The second speaker, Quintus Vibius Crispus, was a gifted politician with a talent for making clever remarks. When he was once asked whether anybody was with the emperor, he replied *"ne musca quidem,"* alluding to Domitian's bizarre habit of stabbing flies with a stylus. According to Tacitus, *Histories* II.10, Crispus belonged *"inter claros magis quam inter bonos."* He is described at length in Juvenal's parody, *Satire* IV.81–93 (see Duff 182–83).

After students have read this passage, ask them what impression of Domitian they have gotten from Messalinus' and Crispus' conversation about him.

Observe how students are coping with examples of the 1st and 2nd persons passive, such as *perturbāris* (line 7), *perturbor* (line 9) and *rogābor* (line 10). If some are having problems, review the forms by asking them to turn to the LI Section, p. 296, and with the tables there, to put together parallel forms on the stems of verbs from Checklists 31–37 (see above, p. 40).

First Language Note (*Indirect Statement with Perfect Active Infinitive*)

Consolidate students' knowledge of this point in some of the following ways:

1 Practice further examples of the perfect active infinitive (formed from verbs in previous checklists), both in isolation (*dūxisse* "to have led") and in the context of an indirect statement (*crēdō Agricolam mīlitēs in Calēdoniam dūxisse* "I believe that Agricola has led his soldiers into Scotland").
2 Compare *puer cantat* and *dīcō puerum cantāre* etc. with *puer cantāvit* and *dīcō puerum cantāvisse* etc.
3 Write some examples of *oratio recta* on the blackboard, e.g. *coquus cēnam parāvit*, for the class (working together with you) to transform into *oratio obliqua* after *dīcō*, e.g. *servus dīcit coquum cēnam parāvisse* etc.
4 Pick out examples of indirect statement from the reading material and ask the class to identify the infinitives and subject accusatives, as in step 5 above, p. 27.

Stage 37

If students recognize the *-isse* ending of the perfect infinitive from their previous experience of the pluperfect subjunctive, confirm that there is a connection between the two forms and compare (with examples) the connection between present infinitive and imperfect subjunctive.

cōnsilium Domitiānī

In the midst of Crispus' conversation with Messalinus, the emperor enters with Epaphroditus. The freedman reads Agricola's letter to the group; Domitian, masking his own feelings on the matter, asks Crispus for his recommendation. The old man, unwilling to commit himself, merely advises "moderation." When the emperor requests him to clarify this ambiguous statement, Crispus is rescued by the bolder Fabricius, who interrupts to suggest that Agricola has underestimated the ease of the proposed invasion of Ireland. Cornelius Fuscus, in his turn, goes still further, declaring that Agricola is wasting his time in Britain with empty conquests of primitive tribes and his Romanization policy. What is needed, says Fuscus, is a firmer hand in the collection of tribute. He concludes that Agricola should be recalled from Britain, and punished. Glabrio is indignant at the trivialization of Agricola's military success, and recklessly praises Agricola as the greatest general of the age, more deserving of a triumph than any other.

Epaphroditus breaks the stunned silence which follows Glabrio's defense of Agricola by pointing out to Glabrio the emperor's "glorious" victory over the Germans. Messalinus, taking his cue from the freedman, adds his support to Epaphroditus' assertions, further suggesting that Agricola, carried away by his own success, might very well be corrupted by power and try to seize the principate; Messalinus compares Agricola to the usurper, Galba. He recommends that Agricola be recalled, praised, and then "removed." Glabrio, grimly aware of the implications of his position as the only dissenter in the group, is alone silent: the others are only too eager to agree with Messalinus. The emperor, however, dismisses the council without dropping his guise of neutrality. He sits alone then, reflecting on the matter of Glabrio and Agricola.

This story, though long, is simple in structure. The emperor poses a question to his council, six speakers give their views, a majority opinion is reached, and the council ends. The illustrations emphasize this basic structure, with portraits of each of the main speakers placed by their opening remarks.

Set the scene and encourage students to anticipate the story's development. They will soon realize that the council is being called to consider Agricola's dispatch, his report of the battle and his suggestion of an invasion of Ireland. Four of the six speakers – Crispus, Glabrio,

43

Epaphroditus, and Messalinus – are already known to the students from their previous reading. Ask them, "What line do you expect each of the four men to take?"

Of the two new characters who participate in the debate Aulus Fabricius Veiento had a reputation as an informer, survived into the reign of Nerva, and managed to keep his position in public life (Pliny, *Letter* IV.22), while Publius Cornelius Fuscus was appointed prefect of the praetorian guard by Domitian and later became commander of a disastrous campaign against the Dacians (a Rumanian tribespeople), A.D. 85–86, in which he died. Veiento and Fuscus are both mentioned in Juvenal's parody, *Satire* IV.111–13 (see Duff 185).

Explain the identity of Galba (II, lines 20–4). He governed Hispania Tarraconensis with great distinction, A.D. 60–68, then marched on Rome after the death of Nero and ruled as Emperor for only a few months before he was overthrown and killed.

Although most students will sense the atmosphere of hypocrisy and the calm but threatening manner of Domitian, accelerate their reading by helping with the harder sentences so that they all can keep pace with the mounting tension in the council meeting. Use questions like the following to draw their attention to motives and feelings:

What is Agricola asking the Emperor for?
Why does Domitian begin by asking Crispus' opinion?
On what grounds does Veiento oppose Agricola's plan? Does he attack him personally?
What effect does Veiento's speech seem to have on the next speaker, Fuscus? Do Fuscus' remarks have anything to do with invading Ireland? What do you think may be the reason for Fuscus' attitude?
Why do you think Glabrio overlooked Domitian's recent campaign in Germany? Do you think he simply forgot? Why?
Why do Epaphroditus and Messalinus now feel that they can safely venture an opinion? How do they exploit Glabrio's outburst? What do you think Messalinus means by *revocandus, laudandus, tollendus est* (II, lines 25–6)?

Discuss the dilemma faced by honest men in public life during the reign of Domitian. Encourage students to suggest some of the different choices open to men like Glabrio. Heroic but futile resistance was one possibility; silent inactivity and a complete "dropout" from public life was another. Tacitus asserted, however, that there was a third option: even under a tyrant (*Agricola* 42.4), a man might live and serve honorably by exercising discretion and forgoing personal ambitions. This, for Tacitus, was one of Agricola's greatest achievements. His assertion may strike some students as an apology for compromise or even a piece of self-justification (Tacitus himself rose to high office under Domitian, as did Pliny). The fact remains, however, that even under a bad emperor, the administration of the empire continued with reasonable efficiency because enough able men were willing to combine political caution with high standards of service.

The presentation of indirect statement is now extended to include the perfect passive infinitive, but contained within easy contexts. There is also a slight extension in II, lines 7–11, in which indirect statements are introduced by verbs in the perfect tense, *nōnne audīvistī* (line 7) and *num oblītus es* (lines 9–10). But because the context strongly suggests "have heard" and "have forgotten," the student is not required to translate the tense of the infinitive differently from before.

The stage contains a number of gerundives; ask students to pick them out and translate them for practice. "cōnsilium Domitiānī" has two examples of the ablative with *ūtor*, and two ablatives of comparison. For further practice, have students study the additional examples in the LI Section, p. 312, paragraphs 6f and g, and pp. 324–25 "Gerund and Gerundive," paragraphs 2 and 3.

Widdess 35 reproduces a coin showing Domitian welcoming Agricola back from Britain.

Second Language Note (*Indirect Statement with Perfect Passive Infinitive*)

Use again here some of the suggestions for consolidation above, p. 19, with perfect passive infinitives in indirect discourse.

Practice the point in paragraph 3 by requiring students to locate participles in paragraph 2, find the nouns they describe, and determine their case, number, and gender.

Use the following additional examples if necessary:

1 *suspīcor tē ab illō mercātōre dēceptum esse.*
2 *Agricola nunc affirmat Calēdoniōs victōs esse.*
3 *amīcus meus dīcit Agricolam revocātum esse.*
4 *audīmus domum patris tuī incēnsam esse.*

Drills

Exercise 1   Type: completion
             Missing item: noun *or* verb *or* participle *or* infinitive
             Test of accuracy: sense and syntax
             Grammatical point being practiced: sentence structure

Stage Commentaries

Exercise 2 Type: transformation
             Grammatical point being practiced: present, future, and
                imperfect passive, introduced in Stages 29 and 34
Sentences 3a–6b test students' ability not only to handle the correct verb form (as in previous exercises of this type) but also to make necessary changes to some of the nouns.

Exercise 3 Type: translation from English, using restricted pool of
                Latin words
             Grammatical point being practiced: perfect passive,
                deponent verbs, purpose clauses, *īdem*, present passive
                infinitive
If students need further practice, refer them to the appropriate pages of the LI Section.

The Background Material

The Emperor's Council. The definitive account of the *cōnsilium prīncipis* is Crook, *Consilium Principis*; there is also helpful information in Millar 119ff., 234ff., 524ff. The chief ancient evidence is Pliny, *Letters* IV.22, VI.22 and VI.31 (see commentary in Sherwin-White 298ff., 381ff., 391ff.), and the parody of a consilium in Juvenal, *Satire* IV (see commentary in Crook 50–52 and Duff 173ff.), in which the *amīcī* of Domitian ponder the question of a giant fish. If you present the Juvenal passage to students, paraphrase and summarize it rather than quote the full translation. The reference on p. 46 of the students' textbook to the *amīcus* who could "slit a throat with a whisper" is from Juvenal, *Satire* IV.110.

Emphasize the ad hoc nature of the *cōnsilium*'s membership, and ask students to suggest reasons for it. A man who normally attended meetings would obviously drop out of the *cōnsilium* temporarily if he were governing a distant province. If the emperor were out of Rome when he summoned his advisers, the *cōnsilium* would naturally be restricted to those who were within call.

There were long-standing precedents in Roman private and public life for the emperor's use of *amīcī*. One of the acknowledged purposes of *amīcitia* was the giving and receiving of advice, often in quite formal ways. A man might call his friends together and ask each in turn for an opinion, on anything from whether a slave should be manumitted to whether a charge of *maiestās* should be faced head on in court or avoided by flight or suicide. Roman magistrates, similarly, were always at liberty to invite *amīcī* to join them either on the bench as associates in court or on their staffs when governing a province. Thus, when an emperor invited his *amīcī* to join him in governing the empire, he was following an established practice.

The term *cōnsilium prīncipis* is applied not only to the group described in the students' textbook, but also to a rather different group established by Augustus with the official task of preparing business for the senate. It lapsed under Tiberius, and to avoid confusion it is not mentioned in the textbook.

The relief on p. 45 is part of the "Plutei Traiani," one of a pair of historical reliefs found in the center of the forum Romanum. The scene is thought to show the Emperor Trajan, possibly granting loans for the support of children in small towns of Italy. The relief shown on p. 48 (also slide IV.27) is from Aquileia and dates to the fourth century A.D. Note the lictors at the front of the procession.

The Senatorial Career. Use some of the following miscellaneous points to bring the basic facts of the *cursus honōrum* to life:

1 The eagerness of the emperors to take *tribūnicia potestās* (see coin on p. 36 of the students' textbook), which they believed helped to create a close tie between themselves and the people in the Roman streets.
2 The absence of any salary for public office, more than compensated for by the great status which it conferred, symbolized by things like the *sella curūlis, toga praetextāta,* and *lictōrēs*.
3 The role of a priesthood as a reward for achieving office and a stepping-stone to further advancement, the religious duties being often purely nominal and the priest's own religious beliefs barely relevant.
4 The difference between *cōnsulēs ōrdināriī* (who held office in January and February, and gave their names to the year) and *cōnsulēs suffectī*. (Often the emperor himself might become a *cōnsul ōrdinārius,* sometimes as a special mark of favor to the man chosen as his colleague, even sometimes an indication that the latter was his intended successor.)

The numbers of office-holders have not normally been included because they varied so much from one period to another. At the time of Domitian there were twenty quaestors and eighteen praetors. This does not mean, however, that all twenty young men who held the vigintivirate could confidently expect a quaestorship or assume a 9 in 10 chance at the praetorship, since advancement of other candidates by imperial favor could thoroughly upset such calculations.

For a full account of Pliny's career, see Sherwin-White 72–82; for Agricola's, see Tacitus (ed. Ogilvie and Richmond) 1–6, 317–20. There are some omissions and uncertainties in the summary in the students' textbook. For example, it is uncertain whether Agricola held the vigintivirate. In fact, there is much controversy whether everyone or

Stage Commentaries

only certain categories of men normally held both the vigintivirate and the military tribunate. Encourage students to compare and contrast the careers of Agricola and Pliny, focusing on the following points:

1 Pliny starts slowly, compared with Agricola; Sherwin-White 73 suggests that after Pliny the Elder's death in the eruption of Vesuvius, Pliny had no close male relative to help him launch his career. But he then accelerates, with the help of various friends, and achieves the consulship before he is forty. The acceleration came mainly under Domitian – a fact which Pliny never mentions in his letters.
2 The comparative tables indicate quite clearly the completeness of Agricola's disappearance from public affairs in the last nine years of his life. Discuss this premature end to Agricola's career, linking it with the story "cōnsilium Domitiānī." See below, "Suggestions for Further Work."
3 The policy of sending a man to the place where his skills and experience would be of most use is well illustrated by the way Agricola was sent to govern a province where he had already twice seen service. Perhaps it was Agricola's previous experience of the province that encouraged him to launch an unexpected assault on the Ordovices (Tacitus, *Agricola* 18) after arriving in Britain at the tail-end of the campaigning season.

Suggestions for Discussion

Elicit from students some of the factors which contributed to success in the *cursus honōrum*. For example:

1 Patronage, ultimately by the emperor but also by other highly placed persons.
2 Family connections, by birth, adoption, or marriage.
3 Wealth (employed, for example, in the presentation of lavish public games, or more crudely for electoral bribery).
4 Distinction in the law courts, or in the performance of public duties in the earlier stages of the *cursus*.
5 Eloquence, especially in political and legal speeches – hence the importance of a good education by the *rhētor*. Tingay and Badcock 86–94 have a useful account of the *cursus*, using Cicero as their example and showing how oratorical ability could carry even a *novus homō* to the consulship.

Words and Phrases Checklist

fīō may require further practice, both of its forms and two of its chief meanings: "become" in the present, future, and imperfect; sometimes "has been done/made" in the perfect and pluperfect. Have students study the LI Section, p. 309 (right-hand column), then (after they close their books) translate random forms like *fit, fīēbant, factī sumus*, and *factus eram*. The verb is further discussed and practiced in a language note of Unit 4, Stage 41.

Suggestions for Further Work

1 Read in translation the story of Agricola's recall, political disappearance, and death (*Agricola* 39–43). If students can be supplied with copies of the translation to study by themselves, they might explore Tacitus' innuendos about Domitian's involvement in Agricola's death and his sinister references to *rūmōrēs*. Ask the class, "What is being suggested in this story? What is actually stated? How is the suggestion built up?"
2 The class might look at particular examples of individual careers, and answer questions like "Is this man an ordinary senator or a 'high-flier'? Does his career suggest that he had any particular skills?" Contrast careers like these with those of known individuals who dropped out of the *cursus honōrum* at an early point, e.g. Ovid, as described in his *Tristia* IV.10.27–40. Contrast examples of equestrian careers, e.g. the career of Pliny the Elder. Lewis and Reinhold II, 122–29 give copious examples of both senatorial and equestrian careers.

STAGE 38: NŪPTIAE

BRIEF OUTLINE

Reading passages } marriage
Background material }
Chief grammatical points   indirect statement with future active and present passive infinitives after present verb of speaking, etc.

Stage Commentaries

NARRATIVE POINTS

A.D. Date	*Setting*	*Characters Introduced*	*Story Line*
90	Rome: house of Flavius Clemens	Titus Flavius Clemens (senator, and relative of the emperor), Flavia (Flavius' wife), Polla (their daughter), Sparsus (Polla's husband-to-be)	Domitian, childless, proposes to adopt Clemens' two sons. He also wants to marry off Polla, Clemens' daughter, aged 14, to 50-year-old senator, Sparsus; Clemens finds this hard, since Sparsus has divorced two wives, but his objections are quickly overruled by Domitian. Polla protests that she loves only Helvidius; her mother advises obedience, since Helvidius' grandfather was killed for offending Vespasian (Domitian's father). Helvidius swears to Polla that he will not allow her marriage to Sparsus to take place. Wedding is interrupted by Helvidius, who is arrested, and sent to emperor to be punished.

GRAMMATICAL POINTS

indirect statement with future active and present passive infinitives after present verb of speaking, etc.
  e.g. *prō certō habeō Quīntiliānum eōs optimē doctūrum esse.*
increased incidence of perfect subjunctive
  e.g. *Helvidius trēs diēs iam abest, neque sciō quō ille ierit.*
deliberative subjunctive
  e.g. *quid faciam?*
gerundive of obligation in future
  e.g. *prius tibi explicandum erit quārē dissentiās.*
dative of possession
  e.g. *est mihi nūlla spēs fugae.*

SENTENCE PATTERNS

ACC + INF + V of speaking, etc.
  e.g. *tē fessam esse videō.*
increased complexity of elements in indirect statement
  e.g. *prō certō habeō Domitiānum eī poenam aptissimam excōgitātūrum esse.*

Title Picture

This drawing (based on a stone relief at Mantua of a marriage ceremony) shows the *iūnctiō dextrārum*. Note the *prōnuba* in the background, the bridal veil, the *tabulae nūptiālēs* in the groom's left hand, and the presence of Cupid, carrying a torch.

Imperātōris sententia

Domitian informs his relative, Flavius Clemens, that since he himself is childless, he will adopt Flavius' two sons as his heirs; further, he will see that they are taught by the great teacher Quintilian. Flavius, who fears the emperor because his brother was killed at Domitian's order, stammers his thanks. Domitian interrupts him to add that he intends also to arrange a wedding between Flavius' daughter Polla, who is fourteen years old, and Sparsus, a middle-aged aristocrat of great wealth. Clemens dares to protest only feebly that this Sparsus has already divorced two wives, but the emperor has made up his mind, and his final words on the matter to Clemens imply that further protest would be dangerous.

Titus Flavius Clemens, who appeared momentarily in Stage 33 as the ex-master of the Christian freedman Tychicus, was related to the Emperor Domitian by both birth and marriage; for he himself was a distant cousin of Domitian, and his wife was one of Domitian's nieces. His brother, Titus Flavius Sabinus, had been put to death by Domitian in A.D. 83 for no apparent reason. Clemens seems to have been an easy-going, complaisant person who managed for some time to avoid any serious conflict with the suspicious emperor. Because by A.D. 90 Domitian had no surviving son of his own, he declared Clemens' two young sons as his heirs and assigned Quintilian to be their tutor, as described in the present story. In A.D. 95 Clemens was consul for four or five months; then suddenly he and his wife were confronted with a charge of atheism. It is possible (as with Glabrio above, p. 23) that the charge related to sympathy with Judaism or conceivably Christianity; more probably it implied some neglect or lack of respect for the official state religion of which the emperor traditionally was head. (Domitian used accusations of this kind more and more to attack actual or potential opponents.) Clemens was executed and his wife deported.

The adoption of the two boys occurred in A.D. 90; thus a gap of six years separates the events of this and the previous Stage. Nothing is known of the boys' fate after Domitian's assassination in A.D. 96. Their sister Polla is wholly fictitious; so is her story.

Expand the comprehension questions in the students' textbook to

Stage Commentaries

probe the situation and behavior of the characters. For example, lines 2–3, referred to in question 1, make it clear that Clemens normally refrains from disagreeing with Domitian. But in lines 22 and 25–26, referred to in question 4, he does disagree with him. Ask the class to explain this divergence from his normal behavior. Do the students think Clemens is likely to respond to Domitian's professed open-mindedness (*haec ... mūtābō,* line 30) and express direct opposition to the proposed marriage? (The answer will emerge in the next reading passage, "Pōlla.") How genuine, in any case, are Domitian's professions of open-mindedness?

Students may observe, either spontaneously or with a little prompting from you, that neither Clemens nor his children are allowed really to contribute to the major decisions being made about their future lives. Encourage the class to attempt a little historical explanation. The passage shows a Roman aristocratic family making dynastic arrangements by the two traditional methods, adoption and marriage. The fact that this is the emperor's family adds to the importance of the decision. The emperor needs an heir to diminish the risk of civil war after his death; and for the same reason he wishes to discourage rivalry between different branches of the *gēns Flāvia* by bringing them together in marriage.

The new grammatical point is the introduction of the future active infinitive into indirect statement, and the picture at the bottom of p. 54 illustrates the first example. Point out that the scene in the inset picture has not yet happened. It is in fact the title picture of the next stage and shows the younger boy reciting to Quintilian, while his brother reads the text. Before the class reads "Imperātōris sententia," review the form of the future participle, contrasting it with the perfect passive participle, e.g. *doctūrus* contrasted with *doctus*. If you discuss a few examples of the compound future tense, e.g. *doctūrus sum*, you will prepare the way for *futūrum esse* in line 29.

Pōlla

In a conversation with her mother, Polla is extremely upset. She does not understand why her father is so inflexible about her marriage to Sparsus, and objects that she is already in love with someone else: namely Helvidius, son of Lupus (who exchanged letters with Glabrio in Stage 35). Her mother reminds her of the antipathy between Polla's own and Helvidius' family, pointing out that Domitian's father, Vespasian, had Helvidius' grandfather killed. She turns a deaf ear to Polla's arguments, insisting that obedience to those more powerful than oneself is the only safe course to follow.

Focus during discussion on the conflicting attitudes of Polla and her mother. Encourage students to understand both points of view. Examine Flavia's comment *necesse est pārēre eīs quī nōs regunt* (lines 6–7). Who are *eīs quī nōs regunt*? Does the phrase refer simply to the emperor and those in political power? Or does *eīs* mean men and *nōs* mean women? In either case, is Flavia's comment justified? How fair is Polla's remark *nihil dē mē cūrās* (lines 11–12)? How sensible is her mother's final advice *melius est ... resistere* (lines 16–17)? Is either Polla or Flavia likely to be persuaded by the words of the other, or are both speakers wasting their breath?

Polla objects to the proposed marriage not only because she dislikes Sparsus, but because she is in love with Helvidius. Polla is the girlfriend of the young man Helvidius mentioned in Stage 35, "vīta rūstica" (see p. 8 of the students' textbook, and above, p. 26, for Helvidius and his family connections, which Flavia here disparages). The conflict between Polla's love for Helvidius and her family's plan for her marriage may raise the question of the advantages and disadvantages of arranged marriages. If any of your students belong to ethnic minorities in which arranged marriages are a present-day reality, handle the discussion with tact.

Indirect deliberative subjunctives have appeared in the material from Stage 28 onwards (Unit 3, p. 128, lines 16–17 *eōs ... rogāvit utrum vim an venēnum adhibēret*). *quid faciam?* in line 4 of the present story is the first example of a direct deliberative and is glossed as such. It recurs in the next story ("prīdiē nūptiārum," line 4), together with another example of an indirect deliberative (*utrum spēret an timeat incerta*, line 45). Do not comment excessively on this point; it will be the subject of a language note in Unit 4, Stage 48.

First Language Note (*Indirect Statement with Future Active Infinitive*)

After students have read the language note, have them pick out and translate examples from "Imperātōris sententia" and "Pōlla." Have students practice the point in paragraph 3 by asking them to pick out the participles in paragraph 2, find the nouns they describe, and state the nouns' gender and number.

Compare indirect statements involving the three active infinitives with each other. For example:

scio servōs dīligenter hodiē labōrāre.
scio servōs dīligenter heri labōrāvisse.
scio servōs dīligenter crās labōrātūrōs esse.

Stage Commentaries

If students find it helpful, compare the corresponding *oratio recta* (*labōrant, labōrāvērunt, labōrābunt* etc.).

prīdiē nūptiārum

On the day before the wedding so hateful to Polla, Helvidius steals into Polla's garden, overhears her lamenting her plight, and passionately urges her to run away with him. When she refuses, declaring that she cannot avoid her fate, he challenges the sincerity of her love for him. Broken-hearted, she assures Helvidius repeatedly that she loves only him, but she can see no way out of her situation. Meanwhile, from inside the house her mother has been calling to her. Moved by Polla's tears, Helvidius seizes her hand, and swears Sparsus will never marry her. He bids her trust him, and as he departs, she is left wondering, caught between hope and fear.

Some Suggested Questions:

What course of action does Helvidius suggest (lines 13–14, 20–22)?
Why does Polla begin to talk more urgently at line 27?
Why, according to Helvidius (lines 31–32), has Polla changed her mind?
What decision has Polla made? Why has she made this decision? Is she right?

priusquam appears in its familiar form in line 11, and as *prius ... quam* in lines 19–20. Analyze *prius ... quam* as "earlier than" or "sooner than" to make the splitting of the word more intelligible to the class.

est mihi nūlla spēs fugae (line 36) is the first example of a possessive dative. The context allows either a literal or an idiomatic translation. Provide students with additional examples, including some in which an idiomatic translation would generally be more suitable than a literal one, e.g. *est mihi magna nāvis*.

The passage contains several verbs in the future tense, both active and passive. Drill students orally in the forms, e.g. have a student translate *ēripiam* in line 14, and then ask other students, "What would *ēripiet* mean? And *ēripiētis*? What would be the Latin for 'we shall praise'? What would be the meaning of *ēripient*? *ēripientur*?" etc.

Second Language Note (*Perfect Subjunctive*)

When students are studying paragraph 4, encourage them to explain in their own words the difference between the forms of the perfect indicative and the perfect subjunctive. Then refer them to the LI Section, p. 299, paragraph 3, to determine whether the same rule applies in the second, third and fourth conjugations.

cōnfarreātiō

On her wedding day, the unhappy Polla is decked out in traditional bridal costume, and goes through the motions of the elaborate pre-nuptial rituals, before she is led off to the ceremony, which is presided over by the emperor himself. As Polla sits beside Sparsus, agonizing over the recollection of Helvidius' promise to rescue her and scarcely hearing the commotion of prayers and sacrifice going on around her, he notices her distraction, but seems to mistake it for merely the anxiety of a young bride. After the rite has been completed, the traditional grain-cake eaten, the wedding contract signed, and the banquet finished, the bridal procession sets out for Sparsus' house, where Sparsus has already gone on ahead to await his bride. During the ceremonies at the door of the house – the exchange of formulaic ritual utterances between the bride and groom and the anointing of the doorposts with oil to avert the evil eye – Helvidius suddenly bursts from the crowd, armed with a dagger. He makes straight for Sparsus, who defends himself from the attack and calls for help, which soon arrives. Helvidius is eventually restrained by some slaves, and led off under arrest, to Domitian. Sparsus, meanwhile, misguidedly attempts to comfort Polla in her distress, by assuring her that Domitian will devise a suitable punishment for this crazed young man whom he recognizes as "most hostile to the imperial family." Polla is, of course, horrified, but she is entirely helpless. Sparsus carries her into his house.

Do this story rapidly at first reading; divide the class into groups and ask each group to prepare a section as homework so that you can cover as much of the story as possible in a single lesson. Use the various hints about Polla's appearance and feelings to make sure that students do not lose the main thread of the story, and bring out the contrast between Polla's internal tension and the outward display of dignified and picturesque ritual. Later, during the discussion, concentrate on the details of the ceremony itself, linking the reading material with points from the background section (students' textbook, pp. 67–71, and below, pp. 57–59). Both pictures here and the title picture illustrate many details: on p. 62 note the sacrificial pig, the *pronuba* standing behind the bride and groom, who are seated on a sheepskin, the bride's veil; and on p. 64 note the pipe-players and torch-bearers, the boys attending the bride, the one behind carrying the spindle and distaff, the children scrambling for the nuts thrown by the bridegroom, the shouting onlookers.

Consider also the character of Sparsus. Does Polla's previous view of him as an ogre seem justified? Might her view have been colored by her feelings for Helvidius? Or is Sparsus in any case likely to be at pains to appear considerate and affectionate on the present occasion, and very

Stage Commentaries

pleased with himself at having secured a bride from the imperial family?

There is a small grammatical advance in I, lines 4, 22–23 and 29 where a verb of speaking, perceiving etc. follows an indirect statement instead of preceding it, e.g. *tē fessam esse videō*. As the examples are all short and straightforward, and in one case illustrated by a line drawing, they are unlikely to cause much difficulty. Make up additional examples if necessary.

The song in II, lines 4–5 and 9–12 is from Catullus 61.

The passage contains many opportunities for reviewing different sorts of participles. There are also several examples of the present tense of the passive. Drill these in the manner described above, pp. 24–25, extending the examples from the present to the future and imperfect tenses, so that *dūcitur*, for example, is contrasted not only with *dūcuntur* or *dūcor*, but with *dūcēbātur* or *dūcētur*. Drill in the same manner some of the deponent verbs whose present tense appears in the story.

For an illustration of a bride being dressed and adorned, see Balsdon *Roman Women* 176.

Third Language Note (*Indirect Statement with Present Passive Infinitive*)

Use the following examples if students require further practice:

amīcus meus dīcit illam tabernam ā lībertō dīvitissimō tenērī.
centuriō crēdit novās cōpiās ab Imperātōre iam mittī.
audiō bellum terribile in Britanniā gerī.
suspicor fīliam meam ā multīs iuvenibus amārī.

Drills and Further Practice

Exercise 1   Type: completion
             Missing item: verb
             Test of accuracy: personal endings
             Grammatical point being practiced: 1st, 2nd, and 3rd
                persons singular and plural, present subjunctive,
                introduced in Stage 36
Exercise 2   Type: transformation
             Grammatical point being practiced: indirect statement with
                present active infinitive, introduced in Stage 35

This stage would be a suitable point to begin consolidation work based on the "Morphology" and "Syntax" parts of the LI Section; see below, pp. 201–209, for commentary. Pay attention in particular to one or two features (e.g. the ablative of comparison) which have appeared occasionally in the readings but have not been the subject of a stage

Stage 38

language note. Consolidation work of this kind is particularly effective when done for a few minutes at the beginning of every period.

During this Stage and the next, review indirect statement, providing practice in all five infinitives encountered so far, but continue to restrict the verb of speaking, believing etc. to the present tense. Use examples in the LI Section, pp. 319–20. Students should discriminate accurately between the different tenses of infinitive and translate them with the correct English forms; in Stage 40 they will be required to handle these infinitives in combination with a *past* verb of speaking.

If time allows, give students practice in listening. Read a passage from the latter part of Unit 3 or an earlier Stage of Unit 4 and have the class follow by ear alone. Pause from time to time and make sure, with comprehension questions, that they are following the story.

The Background Material

In dealing with the immense topic of Roman marriage and the position of women, your greatest problem will be one of selection. Allow, therefore, as much time for research and discussion as time and class interest allow.

There are useful accounts in Paoli 113–18, Cowell 57–63, Carcopino, chapter IV. 2–5, and Balsdon *Life* 82–90, 115–21, and 237–39. Especially valuable are Balsdon *Roman Women* (an excellent general survey), Crook *Law and Life* 99–106 (for the relationship between legal and social aspects of marriage) and Corbett (on the laws and ceremonies). Hammond and Scullard have helpful short articles s.v. "marriage (law of)," "marriage ceremonies" and "*manus*."

Relate the background material where possible to the Latin readings and their accompanying illustrations. Ask the class to pick out from the drawings on pp. 62 and 64 of their textbook as many features as possible that are mentioned in the background material (see above, p. 55). The engagement ring shown on p. 68 dates from the fourth century A.D. and is in the British Museum, London. The photograph on p. 70 shows part of a relief from a sarcophagus of the time of Hadrian in the Louvre, depicting the various stages of childhood. The whole relief is reproduced in C.S.C P. *Pompey and Caesar*, p. 8.

While discussing the topic with students, introduce some of the following points into the discussion:

Early marriage of girls. Agricola's daughter, for example, married Tacitus when she was thirteen; at the same age, Quintilian's wife bore him their first son. Hopkins ("Age of Roman Girls at Marriage" 317) points out some of the social and psychological implications of Roman marriage:

the relatively strong possibility of early widowhood for the wife (since her husband might be much older than she) and early widowerhood for the husband (since his wife might well die in childbirth), and the likelihood that because of infant mortality few if any children would survive to adolescence. Some of the inscriptions in C.S.C.P. *Roman World* (e.g. items 1, 40, 46, 59) vividly illustrate these points.

Marriage "cum manū." Besides *cōnfarreātiō*, the forms of marriage *cum manū* were *coēmptiō*, in which the groom placed copper coins on a pair of scales and claimed ownership of the bride (possibly a relic of bride purchase) and *ūsus*, in which the marriage was established by cohabitation for a year (but under a law of the Twelve Tables, if the wife was absent from the conjugal home for three consecutive nights, the *manus* was nullified, i.e. the marriage reverted to *sine manū*).

Ceremonies. There was much variation in the number and sequence of ceremonies with which a marriage was celebrated. For example, the *iūnctiō dextrārum* and the response *"ubi tū Gāius, ego Gāia"* might occur at various points in the proceedings. Stress that, as far as the law was concerned, the ceremonies were superfluous (except as "evidence") – "If you lived together 'as' man and wife, man and wife you were" (Crook *Law and Life* 101). Similarly, if a couple are married in a present-day religious ceremony, what marries them in the eyes of the law is not the ceremony but the signing of the register.

Restrictions on marriage. Senators were not allowed to marry freedwomen, but a senator could live with a freedwoman in concubinage, a relationship which might differ from marriage only in respect of the two parties' legal status. Slaves were not allowed to marry; nor were soldiers. However, when a soldier was discharged, an existing relationship between him and a woman could become legally recognized, and any children were retroactively legitimized.

The quotations in the students' textbook are from Pliny, *Letters* VII.5 and IV.19; Cicero *ad Atticum* V.1; *C.I.L.* VI.11602, 29580, and 29149. Ask questions about some of these; for example, when students are studying the second quotation, ask, "Why does Calpurnia stay behind a curtain at Pliny's recitatio? Why is she so anxious when he speaks in court?" Further material, both literary and epigraphic, is contained in Lewis and Reinhold I, 59–60, 489, 507–509, and II, 283–86, and in the C.S.C.P. *Roman World* material (see its accompanying Handbook, p. 143). Material on marriage from Martial, Juvenal, and Petronius is excluded from the students' textbook since the distortion of satire may be misleading. But once students have gained some idea of normal

Stage 38

Roman marriage, they may enjoy a caricature (for example, there is a lively translation of Juvenal, *Satire* VI in Massey) – and even caricature must have a connection with reality if it is to be recognizable.

Suggestions for Discussion (Especially for Older Students)

1 The advantages and disadvantages of an arranged marriage in comparison with marriage entered into by choice of the bride- and groom-to-be. (See above, p. 53, under "Pōlla.") As an illustration of the process of arranging a marriage, students might study a translation of Pliny, *Letter* I.14, in which Pliny discusses in detail the merits of a prospective bridegroom.
2 The reasons for the declining birthrate in the Roman senatorial class. Possible explanations include birth control, exposure of unwanted babies, infant mortality, and infertility. Balsdon *Life* 82ff. and *Roman Women* 194–97 has a general skeptical discussion of some interesting views (e.g. that infertility was caused by lead poisoning or by the Roman nobility's tendency to marry their sons to wealthy heiresses, who owed their large inheritance to a lack of brothers and sisters). Hopkins, in a helpful discussion in *Death and Renewal* 69–98, points out a dilemma which faced many Roman *nōbilēs*: if they had only one son, he might die before adulthood, and the family die out with him; but if they had several children, all of whom happened to survive into adulthood, the family property would be fragmented between a multiplicity of heirs.

Words and Phrases Checklist

Take advantage of the Checklist containing four deponent verbs and practice all the inflections of these verbs which students have met so far, including the 1st and 2nd persons singular of the present, future, and imperfect tenses (but not the 1st and 2nd persons plural, which will be introduced in Stage 39). For example, ask the class to translate *polliceor*, *pollicēbor*, and *pollicēbar*, or *verēbantur*, *verēbāris*, and *verēbar*; or ask one of the abler students to give the Latin for, e.g. "he was afraid," etc.

Suggestions for Further Work

By further research the students might supplement the list of ceremonies given on pp. 67–69 of their textbook to produce as complete a list as possible. They might add customs and ceremonies like the dedication by the bride of her toys and *toga praetexta* on the eve of her wedding, the role of the *prōnuba* (a womanfriend of the bride's family), and the

Stage Commentaries

throwing of nuts (see the picture on p. 64). They might investigate some of the explanations (often symbolic) for the various customs; there is much material to be found in a translation of Plutarch's *Quaestiones Romanae*. Students might suggest modern counterparts to some of the Roman customs, and also quote examples where ancient customs still survive. If the class comprises students from a mixture of religious and ethnic backgrounds (Hindu, Sikh, Muslim, Jew, Christian etc.), they might be invited to bring pictures of family weddings for comment and discussion.

STAGE 39: STUDIA

BRIEF OUTLINE

Reading passages	Ovid's flood narrative (introduced by paraphrase, in a lesson by Quintilian)
Background material	Roman authors (social and historical background)
Chief grammatical points	1st and 2nd persons plural: present, future, and imperfect passive (including deponent)
	verse word order: pairs of NOUN+ADJECTIVE phrases (a) juxtaposed; (b) one inside another

NARRATIVE POINTS

A.D. Date	Setting	Characters Introduced	Story Line
90	Rome: palace of Domitian on Palatine Hill	Titus and Publius (biological sons of Flavius Clemens and Flavia, brothers of Polla, and adopted sons of Domitian), Marcus Fabius Quintilianus (rhetor and tutor to Titus and Publius)	Domitian sends for his adopted sons, Titus and Publius, to see how they are doing with their lessons. The boys recite for him a prose version of Ovid's flood myth. Titus startles Domitian and embarrasses Quintilian by talking back to the emperor.

GRAMMATICAL POINTS
1st and 2nd persons plural: present, future, and imperfect passive (including deponent)
   e.g. *cūr nōs ad Imperātōrem arcessimur?*
        sī prūdenter vōs gesseritis, neque castīgābiminī neque pūniēminī.
historical present
   e.g. *"iamque mare et tellūs nūllum discrīmen habēbant…*
        occupat hīc collem, cumbā sedet alter aduncā…" (Ovid)

SENTENCE PATTERNS
verse word order: N+ADJ phrases juxtaposed
   e.g. *"caeruleus frāter iuvat auxiliāribus undīs."* (Ovid)
verse word order: N+ADJ phrases interlaced with each other
   e.g. *"exspatiāta ruunt per apertōs flūmina campōs."* (Ovid)

Stage 39

Title Picture

See notes above, pp. 6 and 51.

hērēdēs prīncipis

Polla's brothers, Titus and Publius, who have recently been named heirs to the emperor Domitian, are studying with their tutor Quintilian. Titus is in the process of narrating a paraphrase version of part of Ovid's flood myth, when the lesson is interrupted by Epaphroditus, who brusquely summons the boys and their tutor to Domitian's presence. This frightens the boys, who assume they are in trouble, but Quintilian assures them that they have nothing to fear if they conduct themselves properly.

On entering Domitian's study, Quintilian and the boys find the emperor stabbing flies with his stylus. He does not acknowledge them at first, and the boys are nervous. Eventually, however, Domitian looks up, and calls the boys into the room with conflicting messages of reassurance and veiled menace. He then asks them how long they have been studying with Quintilian, and what they were taught on the previous day. Publius replies that they have been reading Ovid's poem about the legendary flood. Domitian praises Ovid's eloquence, but adds, to the amusement of Epaphroditus, that the poet deserved his exile, because he led a degenerate life, and offended the emperor. In answer to Domitian's next question, Publius replies that today they have been trying to render Ovid's verse as prose narrative. Quintilian adds that when they were summoned, Titus had been giving his prose version of the wrath of Jupiter, and the emperor, observing that this is a most fitting topic, bids Titus to resume the narrative. Titus does so, and then Publius is given his turn. Pleased with their progress, Domitian declares that if the boys continue to work diligently under Quintilian's tutelage, they will become famous orators and win many cases. Titus, who has forgotten his fear, pointedly asks whether they will not, in fact, win all their cases, simply because they are his heirs. Quintilian turns red, and Domitian is stunned by such directness. Finally he smiles, or feigns a smile, and dismisses the boys and their teacher, whereupon he returns to impaling flies on his stylus.

For Domitian's adoption of Clemens' sons, and his appointment of Quintilian as their tutor, see students' textbook, p. 54, and above, pp. 6 and 51.

At the start of the story, the boys are engaged in producing a paraphrase of Latin verse. This was one of the *progymnasmata* (training exercises) practiced during the transition from *grammaticus* to *rhētor* and described by Quintilian, *Institutio Oratoria* I.9.2: *versus primo solvere, mox*

Stage Commentaries

mutatis verbis interpretari, tum paraphrasi audacius vertere, qua et breviare quaedam et exornare salvo modo poetae sensu permittitur. "First turn the verse into prose and express it in different words, then change it more boldly by means of a paraphrase, shortening some phrases and embellishing others, keeping only to the general sense of the poet's words." For a helpful discussion of this passage and of other *progymnasmata*, see Bonner 255–56.

Some Suggested Questions:

What do we learn about the relative status of Quintilian and the boys from the fact that Epaphroditus interrupts Quintilian at I, line 19, and addresses the boys directly? What is the reason for this difference in status?

Why does Domitian regard (II, line 23) "the anger of Jupiter" as a very appropriate theme for the boys to recite to him?

Why does Jupiter lock up the North Wind and release the South?

What might be the reason for Domitian's long silence (II, line 61)?

What impression do you have of Quintilian's personality?

What do you think Domitian is doing in the picture on p. 74? (Domitian's nasty method of killing flies is described in Suetonius, *Domitian* 3; for Vibius Crispus' witticism on the subject, see above, p. 42).

Titus' final words, though tactless, are well-grounded. During the reign of the more autocratic emperors, it would have been very impolitic to hand down a sentence against a member of the imperial family in court.

The passage provides opportunities for reviewing *fiō* (I, line 4), the connecting relative (II, lines 27 and 32) and the present subjunctive (several examples).

Bonner has several useful illustrations of Roman education, e.g. frontispiece (boy orator); 50 (*grammaticus*); 124 (donkey as master, monkeys as students); 128 (*stilī*); 175 (schoolboy copy of lines from Menander).

The picture on p. 78 shows Domitian describing to the boys their future success in the law courts. The building in the background of the inset picture is the Basilica Julia (see students' textbook, p. 45).

First Language Note (*1st and 2nd Persons Plural, Present, Future, and Imperfect Passive*)

Start discussion from the captioned illustrations (pages 74 and 78 of the students' textbook) and the other examples of the new forms which occur in the readings. When students have read the language note, have them compare sentences with the same meaning but different surface structures. For example, compare *imperātor nōs castīgābit* with *(nōs) ab Imperātōre castīgābimur*; and *centuriō vōs redīre iubet* with *(vōs) ā centuriōne redīre iubēminī*.

versūs Ovidiānī

This is Ovid's rendering, in verse, of the legendary flood that destroyed the world. Jupiter, having rejected the idea of destruction by fire, for fear that the heavens themselves may be scorched, sends a flood to devastate the earth and destroy the human race. With the help of the South Wind, and of his brother Neptune, Jupiter brings down torrential rains and raises tidal waves, until the earth and sea are one, and the shoreline obliterated. The unfortunate humans try by various means to escape: some climb mountains, while others navigate their flooded fields and houses in boats. Fish can be found in trees; wolves, sheep, and lions alike are carried along by the waves; birds fall exhausted into the water; where once goats grazed, now seals disport themselves.

These lines, on which the paraphrase in "hērēdēs prīncipis" is based, are from Ovid, *Metamorphoses* I.253–55, 260–62, 264, 266, 269, 274–75, 283–85, 291–96, 304, 307–308, 299–300. Some lines have been omitted and others transposed, but Ovid's words have not been altered. The passage is divided into five sections.

Even after students have read the earlier paraphrase, they may find these twenty-five lines of unadapted Latin verse fairly difficult, particularly because of the new vocabulary. Begin by asking them what they remember about the flood story from "hērēdēs prīncipis" (using the picture on p. 82 as a reminder, but without turning back to the previous story), and then prepare the way for lines 1–5 by rapidly translating the first section of the paraphrase in "hērēdēs prīncipis" for the class (while the students follow the Latin). Pause periodically and ask students to supply the translation of various words and phrases which will recur in the lines of Ovid; after this, begin with the class the first section of "versūs Ovidiānī." Similarly, preface the remaining four sections with a review of the appropriate part of the paraphrase. Or, alternatively, help students, by referring them to the appropriate vocabulary at the bottom, to translate the underlined noun-and-adjective phrases before they begin reading the whole section.

The passage ends with two lines for students to read or translate "unprepared," i.e. with no corresponding sentence in the previous paraphrase. Encourage the class to see how far they can get with these two lines on their own before helping them. The position of the relative clause before the main clause, and the postponement of *quā* after *modo* in line 24, are likely to pose the chief difficulties.

Stage Commentaries

When answering question 4, some students often pick out the "fish in tree" (line 20) or the "wolf and sheep" (line 21), both of which represent a very picturesque reversal of nature, though Seneca, *Naturales Quaestiones* 3.27.13 stigmatizes the latter line as *pueriles ineptiae*, "childish nonsense." (Attract attention to the reversal in line 21 by asking, "Which two types of animal are represented here as swimming side-by-side? What is their normal relationship?") Other students are more likely to respond to the pathos of the exhausted bird in lines 22–23. After your students have studied question 4, have them examine the picture on p. 82, relating various details of the illustration to the corresponding phrases in the Latin verses.

Discussion of Ovid's "seriousness" (or lack of it) in question 6 could usefully lead to comparison with the Old Testament account in Genesis 7.11–24. If students ask whether the classical version of the myth contains a character corresponding to the Hebrew Noah, confirm that it does and tell the story of Deucalion and Pyrrha from *Metamorphoses* I.313–415.

Compare some of Ovid's phrases with the corresponding words of the paraphrase. For example, comparative evaluation of Ovid's line 13 with "hērēdēs prīncipis" II, line 33 should bring out the superior conciseness and expressiveness of Ovid's phrase *viās ... aquārum*: not only pathways *for* water, but pathways *of* water.

Lee's commentary on the whole passage is invaluable. An excellent extended prose version of the flood episode, including Deucalion and Pyrrha, with useful comprehension questions, can be found in Balme and Greenstock 6–11.

Read aloud part or all of "versūs Ovidiānī" to the class and encourage students to imitate you. Teach verse rhythm first through the ear by reading the verses aloud, and then, if necessary, through the eye by putting an ictus-scheme on the blackboard. Write one of Ovid's hexameters on the blackboard (avoiding for the moment any lines which involve complications like elision), and indicate which syllables are "long" (or "heavy") and which are "short" ("light"). Then invite students to read the line aloud, trying to make each heavy syllable last twice as long as a light one. If some of the students can follow, draw analogies with quarter and eighth notes in musical notation, or with long and short elements of sound or light in Morse code. Indicate the caesura and describe it as a place where one may pause in midline. A class with a good ear for rhythm can pursue the topic further and be introduced to the idea of "feet" (or at least to the regular DACTYL+SPONDEE pattern at the end of each hexameter), but, generally, be satisfied with the students practicing, at this early stage, the idea of syllable length. Finally, reread all or some of the passage aloud, taking care to bring out the underlying hexameter rhythm but not allowing it to distort the natural sense of the words. Allen 89–94 is very helpful on syllable length in general.

Second Language Note (*Verse Word Order*)

Discuss the effect of the word order in some of these examples. Ask the class whether there is a contrast between any pair of words in example 1 of paragraph 2, and whether the word order does anything to emphasize this contrast. Ask whether the word order of paragraph 3, example 1, and paragraph 4, example 4, has anything to do with the meaning of the examples. Elicit the point that the word *iuvenis* is placed in the middle of the phrase *mediōs ... hostēs*, just as the young man is in the middle of the enemy, and the phrase *lupōs ... frementēs* goes around the word *stabula*, just as the wolves go around the sheepfolds. Examples like these may help to make the point that Roman poets employed the various patterns of NOUN + ADJECTIVE phrases for deliberate effect, not just from willful eccentricity or clumsiness.

The English poetry in paragraphs 2 and 3 is by Ogden Nash, and from Henry Wadsworth Longfellow, "Paul Revere's Ride." The parallel with the Latin examples is not an exact one. In the English verse, the pattern of rhyme extends vertically down the line-endings, whereas in the Latin verse, the pattern of half rhyme extends horizontally across a single line. But in both cases, the patterning of words is one of the ways in which a poet can achieve his effect. What do students think is "added" to a poem by rhyme? Is the same effect sometimes achieved in Latin by word order? Some may say (but in less abstract terms than these) that in the lines from "Paul Revere's Ride" the words "church" and "tread" create an expectation in the reader which is fulfilled by the rhymes "perch" and "overhead"; similarly, in example 4 of paragraph 5, the nominative and ablative adjectives *maiōrēs* and *altīs* create an expectation which is fulfilled by the nominative and ablative nouns *umbrae* and *montibus*. In each case, the fulfillment of the expectation is, in some sense, satisfying to the listener or reader.

Drills

Exercise 1   Type: vocabulary
              Grammatical point being practiced: nouns in *-men, -mentum*

Exercise 2   Type: substitution
              Grammatical point being practiced: cases of nouns in different declensions

Follow this with further review of nouns if necessary, e.g. providing

Stage Commentaries

students with an inflected form of one noun and asking them to form the equivalent of another, e.g. give them *mēnsem* and ask them for the equivalent form of *arbor, arboris*. Use nouns from previous checklists which are listed in the Unit 2 Teacher's Manual, p. 68, in the Unit 3 Teacher's Manual, pp. 51 and 74, and for Stages 27–39:

First declension, feminine: *arrogantia* (28); *audācia* (29); *catēna* (31); *causa* (36); *cōpiae* (pl., 38); *corōna* (29); *dextra* (38); *dīvitiae* (pl., 30); *familia* (38); *fuga* (33); *iniūria* (30); *īnsidiae* (pl., 27); *īra* (28); *lectīca* (34); *lingua* (28); *littera* (39); *litterae* "letters" (pl., 39); *patria* (37); *rēgīna* (33); *tenebrae* (pl., 34).

Second declension, masculine: *ager, agrī* (35); *campus* (39); *capillī* (pl., 39); *discipulus* (36); *dīvus* (37); *iocus* (27); *līberī* (pl., 29); *lūdus* (30); *magister, magistrī* (30); *patrōnus* (31); *populus* (29); *praefectus* (37); *stilus* (39); *ventus* (28); *vīcīnus* (35).

Second declension, neuter: *arma* (pl., 36); *aurum* (37); *beneficium* (28); *bracchium* (38); *dubium* (30); *exemplum* (37); *ferrum* (29); *gaudium* (34); *indicium* (34); *initium* (37); *iussum* (27); *odium* (37); *officium* (35); *ōsculum* (27); *praemium* (27); *proelium* (37); *sepulcrum* (30); *silentium* (27); *studium* (39); *supplicium* (35); *tēctum* (33); *testāmentum* (28); *vestīmenta* (pl., 34).

Third declension, m. or f.: *arbor, arboris* f. (39); *auctor, auctōris* m. (34); *avis, avis* f. (32); *cliēns, clientis* m. (31); *comes, comitis* m. or f. (27); *coniūnx, coniugis* f. (37); *dolor, dolōris* m. (29); *dux, ducis* m. (31); *favor, favōris* m. (31); *fax, facis* f. (27); *fīnis, fīnis* m. (36); *fragor, fragōris* m. (39); *fraus, fraudis* f. (31); *hērēs, hērēdis* m. or f. (28); *ignis, ignis* m. (36); *labor, labōris* m. (32); *lēx, lēgis* f. (38); *lībertās, lībertātis* f. (32); *lūx, lūcis* f. (29); *mēns, mentis* f. (38); *mēnsis, mēnsis* m. (39); *mōs, mōris* m. (31); *occāsiō, occāsiōnis* f. (37); *opēs, opum* f. (pl., 28); *ōrātiō, ōrātiōnis* f. (39); *pavor, pavōris* m. (30); *pontifex, pontificis* m. (38); *potestās, potestātis* f. (33); *praecō, praecōnis* m. (31); *quiēs, quiētis* f. (29); *ratiōnēs, ratiōnum* "accounts" f. (pl., 31); *regiō, regiōnis* f. (36); *salūs, salūtis* f. (29); *sēdēs, sēdis* f. (30); *sōl, sōlis* m. (30); *soror, sorōris* f. (30); *sors, sortis* f. (29); *tempestās, tempestātis* f. (30); *timor, timōris* m. (30); *ultiō, ultiōnis* f. (34); *vestis, vestis* f. (38); *virgō, virginis* f. (35).

Third declension, neuter: *carmen, carminis* (29); *certāmen, certāminis* (27); *corpus, corporis* (28); *discrīmen, discrīminis* (39); *genus, generis* (39); *līmen, līminis* (38); *opus, operis* (30); *rūs, rūris* (35); *scelus, sceleris* (29); *tempus, temporis* (31).

Fourth declension, m. or f.: *aditus* m. (27); *adventus* m. (27); *cāsus* m. (32); *cōnsulātus* m. (34); *cursus* m. (29); *exercitus* m. (37); *gemitus* m. (28); *manus* "band (of men)" f. (27); *metus* m. (28); *strepitus* m. (30); *vultus* m. (31).

Fifth declension, feminine: *rēs (adversae), rērum (adversārum)* (pl., 32); *spēs, speī* (28).

Exercise 3   Type: completion
            Missing item: verb
            Test of accuracy: sense
            Grammatical point being practiced: 1st and 2nd persons
               singular, present, future, and imperfect passive,
               introduced in Stage 35

Exercise 4   Type: transformation
            Grammatical point being practiced: indirect statement with
               perfect active and passive infinitives, introduced in Stage
               37

On the need to consolidate indirect statement at this point, see above, p. 27. Have the class, with your help, practice turning some of the direct statements in Stages 38 and 39 into indirect statements after a present verb of speaking etc. (e.g. *Ovidius dīcit, Titus affirmat* etc.). Note that students have not met the future passive infinitive, and are unlikely to do so for some time.

The Background Material

Kenney and Clausen 3ff. are invaluable. There is helpful material in Ogilvie 11–17, and in the accounts referred to on p. 36 above. A selection from the following points may be useful in supplementing the background material (the sub-headings follow roughly the order in which information is presented in the students' textbook):

Publishing. Emphasize that in classical times there was no such thing as "publishing" in the modern sense. To a Roman author, "publishing" meant "allowing one's work to circulate freely and be copied." Students might consider the changes which resulted from the invention of printing.

Lack of payment for authors. As there was no law of copyright, it was open to anyone to make as many copies as he wanted of any book to which he had access (hence Martial's gibe at the bookseller Tucca on p. 23 of the students' textbook). Juvenal and Martial grumble frequently about the poor financial rewards for writers (e.g. Juvenal, *Satire* VII; Martial, *Epigram* III.38).

Patronage and imperial favor and disfavor. For Horace's introduction to Maecenas, see *Satire* I.6.56ff. While discussing with students the different ways in which authors reacted to the dangers of expressing outspoken opinions under the principate, draw a contrast between Martial and Statius (both of whom took care to flatter Domitian), Pliny, Tacitus, and Juvenal (who published nothing during Domitian's reign), and Lucan (whose outspokenness led to a quarrel with Nero and eventually to Lucan's execution).

Stage Commentaries

Public awareness of literary work. Emphasize the point made in the students' textbook, that close acquaintance with Latin literature was the exclusive preserve of a highly educated minority. On the other hand, the presence of occasional literary quotations among the graffiti of Pompeii (e.g. *conticuēre omnēs* from Vergil *Aeneid* II.1) suggests that some snippets of Latin verse may have been widely familiar even among the uneducated (cf., in English, "To be or not to be..."). The public libraries (see Hammond and Scullard, s.v. "libraries") provided some opportunities for those who were interested in reading literary works but could not afford to have copies made for themselves.

Quintilian's comment on Ovid. This occurs in *Institutio Oratoria* X.1.88, in the course of Quintilian's survey of Greek and Roman authors.

Greek literature. The link between Greek and Latin literature could be demonstrated by listing the names of any Greek and Roman authors known to the students, writing them on the blackboard with Greek authors in one column and Roman authors in another, and pointing out links between particular Roman authors and particular Greek predecessors (e.g. Vergil and Homer).

Reading aloud. Saint Augustine's description of Saint Ambrose reading to himself comes from *Confessions* VI.3.

In addition to the example quoted on pp. 90–91 of the students' textbook, demonstrate other stylistic consequences of the spoken nature of Latin literature, such as the tendency of Silver Age writers to round off a paragraph or section with a short striking *sententia* (e.g. *solitūdinem faciunt, pācem appellant,* Tacitus, *Agricola* 30), crisply summing up the previous argument and signaling the end of a section and a moment for applause (like a coda in music, or the closing of a theater curtain). Students can observe the same tendency in present-day political speeches, where each section of argument may end with a cue-like slogan which can often prompt wild applause from the audience. Students might compare the content of political speeches on television and the reports of these in newspapers. "Do the newspaper reports emphasize the content of a speech or simply repeat and comment on the slogans? What part(s) of the spoken speech is missing from the newspaper report? What are some of the differences between a spoken and a written speech?"

Suggestions for Discussion

1 "Why did an author allow booksellers to copy his work if it brought him no financial profit?" Encourage students to explore the various

explanations: that the booksellers' copyists enabled a man to bring his work before a larger public; that a politician like Caesar might write accounts of his exploits in order to propagandize for his policy; and that for many writers, fame (immediate or posthumous) was a far more powerful incentive than financial reward. Link the last point with previous discussion of *dignitās* and illustrate it from a passage such as Lucretius I.922ff.; Horace, *Odes* III.30; Ovid, *Amores* I.15 or *Metamorphoses* XV.871ff.

2 Ask students who dislike the notion of a poet flattering his patron, or criticize the practice of literary patronage because it encourages hypocrisy or servility, to explore some of the underlying issues. For example, is it necessarily wrong for a poet to express sentiments which he knows will be shared by his patrons or intended readers? Does this apply equally to jingoistic poets, nature poets, or rock-and-roll lyricists? While discussing with students literary patronage in its classical Roman context, mention considerations like the poet's obligation to repay his patron for favors received, the long-established tradition that praise of a ruler or other individual was an appropriate theme for poetry, and (in the case of the Augustan poets) genuine relief that the *pāx Augusta* had brought civil war to an end.

The relief shown on p. 89 dates to the third century A.D. from Neumagen, Germany, and is now in the Trier Museum (see slide IV.25). For more information on Roman education, see Unit 1, Stage 10, and Unit 1 Teacher's Manual, p. 87. The relief on which the seventeenth-century drawing on p. 91 was based is now lost but also came from Neumagen. It shows how books were stored; note the labels missing from some of the rolls (see students' textbook, p. 31).

Words and Phrases Checklist

Comment on some of the words in this Checklist, e.g. the connection between *littera* and *litterae*, or the different meanings of *discrīmen* and *studium*.

Have students practice the cardinal numerals in the Checklist by giving them Latin arithmetic problems, e.g *"quot sunt duo et trēs?"* and *"quot sunt bis quattuor?"* and the like.

Stage Commentaries

STAGE 40: IŪDICIUM

BRIEF OUTLINE

Reading passages — the trial of Salvius
Background material — Roman law courts
Chief grammatical points — indirect statement with present active and passive, perfect active and passive, and future active infinitives after past verb of speaking, etc.
gerundive with *ad*

NARRATIVE POINTS

A.D. Date	*Setting*	*Characters Introduced*	*Story Line*
Switchback: 87	Rome: Curia (Senate House)	Lucius Ursus Servianus (presiding judge), Vitellianus (son of Salvius and Rufilla)	Salvius is accused by Glabrio of forging Cogidubnus' will and of other crimes in Britain. Memor is one of the chief witnesses against him. Domitian keeps a low profile at first, hoping that Salvius will not implicate *him*. Domitia, restored to favor, plots revenge on Salvius. Quintus, who has come to Rome from Britain, testifies against him; an angry mob is now out for his blood; Rufilla abandons him; their son stands by him. Salvius decides not to reveal Domitian's involvement in his own crimes, so as not to endanger his son further; he makes his will and attempts suicide, but is thwarted, and condemned to five years in exile. Haterius bravely accompanies his old patron. Glabrio and Quintus are rewarded with the favor and support of the emperor. Myropnous declines an offer of freedom, satisfied that Paris has been avenged at last.

70

Stage 40

GRAMMATICAL POINTS

indirect statement with present active and passive, perfect active and passive, and future active infinitives after past verb of speaking, etc.
  e.g. *prīmus accūsātor affirmāvit multa scelera ā Salviō in Britanniā commissa esse.*
gerundive with *ad*
  e.g. *magna senātōrum multitūdō ad causam audiendam in cūriā convēnit.*

SENTENCE PATTERNS

increased complexity in indirect statement, including:
  gerundive of obligation
  e.g. *aliī exīstimābant Domitiānī īram magis timendam esse quam minās accūsantium.*
subordinate clauses
  e.g. *dīxit Salvium domī statuam suam in locō altiōre quam statuam prīncipis posuisse; imāginem dīvī Vespasiānī quae aulam rēgis Cogidubnī ōrnāvisset ā Salviō vīlī pretiō vēnditam esse.*
further examples of verb of speaking, etc., placed after indirect statement or omitted
  e.g. *affirmāvit Salvium superbē ac crūdēliter sē in Britanniā gessisse; cōnātum esse necāre Ti. Claudium Cogidubnum, rēgem populō Rōmānō fidēlissimum et amīcissimum; rēge mortuō, Salvium testāmentum finxisse; poenās maximās meruisse.*
perfect infinitive deponent
  (see example immediately above)

Title Page

This shows Quintus speaking at Salvius' trial in the curia. (Quintus is not named in the students' textbook until p. 98, and you may not want to identify him until then.) Note the scribe of the court in the left foreground; Glabrio, the first accuser, holding his scroll, next to him; Ursus Servianus, the presiding magistrate, seated on the tribunal at the end; the accused man, Salvius, standing in front of his chair; and the senators sitting on benches down the side.

Model Sentences

These sentences, like the reading material, deal with the trial of Salvius Liberalis. Salvius and two of his accusers, having appeared in the title picture in a general scene of the trial, are now presented making their speeches. The captions give their words in *ōrātiō rēcta* and then repeat them in *ōrātiō oblīqua*.

Students have so far met examples of indirect statement in which the verb of speaking etc. is in the *present* tense; because they now have to deal with examples where the various infinitives are used with verbs of speaking etc. in the *past* tense, they must adjust the way they have been translating the infinitives. Initially, encourage students to follow the contextual clues and translate as the sense requires; if they mistranslate, guide them to the required version by emphasizing the meaning rather

71

than by quoting the grammatical rule. For example, if they translate the first caption as "The first accuser declared that many crimes were committed..." etc., accept this translation, but also ask which happened first, the committing of the crimes or the speech of the accuser, and so encourage the rephrased version "...declared that many crimes *had been* committed...". If they translate the final caption as "Salvius said that he is innocent," ask them, "Do you mean the trial is still going on?" and so elicit the correction "...*was* innocent." When students have met further examples of this type of indirect statement and can cope with it adequately, introduce some discussion of tense sequences and take the class through the language note on pp. 99–100 of their textbook.

accūsātiō

Note: The final set of stories is different in style from those of the preceding Stages. It is written in an annalistic style reminiscent of Tacitus, and as if by an author who is on the periphery of events, and is less familiar with the characters than readers of the previous Stages will be.

After Salvius completed his consulship, he was accused by Glabrio of forgery. Alarmed, he asked his friends for advice on how to proceed. After hearing their recommendations, he decided to wait and see how the emperor would act. The accusers, meanwhile, prepared their case with assistance from Lucius Marcius Memor, Salvius' former accomplice (in Britain), and presented it to the emperor. Domitian responded cautiously, for fear that his own involvement in Salvius' activities in Britain might come to light. He indicated by his behavior toward Salvius that the accused man had not fallen out of imperial favor.

The emperor's wife Domitia, however, had meanwhile been reinstated, and had learned from Myropnous, the slave of Paris, that it was Salvius who had arranged the plot which resulted in Paris' death and her own divorce. She urged on the prosecutors, who demanded that Salvius be tried by the Senate. Rumors began to spread that Salvius had poisoned the king and had used curses and black magic against him, and these rumors made Salvius increasingly unpopular with the citizens of Rome. This, along with the seriousness of the charges, caused Salvius so much anxiety that he put on mourning clothes and went to solicit the help of his friends. All of them, to his great dismay, turned him away.

The trial of Salvius is historical, though the details in the students' textbook are for the most part fictitious. Pliny, *Letter* III.9.33, says that Salvius was prosecuted during the reign of Domitian, but does not

Stage 40

mention the charge; Salvius' name is missing from the attendance lists of the priestly college of the Arval Brotherhood for the years A.D. 89–91 (the list for 88 is lost), which may indicate a period of exile following his trial. He returned to Rome and resumed his legal career, though he declined the proconsulship of Asia when it was offered to him. For more information on Salvius, see the Unit 2 Teacher's Manual, pp. 5–6 and 23–24.

The students' textbook envisages the trial as taking place in A.D. 87, which would be consistent with the evidence cited above (it therefore slightly antedates the events of Stages 38 and 39, which are set in A.D. 90; see "Time Chart of Events in the *C.L.C.*, States 1–40" in Appendix E below, pp. 246–49). The story imagines a charge of forging the will of King Cogidubnus; Acilius Glabrio, who has appeared from time to time in this Unit, initiates the prosecution, and Quintus Caecilius is the chief witness on the forgery charge. Various other characters who appeared in earlier Units reappear here as a kind of reprise in this, the final Stage of the facsimile Latin readings. First the soothsayer Memor, then Salvius' wife Rufilla, then his son Vitellianus, and finally the builder Haterius show themselves in their true colors, sometimes in unexpected ways.

On the Roman habit of consulting one's friends formally in times of crisis, see above, p. 46. The students should be able to recall from earlier Stages some of the characters and events mentioned here; the crimes of Salvius, in which Domitian fears he is implicated (I, lines 17–18), include not only the poison-plot against Cogidubnus, but also the trap set for Paris and Domitia in Stage 34. Ask students also about some of the details, for example, "Why does Salvius put on mourning clothes?" (II, line 15) – an answer is suggested in the students' background material, p. 109.

Drill one or two language points after students have read the story. For instance, the DATIVE NOUN + PARTICIPLE phrase *Salviō rogantī* (I, line 5) provides a starting-point for further practice of this feature (cf. paragraph 2, and sentence 5 of paragraph 5 in LI Section, pp. 315–16; another example occurs in the next story, "cognitiō," line 22). The connecting relative is used as an adjective at I, lines 3 and 15; if this causes students difficulty, they might examine some easier examples, e.g. *quibus verbīs dictīs, nuntius discessit.*

cognitiō

On the day of the trial, Salvius and his son entered the senate house and approached the emperor as suppliants. Domitian received Salvius with his usual impassivity, which concealed whatever he might actually be feeling. The emperor read the charges, added a few details concerning

Stage Commentaries

Salvius' service under him (Domitian) and his father Vespasian, and then appointed Lucius Ursus Servianus as the presiding judge. On the first day, Glabrio presented such inconsequential evidence (such as the charge that Salvius had placed a statue of himself in a higher place than one of the emperor) that Salvius' hopes for acquittal rose, only to be dashed by the events of the second day, when Quintus appeared as a witness. Quintus recounted Salvius' crimes in a vigorous, passionate speech. Salvius, although he calmly dismissed as absurd Quintus' allegations that he had murdered Cogidubnus, had no reply to the charge that he had falsified the king's will. The sudden uproar of an angry mob outside the senate house clearly showed how public opinion had swung against Salvius. The emperor sent soldiers to disperse the crowd; Salvius was escorted home by a tribune, and no one could say whether the tribune had been sent as an escort or as an executioner.

Some Suggested Questions:

Do the emperor's opening remarks suggest favor towards either the prosecution or the defense, or is he strictly neutral?
Why do you think Quintus adds that Cogidubnus was "*populō Rōmānō fidēlissimus et amīcissimus*" (lines 19–20)?
What are the strongest and weakest points of Salvius' defense?
What indications are there of the general public feelings towards Salvius? What might have been the cause of these feelings?

On the torture of slaves (line 26), see Unit 3 Teacher's Manual, p. 52.
 The story contains one example of a conditional clause in *oratio obliqua*: *sē ipsōs Salvium interfectūrōs esse sī poenam scelerum effūgisset* (lines 28–29). There is probably no need to explain fully the complexities of this construction, as students may take it in their stride and produce the appropriate English idiom: "...would kill Salvius if he escaped...". If they ask why the pluperfect is being used in Latin, point out that if the people were to kill Salvius, that would imply he *had* escaped previously.
 The gerundive with *ad*, which has been translated in the students' textbook on its previous two occurrences in the text, appears unglossed in lines 6–7, *missum esse ad Britanniam administrandam*. If students are hesitant about its meaning, ask comprehension questions such as "What had he been sent to do?" Additional examples of this construction appear in the following stories, and it is discussed in a language note towards the end of the Stage.
 There are examples of *quī* used in purpose clauses at lines 8 and 33,

and of the participle used as a noun in line 28. After students have read the story, have them practice these points further, using the examples in the LI Section, p. 316, paragraph 3, and pp. 315–16, paragraphs 4 and 5 (sentence 2), adding further examples if necessary.

First Language Note (*Indirect Statement after Past Verb of Speaking etc.*)

Comparison of paragraph 1 with paragraph 2 should establish that in pairs of sentences such as *puer dīcit custōdem revenīre* / *puer dīxit custōdem revenīre*, the Latin tense varies at only one point (*dīcit* / *dīxit*), whereas in the corresponding English sentences, the tense changes in two places ("The boy *says* that the guard *is* returning" / "The boy *said* that the guard *was* returning"). Invite the class to account for the absence of variation in the Latin infinitive, guiding them if necessary to the left-hand columns of paragraphs 1 and 2, which contain examples of the corresponding direct statements. Encourage students to make, in their own words, the point that the tense of the Latin infinitive is the same as the tense of the original direct statement. Have them practice the point with an example: take an indirect statement like "He said that the enemy were coming," ask what the words of the original speaker were, paying particular attention to their tense, and then ask what tense of infinitive Latin would use in the indirect statement.

Some students (but not all) are helped by a general rule that if the verb of speaking etc. is in the past, then the tense of the infinitive goes back one step in time when translated into English, so that a perfect infinitive is translated by "had ...", instead of "has ...", a present infinitive by "was..." instead of "is...", and a future infinitive by "would..." instead of "will...".

Perhaps the hardest examples are those in which a past verb of speaking is followed by a *present* infinitive, requiring such translations as "he said he *was* living," "he believed they *were* governed" etc. Some students will grasp the point fairly easily, while others will not be secure until they have met many more examples in their reading. The difficulty, however, may not result from the Latin, but from the students' unfamiliarity with standard English expressions. If they translate example 10 of paragraph 3 (for example) as "The citizens knew that Domitian is often alarmed," say "Do you mean that the first-century Roman citizens knew that Domitian is often alarmed *now*?" thus guiding the class to the version "... knew that Domitian *was* often alarmed."

Stage Commentaries

dēspērātiō

Salvius' wife Rufilla, having promised at first to see him through his difficulties, on obtaining a secret pardon from Domitia promptly abandoned him. Salvius' son, however, remained with him and tried to encourage him, but Salvius declared that his case was hopeless. It was rumored that a certain document seen in Salvius' hands was a letter containing evidence of Domitian's involvement in Salvius' intrigues in Britain. Friends of Salvius urged him to bring forth any such evidence, but Salvius, mindful of his son's welfare, refrained. Instead, after making his will, he broke his signet ring, so that it could not be used against others in the future, and wrote a letter to the emperor, in which he stated that he had been loyal to the end, despite the machinations of his enemies, and begged clemency for his son.

That night, after freeing some of his slaves and giving money to others, he got into his bath, and opened his veins. Domitian, however, having caught wind of Salvius' intentions, sent soldiers to prevent his suicide. They lifted Salvius, by now unconscious, from his bath, and bandaged up his wounds.

While students are discussing Rufilla's actions in lines 1–5, they may be able to recall from Unit 3, Stage 34, that Rufilla's sister, Vitellia (the wife of Haterius), was a friend of Domitia.

Encourage full answers to the questions, some of which seek to probe character and motive. Help the class, if necessary, with the idea behind question 3, that the seal on someone's ring can be fraudulently affixed to forged documents and thus be used to incriminate others. The breaking of the ring, and some of Salvius' other actions, are modeled on Tacitus' account of the last hours of Petronius Arbiter, *Annals* XVI.19.

Students have already met the predicative datives *auxiliō*, *cūrae*, and *odiō*. Part I, line 18, introduces a further example: *ūsuī*. The point is practiced in the LI Section, p. 311. Discuss the literal and idiomatic translations of *licet* (I, line 21) and have students practice them in further examples; compare them with the literal and idiomatic translations of *placet*. Note the position of *cognōvit* in II, line 7, placed after the indirect statement which it governs; if students have difficulty with this word order, remind them of examples which they have met earlier, such as *Sparsus Pōllam perturbārī animadvertit*, or make up fresh examples, such as *nūntius oppidum hostium oppugnārī dīxit* or *cēnam parārī putābant*.

The drawing of the seal on Salvius' ring (p. 101 of the students' textbook) shows him in oratorical pose, with the basilica behind him. Note his initials C S L.

damnātiō

The day after Salvius' suicide attempt, the judge pronounced sentence on him. Salvius' name was to be erased from the *Fasti* (list of consuls); part of his property was confiscated, and the remainder passed to his son; Salvius himself was exiled for five years, and left Rome as soon as his wounds were healed. In a singular act of loyalty, Haterius voluntarily accompanied his former patron into exile. Following the trial and sentencing of Salvius, a prestigious priesthood was conferred on Glabrio, although many believed that the prosecution of this case had seriously offended Domitian. Quintus received a promise of the emperor's support in seeking office, with a warning not to aspire too high. Myropnous was offered his freedom, but declined, because, he implied, he was better off as a slave. It was enough for him, he said, finally to have avenged the death of his friend and master, Paris.

The story provides various opportunities to discuss motive and character. What, for example, might have been the reason for Haterius' acting as he did? Which characters have emerged with credit from the stories of this Stage, and which have appeared in a poor light? What do students think of the behavior of Salvius himself? Have they changed their opinion of his character in any way during this Stage? Why does the emperor behave in so ambivalent a way?

For Myropnous' vow never to play the pipes again until his friend Paris had been avenged, see Unit 3, p. 251.

The final paragraph provides practice in sentences beginning with a noun in the dative case; sometimes the subject of the sentence is expressed, sometimes not. Note how students manage with this point, and give further examples, if necessary, after they have read the story.

The drawing of Myropnous is based on a Florentine tombstone of the late second century A.D. (see Bieber 236 and 305).

Second Language Note (*Gerundive with* ad)

In this note, the gerundive is initially translated in a painfully literal way as "for the purpose of Salvius being accused" etc. to emphasize that *accūsandum* is an adjective agreeing with *Salvium*; ask students to find the noun described by each of the gerundives in paragraphs 1–3, and to note the agreement in gender and number. Once they have grasped the principle of agreement, encourage them to move as quickly as possible away from un-English literalism towards the flexible handling of a range of idiomatic versions.

The gerund with *ad* will appear in Stage 41, to be followed by other cases of the gerund in later Stages.

Stage Commentaries

Drills

Exercise 1   Type: vocabulary
            Grammatical point being practiced: antonyms
Discuss the pairs *gravis–levis, dūrus–mollis* in their metaphorical aspects as well as their literal ones.

Exercise 2   Type: translation from English, using restricted pool of
              Latin words
            Grammatical points being practiced (Stage number of
              relevant language note is in brackets): 1st person singular
              imperfect passive (35), indirect statement with future
              active and present passive infinitives (38), indirect
              command with *nē* (29) and present subjunctive (36),
              ablative absolute (31), perfect passive (30)
Provide practice in any of these features which cause especial difficulty; in some cases, the LI Section will be found to contain suitable examples.

Exercise 3   Type: substitution
            Grammatical point being practiced: relative pronouns
In this exercise, students have to combine two sentences into one by using the relative pronoun in its correct case (as in Stage 35, exercise 3) and also adjusting the word order appropriately.

The Background Material

Crook *Law* 68–97, 268–78 is full of interesting material; there is also much useful information in Balsdon *Life* 24, 79–81, 211–13, Paoli 191–204, Cowell 128–30, 161ff., Carcopino chapter VII.3, and Millar 228–40, 516–37.

The survey in the students' textbook is inevitably incomplete. As time went on, the legal machinery at Rome came to involve further officials of the emperor, such as the *praefectus urbī* and the commander of the praetorian guard (who might, as Crook *Law* 72 points out, be very much quicker than the *quaestiōnēs* at settling cases). The jurisdiction of the emperor and his officials was known as *cognitiō extrā ōrdinem*, and the emperor's role gradually extended from the hearing of appeals (such as the appeals of citizens like St. Paul against sentences of death or flogging) to the hearing of actual cases, sometimes in his *cōnsilium* as described in the students' textbook, sometimes in the more sinister private trials *intrā cubiculum* (for an example of which, cf. Tacitus, *Annals* XI.2–3).

Some Supplementary Points

Reward for successful prosecutors. This custom was open to abuse, most notoriously under the reigns of Tiberius and Domitian, and encouraged the activities of *dēlātōrēs* "informers."

Payment to lawyers. Under a decree of Claudius, any payment to lawyers was strictly at the client's discretion, and was in any case not to exceed 10,000 HS. Cf. Pliny, *Letter* V.9 for the consternation caused by a praetor who announced his intention of enforcing this decree strictly.

The description of the *cause célèbre* on p. 108 of the students' textbook is from Pliny VI.33 (translation adapted from Crook *Law* 33); the illustration on p. 78 of Stage 39, although it represents a less crowded occasion, may help the class to imagine the scene, especially the spectators in the upper galleries. The sources for the anecdotal details in the students' textbook are Pliny VI.2 (gimmicks of Regulus); Pliny II.14 (hired claqueurs); Pliny IX.23 (standing ovation); Pliny II.11 and Martial, *Epigram* VI.35 (water-clocks); Quintilian, *Institutio Oratoria* XII.5.5 (the man with the big voice); Martial VI.19 (she-goats); and Pliny IV.19 (the anxious wife). Quintilian XII.7 and 8 has some very practical and occasionally amusing advice to lawyers; and the belief that oratory declined after the fall of the Republic is discussed in Tacitus, *Dialogus* 36ff.

Students have already met two meanings of *patrōnus*, "patron" and "ex-master"; introduce them to a third sense, "advocate," and consider the links between the three meanings.

Emphasize that the man trying a case might well be a complete amateur in legal matters, and might therefore need to invite *assessōrēs* to join him in court (cf. the role of *amīcī* in giving advice, for example at the emperor's *cōnsilium*), and to obtain opinions from *iūriscōnsultī* ("men learned in the law"), who would give advice on what the law said and how it should be interpreted (Crook *Law* 25–27, 88–89). The systematic and consistent nature of Roman law owed much to these *iūriscōnsultī*.

The coin on p. 109 is a silver denarius, showing the praetor's judgment seat, the jurors' voting urn, and the letters A (= ABSOLVŌ) and C (= CONDEMNŌ).

Words and Phrases Checklist

The inclusion of *meditor, minor, ūtor,* and *videor* in the list may provide a convenient opportunity to practice these and other deponent verbs. Repeat the exercise suggested above, p. 56, with the addition of the 1st and 2nd person plural endings of the present, future, and imperfect

Stage Commentaries

tenses, which students have now met. Follow this by study of the tables in the LI Section, pp. 303–04.

Suggestions for Further Work

1 Students might look at examples of actual Roman laws. There is helpful illustrative material in Lewis and Reinhold, e.g. I, 102–109 (the Twelve Tables, the oldest Roman laws); I, 408–28 (Caesar's legislation at Rome and elsewhere); and II, 533–51 (principles of law, including the rules of evidence). Observe how the *iūriscōnsultī* and others applied the law to particular cases, either real or imaginary. The Lex Aquilia (injury through negligence) provides some picturesque instances; for example, students might study the case of the barber's customer, injured when the barber's elbow was jogged by a ball thrown from an adjacent palaestra (Crook *Law* 162–65; C.S.C.P. *Roman World* (Items 97–100)), and compare their own view with those of the *iūriscōnsultī*.
2 Read the class a description of the hearing of an actual case, taken (in excerpted form) from the translation of one of Pliny's letters, e.g. II.11 (trial of Priscus) or III.9 (trial of Classicus), in each of which Salvius makes an appearance; or read aloud extracts from the translation of one of Cicero's forensic speeches, e.g. *in Verrem* V.160–64 (the illegal crucifixion of a Roman citizen).
3 If students are older, read to them, in translation, Tacitus' account of Petronius Arbiter's easygoing character and leisurely suicide (*Annals* XVI.18–20 = pp. 389–90 in the revised Penguin translation of the *Annals* by Michael Grant), and then play the relevant segments from a video of Joseph Mankiewicz's film *Quo Vadis* (the action takes place under the Emperor Nero), based on a novel of the same name by Henryk Sienkiewicz. Because the film's portrait of Petronius is particularly vivid, compare it with Tacitus' portrait in *Annals* XVI.18–20. Finally, compare the attitude of Tacitus' Petronius at his suicide with that of Salvius in Stage 40, "dēspērātiō" II.

STAGE 41: BĪTHȲNIA

BRIEF OUTLINE	
Reading passages	Pliny, *Letters* X.17–20, 37–38, 29–30, 33–34 (adapted)
Background material	Roman provincial government
Language notes	gerund with *ad*
	fīō
	present subjunctive passive and deponent

DIGEST

The five pairs of letters in this selection provide a first-hand picture of Roman provincial government in action. They were written circa A.D. 110 to the Emperor Trajan by Pliny the Younger while he was governor of the province of Bithynia and Pontus (Asia Minor). The letters show some of the problems Pliny had to deal with, the ways in which he handled them, and Trajan's responses. They may also give students some impression of both men's personalities.

GRAMMATICAL POINTS

ad + gerund
  e.g. *melius est pūblicīs servīs ad vigilandum in carcere ūtī.*
fīō, fierī, factus sum
  e.g. *mēnsōrēs vix sufficientēs habeō etiam eīs operibus quae aut Rōmae aut in proximō fīunt.*
present subjunctive passive and deponent
  e.g. *cūrandum est, ut aqua in oppidum Nīcomēdīam perdūcātur.*
increased incidence of conditionals using the indicative
  e.g. *sī quid adversī acciderit, culpam mīlitēs in servōs, servī in mīlitēs trānsferre poterunt.*

SENTENCE PATTERNS

increased complexity in indirect discourse: indirect discourse containing an indirect statement or indirect question
  e.g. *dispice, domine, num necessārium putēs mittere hūc mēnsōrem ad opera pūblica īnspicienda.*
increased incidence of the alternative indirect question (including the third alternative)
  e.g. *incertus enim sum utrum carcerem custōdīre dēbeam per pūblicōs servōs (quod usque adhūc factum est) an per mīlitēs.*
omission of forms of *esse*
  e.g. *rēfert autem utrum voluntāriī vēnerint an lēctī sint vel etiam vicāriī ab aliīs datī.*

Title Picture

Pliny on his tribunal, dispensing justice.

adventus I (*Letters* X.17a–b)

On Pliny in Bithynia, Sherwin-White's commentary is full of useful information. Also helpful (and suitable for students as well) are Sherwin-

Stage Commentaries

White's *Greece and Rome* article (especially 86–88) and Richardson 74–78.

The "special status and special job" referred to in the introduction on p. 112 of the students' textbook can be left to emerge from the reading of "adventus" II.

Notes

(Numbers refer to lines.)

8	**excutiō:**	a lively metaphor from shaking out a bag. Draw students' attention to this verb and tell them to anticipate Trajan's double repetition of it in his reply.
9–10	**multae ... retinentur:**	refers to embezzlement of public money by private citizens who were awarded public contracts (cf. the reference to *cūrātōrēs pūblicōrum operum* in line 13), also perhaps to payments for work not done.
10–11	**quaedam ... impenduntur:**	illegal expenditures, such as pay-offs by communities to individuals.
11–14	**dispice ... agantur:**	These lines are taken from a second letter (X.17b) sent off by Pliny when he discovered the need for a *mēnsor*.
12	**mēnsōrem:**	A *mēnsor*'s main tasks were land measurement and quantity surveying (see Dilke, *Roman Land Surveyors*, especially 15–16). Pliny needs somebody to see whether the buildings have been built in accordance with the contract, thus uncovering any cases of collusion between the builders and the *cūrātōrēs operum* who employed them.

In this, as in other letters, encourage the students to interpret the text as a historical document and visualize the reality which it reflects. For example, Pliny's journeys can be tracked on the map on p. 112: he crosses the Adriatic and rounds the dangerous southern tip of Greece, then travels over the Aegean to Ephesus, site of the temple of Artemis which was one of the Seven Wonders of the World (encourage the students to contribute such details as these from their own knowledge where possible, to prevent the itinerary from becoming a bare list of names); then he switches over to a carriage, supplied as part of the *cursus pūblicus* which students may recall from Unit 3 (p. 66); overcome by heat, he pauses to recover at Pergamum (where appropriately there was a shrine of Aesculapius, god of healing) and turns back to the sea, probably at Elaea, where the etesian (modern *meltemi*) winds which blow steadily from the north from mid-June to September delay him further; his port of disembarkation is probably Cyzicus, from where he travels to Prusa (modern Bursa, Turkey) to begin his duties. Since the main administrative units in the province were cities, Pliny's governorship took the form of a continual tour from city to city.

Ask the students in what way the letter's subject matter changes at

Stage 41

line 8. They may be surprised that the personal details about the journey are included in the same letter as the official report.

The picture of prompt and busy activity conveyed in lines 8–15 may be designed by Pliny (as is suggested in question 8 of the students' textbook) to counteract any unfortunate impression made on Trajan by the belatedness of Pliny's arrival; but this interpretation should not be pressed on the students as the only "correct" one. They may have alternative explanations of their own. Encourage idiomatic translations of *ipsō* (line 14).

Slides IV.42–45 show Ephesus, a carriage, Pergamum, and the Peutinger table (diagrammatic map of the Roman empire). See also the students' textbook, pp. 113, 134–35, 136.

Vocabulary Check: (described on pp. 20–21 above) *inde* (line 2); *iter* (3); *coepī* (3); *etiam* (4); *retineō* (6, 10); *spērō* (7); *ratiōnēs* (8); *magis ac magis* (8); *videor* (9); *praetereā* (10); *quīdam* (10); *putō* (11).

adventus II (*Letters* X.18)

The evidence collected by Sherwin-White 536–46 suggests that Trajan took an active part in drafting the replies to Pliny's letters, deciding the point at issue himself and usually dictating the actual wording of the reply to the secretary *ab epistulīs* or other assistant. (Millar 213–28 reaches similar conclusions for imperial correspondence generally.) The reply would then go off to Pliny by the *cursus pūblicus*.

Notes

4   **quī ... mittāris:** This is the first time students have met the 2nd person singular form of a passive subjunctive, and its occurrence in a purpose clause with *quī* is likely to cause trouble. Give help initially, if necessary, with a comprehension question such as "For what purpose has Trajan chosen Pliny?" and analyze the verb form more fully later, when the whole letter has been read.
    meī locō: (referred to in question 1) emphasizes that Pliny is the emperor's personal representative. Unlike previous governors of Bithynia, he has been personally appointed by the emperor, and his added *dignitās* is symbolized by his title (*lēgātus Augustī prō praetōre prōvinciae Pontī et Bīthȳniae cōnsulārī potestāte*) and an extra *lictor*.

6   **tibi ratiōnēs ... excutiendae:** If the gerundive causes trouble, a simpler example may help, e.g. *tibi cēna est paranda* or an intransitive example like *tibi currendum est*.

8   **eīs ... quae:** first of several examples of *is quī* etc. in this Stage.
    operibus: The drawing on p. 115 of the students' textbook shows an

83

Stage Commentaries

example of Trajan's huge building works in Rome. In the center of the picture is Trajan's Forum, flanked by colonnades and semi-circular exedrae; on the right is the entrance, the triumphal Arch of Trajan, and facing it the Basilica Ulpia. To the left of the Basilica is Trajan's Column with libraries on either side, and on the far left the Temple of Trajan. The semi-circular building at the top of the picture formed part of Trajan's Market. See also slide IV.40. Trajan also built the great hexagonal harbor at Ostia (slide IV.41), and another at Centum Cellae, and the *via Trāiāna* running from Beneventum to Brundisium (slide IV.39).

11 **excutiēs:** Trajan's second repetition of Pliny's verb *excutere*; perhaps he is deliberately, and teasingly, turning Pliny's own wording against him to justify the refusal to send a *mēnsor*.

The concern of emperors for their public image could be brought out by asking, as a follow-up to question 2, "Did it really matter to Trajan what the Bithynians thought about him? If so, why? Would the Bithynians have even known the emperor's name, or known what he looked like?" The latter question might lead to discussion of the emperor's use of the coinage for propaganda purposes (see p. 196 below).

Sherwin-White 527 distinguishes three problems which faced Pliny: a turbulent element in the mass of the population; feuding between members of the governing class; and a financial problem, with which Pliny was especially concerned. Some public money was in private hands, while public funds were being spent illegally (cf. "adventus" I); inter-city rivalry was leading to wasteful, competitive construction projects (cf. "aquaeductus" I); private individuals were failing to pay donations which they had promised (cf. Pliny X.40). Discussion of question 4 might include a second look at the details of Pliny's *cursus* (previously met by students in Unit 4, Stage 37, p. 50), especially the two treasury prefectships. Do your students think it would have been practical to send Pliny to govern Britain, or Agricola to Bithynia?

Suggestions for Consolidation: predicative dative (line 4; cf. *odiō est*, *auxiliō est*).

Vocabulary Check: *cognōscō* (2); *brevis* (3); *ēligō* (4); *ratiōnēs* (6); *vix* (8); *etiam* (8); *fīō* (9); *inveniō* (9); *ideō* (10); *vereor* (10).

carcer I (*Letters* X.19)

Notes

3   **carcerem:** for custody, not punishment. The prisoners are held in the jail of their town until Pliny, the governor, arrives and conducts a trial.
    pūblicōs servōs: owned by the state, as their name suggests. They were employed as clerks and ordinary workers. Unlike most slaves, they received a (small) wage.

Stage 41

4 **mīlitēs:** Pliny had at his disposal at least two auxiliary cohorts and a coastal force under the *praefectus ōrae Ponticae*. The duties of the small detachment of soldiers specifically assigned to the governor's staff are described by Watson 85ff.

8–9 **nam ... poterunt:** Encourage students to read the sentence all the way through to the end at least twice before attempting to translate or answer comprehension questions.

Center discussion on the nature of Pliny's problem: Why should he worry about an arrangement that has worked well up to now? (Are the jails particularly congested and difficult to guard at present?) Why does he regard the public slaves as potentially unreliable? From what duties might he be diverting soldiers? (The class may recall examples of jobs from Unit 3, p. 84; see also Watson 72–74, 222–31.) What consequences does Pliny fear from possible *neglegentia* (inefficiency? riot? escape?)?

Encourage the class to put themselves in Trajan's place and say what they would have done; they might compare their decision with the one actually made by Trajan. Invite them to suggest solutions of their own, such as the use of a very limited number of soldiers as supervisors of the *pūblicī servī*.

Suggestions for Consolidation: meaning and morphology of *fīō* (4); fearing clauses (4–6 and 7–8; cf. "adventus" II, p. 114, line 10).

Vocabulary Check: *cōnsilium* (2 and 7, different meanings); *ūtor* + ablative (4 and 5); *vereor* (4 and 5); *interim* (6); *accidō* (8).

carcer II (*Letters* X.20)

Ask students "What do we learn from this letter, especially from line 5, about the way in which Trajan wants Pliny to carry out his duties?" Compare Trajan's disciplinarianism with his instructions to Pliny in "adventus" II to project an image of a benevolent and paternal emperor. Does the class believe that Trajan is being inconsistent?

Trajan probably fears that the withdrawal of troops for duties of this kind will disrupt training and interfere with more important work; there is no suggestion that it would involve an immediate military risk. Discuss the various duties on which detachments of soldiers might be sent, described in Unit 3, pp. 84 and 86, and Watson 72–74, 222–31, unless the class already discussed these in connection with "carcer" I.

Note how the students cope with *ad pugnandum* (line 9); it is the third gerund in this Stage, and the first to be left unglossed. A language note follows.

Suggestions for Consolidation: fearing clauses (7).

Stage Commentaries

Vocabulary Check: *ūtor* + ablative (5); *vereor* (7); *nōs oportet* (7); *pōnō* (8).

First Language Note (*gerund with* ad)

For some students, who would be merely confused by detailed exploration of the difference between gerund and gerundive, it will be enough if you take them through the examples in paragraphs 2 and 3, check that they can translate both gerund and gerundive idiomatically, and omit the final question in paragraph 3 or treat it cursorily. Older students, however, will find discussion of the difference between gerund and gerundive helpful, and can profitably explore the final question in paragraph 3. It is far better for the students to try to detect and describe the difference themselves, than for you to supply the explanation. The class will usually spot fairly quickly that the gerundive is used with a noun, and can often detect that the two are in agreement. (Prompt students if necessary by such questions as "Why does sentence 4 have *īnspiciendās* and not *īnspiciendum*?") Use the literal translation of the gerundive to elicit the point that the gerundive is passive; but if the students show signs of confusion over this, suspend further exploration for the moment and re-emphasize that, for an idiomatic translation, gerund and gerundive are generally translated in exactly the same way.

aquaeductus I (*Letters* X.37)

Notes

3   [XXX]CCCXVIII ... CC: The sums are described as "considerable but not enormous" by Sherwin-White 614, who compares the cost of the aqueduct at Troas, nearly ten times greater than that of the Nicomedians' first effort. Evidently, the second attempt had not proceeded far before it was abandoned. Encourage the class to cite any sums they know as a yardstick for comparison, e.g. the property qualification for membership of the *ōrdō senātōrius* (1,000,000 sesterces) or a legionary's annual pay (1,200 sesterces).

6   **ipse pervēnī ad fontem:** Pliny's curatorship of the river Tiber in A.D. 104–106 had given him practical experience in hydraulic engineering, and a number of his letters indicate interest in hydrostatics and mechanical engineering generally (cf. his canal proposal in X.41 and his speculations about the cause of a tidal spring in IV.30).

10–11   **lapide quadrātō ... testāceō opere:** illustrated on p. 121 of the students' textbook.

11–12   **agenda erit:** first occurrence of gerundive of obligation with future verb.

Stage 41

Roman engineering skill achieved some famous and impressive aqueducts, especially in the western provinces. (Some students will know about the Pont du Gard near Nîmes, France (slide III.32), and others of the fine aqueduct at Segovia, Spain; for a clear and interesting account, suitable for students, see Hamey 8–18.) Nevertheless, the Romans sometimes bungled their aqueducts (cf. *Omnibus* II, 5–6, reprinted in *Omnibus Omnibus* 40–41, for an example), and the bungling was all the worse when inexperienced and incompetent provincial authorities attempted over-ambitious projects.

Pliny's *mandāta* may have instructed him to refer all proposals for major building schemes back to the emperor. To judge from the correspondence, both Trajan and Pliny were worried because inter-city rivalry was frequently resulting in pretentious, overpriced projects (cf. X.39 for another example: a jerrybuilt and uncompleted theater at Nicaea, costing 10,000,000 sesterces). For the prestigiousness of building projects apart from their utility, cf. lines 14–15 of the present letter.

Follow up on Pliny's argument in lines 8–9 to make sure that the students grasp the point that water in an open channel unsupported by arches would have reached only the lower parts of the city. An alternative method, with which Pliny would certainly have been acquainted, would have been to use a closed pipe and let the water under pressure find its own level. But without cast iron the Romans lacked the technology for constructing a pipe on the required scale, capable of resisting a huge volume of water under high pressure.

Suggestions for Consolidation: present infinitive passive (7,10,13); perfect and pluperfect passive (3–4,4,8); *id quod* (13); Roman numerals (3–5; students could practice additional examples, including some involving the horizontal and vertical bars).

Vocabulary Check: *impendō* (2); *videor* (7 and 11); *dēbeō* (7); *sīcut* (7); *tantum* (8); *complūrēs* (10); *lapis* (10); *vīlis* (12); *accidō* (13); *dignus* + ablative (15).

aquaeductus II (*Letters* X.38)

Notes

3–4   **medius fidius:** This expletive is derived from the jussive clause *me dius fidius (iuvet)!* "may the god of truth help me!" and therefore has no connection with *medius* "middle."

5   **quōrum vitiō:** If students need help, ask "What does Trajan want Pliny to find out?"

Stage Commentaries

Some Suggested Questions

What arrangement does Trajan suspect has been made between the builders and the officials of the Nicomedian council? What has happened to the money? (cf. the activities of the *cūrātōrēs operum* in "adventus" I).

Does any phrase in the letter seem rather different in tone from the rest? (When students have identified *medius fidius*, ask them what they think provoked this little flare-up of imperial anger – the Nicomedians? the city's gougers? Pliny's naiveté?)

Suggest reasons why Trajan is so unhelpful to Pliny over the request for an *aquilex*.

Vocabulary Check: *efficiō* (3); *īdem* (4); *ūtor*+ablative (4); *cognōscō* (4 and 7); *tantus* (5); *ideō ... ut* (6); *tot* (6).

supplicium I (*Letters* X.29)

Watson 38–53 is invaluable for this letter and Trajan's reply.

Notes

2   **Semprōnius Caeliānus:** known only from this letter. Evidently he was the local officer in charge of recruitment for the army.
    servōs: Slaves were excluded altogether from both auxiliary forces and legions. Only Roman citizens were allowed to serve in the legions; non-citizens could serve in the *auxilia* if they were freemen, and received citizenship on discharge. The slaves referred to here were thus engaged in an illegal attempt to earn their freedom and (immediate or eventual) Roman citizenship.

2–3 **duōs servōs ... ad mē:** Use question 1 in the students' textbook to establish the meaning, and discuss the agreement of the participle *repertōs* later during consolidation.

3   **mīsit:** Cases involving capital punishment had to be referred to a magistrate with *imperium*.
    quōrum: connecting relative in unfamiliar form.
    supplicium: Slaves who falsely declared their legal status were liable to the death penalty. But Pliny is uncertain about the present status of the slaves (cf. lines 5–6) and seems to think this will affect the kind of sentence (*modus poenae*) they should receive.

5–6 **quamquam ... distribūtī sunt:** The slaves had been enlisted (*probātiō*) and had taken their oath (*sacrāmentum*), but had not yet been assigned to their unit nor had their names been registered in its roll (for all these procedures, see Watson 38–53). Pliny's problem is: do the would-be recruits have to be regarded as soldiers now, and if so, how does this affect their punishment?

Stage 41

5   **sacrāmentum:** oath of loyalty to the emperor, sworn by the recruit upon enlistment. Watson 49–50 gives examples.

First focus discussion on the nature of the slaves' offense (see on line 2, *servōs*, above). Students might consider why slaves should be willing to run the risk of execution. The benefits (freedom and citizenship) were considerable, and once they were in the army the chances of detection were probably low, since it was likely that they would be sent away from their home territory.

Next, ask the class to consider the legal technicality that bothers Pliny (see on lines 5–6 above): should the slaves be considered soldiers or not? As with other texts in Stage 41, ask "What would you do in Pliny's situation?" Some students may reach Trajan's conclusion that there is more than one person or group of persons who could be at fault here.

On enlistment procedures, review with students some details from Unit 3, p. 82, which can be supplemented from Watson.

Vocabulary Check: *reperiō* (3); *supplicium* (3); *ideō* (4); *nōndum* (5); *dēbeō* (7); *praesertim* (7).

supplicium II (*Letters* X.30)

Notes

4–5 **voluntāriī ... datī:** Whether the Roman army outside Italy depended mainly on draftees or volunteers is a matter of scholarly debate; but it is clear from this letter that in Bithynia both volunteers and draftees were enlisted. It was also possible for a draftee to send a substitute in his place, provided that the substitute was a freeman and met the required physical standards.

5–6 **illī ... ēlēgērunt:** Selection of recruits included an examination process at the *probātiō*, at which the recruit underwent a medical examination and his legal status was (or should have been) investigated; it is the latter point which concerns Trajan here.

9   **quod:** "(the fact) that..."

Focus in discussion on Trajan's argument. He makes it clear in lines 8–11 that Pliny should not worry about the technical question of whether the slaves are in the army or not; an offense had been committed at the *probātiō* and all subsequent steps in the enrollment procedure are therefore null and void. The class may believe that Trajan is sharper than Pliny in considering the cause of the mistake and the possible guilt of other people as well as or instead of the slaves. They may also believe that the sentence is excessively harsh; if so, encourage them to suggest explanations, e.g. that the ancient world in general did

Stage Commentaries

not set a high value on human life; that slaves were regarded as expendable; that the Romans guarded their citizenship jealously; that strict discipline is essential in an army.

In military matters, as here and in "carcer," Pliny is relatively inexperienced and needs Trajan's help. However, on financial matters his expertise is greater than Trajan's; hence, as Sherwin-White points out (553), there are few letters asking Trajan's advice on the main problem Pliny was sent to handle, financial mismanagement.

Suggestions for Consolidation: indirect question with *num* (3; cf. "adventus" I, p. 114, line 11) and *utrum ... an* (4; cf. "carcer" I, p. 116, lines 2–4); gerundive of obligation with verb in future and past tenses (8 and 11; for more examples, see Unit 4 students' textbook, Language Information Section, "Review Grammar," p. 325); predicative nominative *voluntāriī* and *vicāriī* (4, 5, 6; cf. *servus mortuus prōcubuit* etc.). The perfect subjunctive passive in lines 4–5 is translated in the facing vocabulary and need not be discussed at this moment; its next occurrence is in Stage 48, where it is the subject of a language note.

Vocabulary Check: *reperiō* (3); *tē oportet* (3); *cognōscō* (3); *supplicium* (3); *videor* (4); *ēligō* (6); *culpa* (6); *nōndum* (9); *patefaciō* (11).

Second Language Note (fīō)

You may find it convenient to lead students through this note on two different occasions, concentrating on the morphology and paragraphs 1–2 in one lesson and postponing to a second lesson paragraphs 3–4 and the more difficult (but more important) point about flexibility in translation. If students ask about the 1st and 2nd person plural forms of the present tense, confirm that they exist but are extremely rare.

Examples of *fīō* already met in Stage 41 (two more will be met in "incendium" II, lines 3 and 6):

1 *mēnsōrēs ... in proximō fīunt* ("adventus" II, lines 8–9, also used as caption to illustration on p. 115 of students' textbook).
2 *quod ... factum est* ("carcer" I, lines 3–4).
3 *perīculum ... neglegentiōrēs fīant* ("carcer" I, lines 7–8).

Further examples:

1 *multa opera in hāc urbe fīunt.*
2 *quid nunc fīet?*
3 *mīlitēs miseriōrēs fīēbant.*
4 *fīliī imperātōris numquam cōnsulēs factī sunt.*

Stage 41

incendium I (*Letters* X.33)

Notes

4 **Gerūsiān:** a civic center, often organized around a gymnasium, for older men, usually of aristocratic birth and active in politics.

8 **sīpō:** cf. English "siphon" (both the Latin **sīpō** and the English "siphon" are derived from the Greek σίφων "straw, tube") which works on the same principle; for its operation, cf. the photograph and diagram on p. 127 of the students' textbook. The pump stood in water, presumably in a large bucket or tank. The pistons were operated alternately by means of a handle. When each piston (see cylinder on left) was raised, a vacuum was created in the cylinder. The pressure of the water then opened the valve at the bottom of the cylinder and the water entered it. When the piston was lowered again (see cylinder on right), the water pressure in the cylinder closed the valve at the bottom and opened the valve in the crosspipe. The water was thus forced up the pipe. (Pumps probably were not used *inside* houses for domestic water supply.)

8–9 **nūllum ... īnstrūmentum:** Equipment at Rome included not only *hamae* (water buckets made of tightly-woven rope smeared with tar) but also *spongiae* (sponges, perhaps for squeezing water over walls near to the fire, as a preventive measure), *centōnēs* (pieces of quilt or blanket soaked in vinegar, to smother small fires), *dolābrae* and *secūrēs* (pickaxes and hatchets), *scālae* (ladders), and *formiōnēs* (gigantic wicker mats to catch and break the fall of those jumping from upper storeys – precursors of modern canvas trampolines).

10 **parābuntur:** The tense indicates that the equipment has not yet been purchased (Pliny may not have had much time, of course), but Pliny glosses over this by claiming he has the matter in hand (*ut iam praecēpī*).

11 **collēgium:** The word can mean either an association of full-time or part-time craftsmen, as here, or a cooperative association of poor men organized around a religious cult, often combining the functions of a luncheon club like the Rotarians and a burial-insurance society like the Masons. For the political factionalism in some of the craftsmen's associations, see p. 92 below, on lines 4–6 of "incendium" II.
fabrōrum: a troop of civil volunteers (as organized in Italy and in the western, but not the eastern, provinces), similar – *mutatis mutandis* – to the Guardian Angels or members of a Neighborhood Watch. The fire department (*vigilēs*) in Rome, on the other hand, was a branch of the army.

For the danger of fire in ancient cities, cf. Juvenal *Satires* III.197ff. (making allowance for satirical exaggeration; translation in Massey 17) and for fires at Rome, Tacitus, *Annals* IV.64, VI.45, XV.38ff. (translation in Tingay *Empire* 84–86). Some students may know of the great Neronian fire of A.D. 64 from having seen the film *Quo Vadis*, and may be able to suggest reasons why fires were so frequent. Hardy, in his

Stage Commentaries

commentary on Pliny's *Letters* X.33, suggests height of houses, narrowness of streets, and wooden projections from lower storeys.

The division into A and B questions, described on p. 13 above, is here used for the first time. Question B1 suggests that Pliny is discreetly covering himself with an alibi to protect himself against any possible blame for failure to deal with the fire. After discussing question B2, students might consider Sherwin-White's suggestion (607) that "perhaps the masses were not sorry to see the palaces of the wealthy burning." Discussion of B3 and B4 may well overlap. Students are likely to say that Pliny's suggestion is good common sense, and to wonder why he bothers Trajan about it at all. But Pliny's implied promise to keep the volunteer fire department relatively small (*dumtaxat hominum CL*), his earnest efforts *nē quis nisi ... nēve fabrī ... ūtantur*, and his assurance *nec erit difficile custōdīre tam paucōs* may suggest to them that Pliny is defending himself against any and all objections. Ask the students what they think the imperial objection might be, and see whether they can anticipate Trajan's reply; this is difficult, but perhaps *nē quis nisi faber* will give them a clue.

Vocabulary Check: *dēleō* (4); *opus* (4); *quicquam* (7); *praetereā* (7); *ut*+indicative (10); *putō* (11); *efficiō* (12); *ūtor*+ablative (13).

incendium II (*Letters* X.34)

Notes

4   **factiōnibus:** Trajan's statement is supported by evidence of political feuding, both in other letters of Pliny, e.g. X.58; X.81, and in the aggressive speeches of Dio Chrysostom, a prominent and controversial orator in Prusa at the time of Pliny's governorship.

6   **hetaeriae:** For the development of a political role by *collēgia*, compare their possible involvement in the riot between the Pompeiani and Nucerini (Tacitus, *Annals* XIV.17; see also Unit 1, p. 130) and the disturbances caused by *collēgia* in Rome at the end of the Republic. For a full account, see Crook 264–68. Students may recall the turbulence of Pompeian elections from Unit 1, Stage 11, and readily recognize the possibility that professional associations could easily develop into strident lobbying groups or, worse, political gangs. Pliny had been instructed in his *mandāta* from Trajan to ban *collēgia* in Bithynia, though exceptions were made for the *collēgia tenuiōrum* (poor men's burial-cum-dining clubs). Because there was a particular danger that *collēgia* might attract inveterate rabble rousers, Pliny was eager to assure the emperor, in "incendium" I, *ego efficiam nē quis nisi faber ... admittātur*.

8   **admonendī ... sunt dominī:** The word order may cause problems. A simpler example may help, e.g. *paranda est cēna*.

9–10 **auxilium ... est petendum:** Trajan seizes upon Pliny's comment in "incendium" I, lines 6–7, and cunningly uses it to back up his own counterproposal to Pliny's suggestion.

After students have discussed some of the background to Trajan's refusal of Pliny's request, using some of the information given above on lines 4 and 6, they might consider question 4 and discuss the adequacy or inadequacy of Trajan's reply. Encourage students to produce their own ideas, stepping in with a contribution only if the discussion seems to be flagging. If the class is large, divide it into break-out groups and allow the groups to discuss the question among themselves. Afterwards, a spokesperson for each group should report back to the rest of the class.

In support of Trajan's view, students might decide that a militant *collēgium* could be even more dangerous than a fire, and that property owners might grow careless if they thought that the state would always come to their aid when needed; also that "the close building and crowded streets must have made it difficult to bring fire-brigades into action" (Sherwin-White 610). Against Trajan, students might argue that large and rapidly spreading fires could only be dealt with by something like Pliny's plan, and that Trajan's advice is not specific enough. Who, for example, is to set about obtaining *ea quae ... auxiliō esse possint*, and what happens if the *dominī praediōrum* are incapable of extinguishing the flames?

Suggestions for Consolidation: gerundive of obligation (8 and 10); *is quī* (5 and 7); for further examples, see the Unit 4 students' textbook, LI Section, "Review Grammar," p. 292, first half of paragraph 9; also p. 201 of this Manual.

Vocabulary Check: *sīcut* (3); *fīō* (3 and 6); *nōs oportet* (3); *meminī* (4); *brevis* (6); *comparō* (7); *auxiliō est* (7); *admoneō* (8); *opus est* (9).

Third Language Note (*Present Subjunctive Passive*)

The main point to establish from either paragraph 1 or paragraph 2 is that the personal endings of this tense, *-r*, *-ris*, *-tur*, etc., are exactly the same as those met previously in the present and imperfect indicative passive. Students can practice the point for themselves by turning examples of the present subjunctive active such as *laudent*, *salūtem*, *dūcāmus*, etc., into the corresponding passive forms *laudentur*, *salūter*, *dūcāmur*, etc., noting the translation of the new form. Use the tables in the Unit 4 students' textbook, LI Section, "Review Grammar," p. 299, to establish that the first conjugation differs from the others in having "e" where they have "a," and that the students have met this difference

Stage Commentaries

already, when they learned the present subjunctive active forms ("Review Grammar," p. 298). Use the tables of the deponent verbs in the "Review Grammar," p. 305, to elicit the point that the present subjunctive of these verbs follows the normal rule in having passive endings but active meanings; an example with *cōnentur* is given in the caption to the illustration on p. 129 of the students' textbook.

Practice syntax by asking the class why the subjunctive is being used in the various examples in paragraphs 1 and 3.

Drills

Exercise 1   Type: classification
　　　　　　 Grammatical point being practiced: forms of present and
　　　　　　 　perfect tense

Exercise 2   Type: completion
　　　　　　 Missing item: verb
　　　　　　 Test of accuracy: sense
　　　　　　 Grammatical point being practiced: 1st and 2nd persons
　　　　　　 　plural, present, future, and imperfect passive, introduced
　　　　　　 　in Stage 39

Future passive forms of 3rd- and 4th-conjugation verbs are excluded; they will be practiced in Stage 42, exercise 2.

Exercise 3   Type: completion
　　　　　　 Missing item: clause *or* infinitive phrase
　　　　　　 Test of accuracy: sense, based on "aquaeductus" and
　　　　　　 　"supplicium"

The Background Material

For teacher reference, Garnsey and Saller 10–20 is invaluable, and for students, Richardson 59–86 and Tingay and Badcock 165–73. There is copious source material in Lewis and Reinhold I.308–78, II.319–418.

The students might begin by studying the map on p. 133. They should quickly notice that the imperial provinces are generally the frontier ones; if the teacher reads them a translation of Tacitus, *Annals* IV.5, they will also notice that the emperor's provinces contained the greatest concentration of legions, with *auxilia* used in a supporting role. (Britain, which was not in the empire at the time described by Tacitus, became an imperial province with, at different periods, three or four legions.) Encourage the class to comment on this arrangement, and compare the remark of Dio Cassius (quoted in Lewis and Reinhold II.32) that "Augustus' real purpose was that the senators should be unarmed and peaceful, while he alone had arms and maintained soldiers."

The map indicates that some provinces, such as Gallia and Hispania, were subdivided, and that some areas, such as Dacia, were temporarily conquered by Trajan, giving a total number of provinces in excess of the twenty-eight mentioned in Unit 4, Stage 37, p. 48. Of the ten provinces which could only be governed by ex-consuls, eight (including, for example, Syria and Britannia) were imperial; the two most prestigious senatorial provinces were Africa and Asia, traditionally awarded to the two senior ex-consuls who were willing to accept the governorship and had not previously held it. (Coincidentally, the two leading historical characters in the students' earlier reading material, Agricola and Salvius, both at different times turned down the governorship of Asia; for Agricola's refusal, see Tacitus, *Agricola* 42).

A selection from the following points may be useful in supplementing the students' textbook (the subheadings follow roughly the order in which information is presented in the students' textbook). Encourage students to recall points they have met earlier in the Course, in either the reading passages or the background material, which illustrate or are linked with the present topic. Where time allows, let students turn up some of the information from their own researches, working in small groups and using either such handbooks as Richardson or (under the teacher's guidance) translations of primary sources, e.g. in Lewis and Reinhold.

Length of governorship. Governorship of a senatorial province was normally for one year. Governorship of an imperial province normally lasted for three years, but could last longer; for example, Agricola governed Britain for seven years, and Poppaeus Sabinus (grandfather of Poppaea, the *femme fatale* of Stage 48) was kept in his position by Tiberius for twenty-four.

Special expertise of Agricola and Pliny. The *cursūs* of both men were given in the Unit 4 students' textbook, p. 50. Encourage students to recall that Pliny served in two treasury offices and Agricola had experience in Britain both as military tribune and as legionary commander before he was sent there as governor.

Saint Paul. For Paul's trials before two Roman governors, Felix and Festus, see Acts 24–25, and for his adventures on route to Rome, Acts 27–28.

Position of "iūridicus." A *iūridicus* was subordinate to the governor. The students have read a fictionalized presentation of a clash between a

Stage Commentaries

governor and a *iūridicus* in Unit 3, pp. 96–97, where Agricola claims *summa potestās* (and legally is in the right) but his *iūridicus* Salvius has more actual power, since he enjoys more of the emperor's confidence.

Unsuccessful building projects. Slide IV.50 shows the remains of one such project, the botched vaulting of the theater at Nicaea, about which Pliny writes in X.39.

The final quotations are from Tacitus, *Agricola* 21 and 30.

Mention the Romans' use of client-kings and buffer-states as alternatives to occupying territory and turning it into a province. Sometimes a native ruler, such as Cogidubnus among the Regnenses in Britain and Herod in Judaea, became a "client-king" and enjoyed considerable independence in governing his people, provided he did not act against Rome's interests; at other times, Rome might sign a treaty of friendship with a friendly "buffer-state" like Armenia, who then received Roman backing against more dangerous neighbors.

The Peutinger Table (Unit 4 students' textbook, pp. 134–35) is the kind of map which Pliny might have used. Students may be interested in comparing it with the modern map on p. 133. The Peutinger Table is a medieval copy of an itinerary of the Roman empire, in pictorial form – a diagram rather than a map, for there is considerable distortion in the drawing of geographical features. It is intended to show the cities and posting-stages reached by the major roads and the distances between them. Fixed symbols were used to indicate the sizes of the towns and the facilities available in them. As in a modern travel guide, a good inn, for example, is indicated by a house with a twin-peaked roof, and a very basic accommodation, by a single house. For further details see Casson, 186–88 and Dilke, *Greek and Roman Maps* 112–20 and 193–95. The original may have been compiled in the fourth century A.D., perhaps on the basis of older works. The Table is a parchment roll in Vienna, but there is a facsimile in the Museum of Classical Archaeology, Cambridge, England. Part of this facsimile is shown on slide IV.45.

The photograph on p. 136 of the students' textbook shows a messenger traveling by the *cursus pūblicus* (described in Unit 3, p. 66). Pliny puts various queries to Trajan (e.g. X.45; X.64; X.120) about the correct use of the *cursus pūblicus* and the issuing of official passes (*diplōmata*) to travelers.

Suggestions for Discussion

1 When Tiberius' advisers suggested he should extort all the money he could from the provinces by taxation, he replied (Suetonius, *Tiberius*

32) "A good shepherd shears his sheep; he doesn't skin them." What did he mean by this? Was he being kind or calculating?
2 Suggest reasons why a king might deliberately choose to bequeath his kingdom to the Romans.
3 Why did such an important province as Egypt only have an equestrian governor? (To emphasize that Egypt was a politically sensitive province, inform students that no senator was allowed even to visit it without special permission. The students may be able to recall Rome's heavy dependence on Egyptian grain, and some students may have heard of Antony and Cleopatra's use of Egypt as a base in the civil war with Augustus.)
4 Augustus, in his will, advised his successors not to enlarge the empire beyond its existing size (Tacitus, *Annals* I.11). Suggest reasons, either honorable or dishonorable, why he gave this advice. (Tacitus' suggestions are *metus* and *invidia*. Claudius' invasion of Britain was the only important example of disregard for Augustus' advice until the time of Trajan.)
5 How justified is Tacitus' cynicism in his comment (*Agricola* 21, quoted on p. 137 of the students' textbook) that the trappings of Roman civilization, such as colonnades and baths, were in reality part of the Britons' slavery?
6 Compare Calgacus' attack on Roman imperialism (Tacitus, *Agricola* 30–32) with the defense made by Cerialis (Tacitus, *Histories* IV.73–74).

Vocabulary Checklist

Students are likely to need help with the Checklists in this and subsequent Stages, as they contain some words met only once or twice in the Course. Discuss some of the words in the Checklist before assigning the list as homework; for example, remind the students of the contexts where they met *iūs* ("incendium" I, p. 126, line 13) and *opus est* ("aquaeductus" I, p. 119, line 5; "incendium" II, p. 128, line 9), and practice the two different ways of translating *nec*.

Some cognate words, both new and familiar, and familiar Latin synonyms (– "Synonym Search") are added at the end of each Checklist in this and subsequent Stages so that students can practice the principles of word formation and semantic overlapping. Remind students that if they know the meaning of a given word, they will often find it helps them to understand a number of other related or synonymous words. If a particular suffix causes them trouble (e.g. *-tās* in *vīlitās*), remind the students of some simpler or more familiar examples (*crūdēlitās* from *crūdēlis*, *tranquillitās* from *tranquillus*, etc.).

Stage Commentaries

Suggestions for Further Work

1 Ask students to describe one of the situations in Stage 41 through the eyes of a newspaper reporter. Encourage them to mix narrative, reported interview, and editorial comment, and to compose headlines which reflect the writer's sympathies ("Pliny Uncovers Slave Scandal" or "Public Uproar at Veto of Fire Safety Plan"). If the students have access to a suitable translation, extend this exercise to letters in Book X other than those in Stage 41.
2 The students could consider the much-discussed question of Pliny's competence as a governor. Does his correspondence indicate efficiency or fussiness, conscientiousness, or lack of initiative? Which of the letters in Stage 41, if any, strikes the students as unnecessary (cf. Sherwin-White 546–55)?
3 Ask students to compose a letter, supposedly by Pliny to a friend, in which he describes either his life in Bithynia or one of the Stage 41 situations more informally and frankly than in his letters to Trajan.

STAGE 42: CARMINA

BRIEF OUTLINE	
Reading passages	Phaedrus, *Fables* I.1
	Catullus, *Poems* 39 and 101
	Martial, *Epigrams* IV.69; VII.83; X.8
	Ovid, *Ars Amatoria* I.469–78
	Vergil, *Aeneid* III.192–206
Background material	time chart (poets and historical events)
Language notes	conditional clauses: imperfect subjunctive
	poetic word order: interlacing of noun + adjective phrases

DIGEST

An introduction to Latin poetry, with short selections from Phaedrus, Catullus, and Vergil, as well as from Martial and Ovid, whose poetry was introduced in Stages 36 and 39 respectively. The poetic passages in this Stage have been chosen as short but characteristic samples of works in different styles and genres, including fable, elegy, epigram, didactic (parodied), and heroic epic.

GRAMMATICAL POINT
conditionals: imperfect subjunctive (one occurrence)
    e.g. *sī urbānus essēs ... tamen renīdēre usque quāque tē nōllem.*

SENTENCE PATTERN
interlocking and interlacing of two noun-and-adjective phrases in verse word order
    e.g. *dūra tamen mollī saxa cavantur aquā.*

Title Picture

Vergil composing the *Aeneid* (based on a mosaic from Tunisia). The scroll bears the invocation to the Muse, *mūsa, mihi causās memorā, quō nūmine laesō quidve* ... (*Aeneid* I.8–9).

Phaedrus (*Fables* I.1)

Notes

2–3 **superior ... īnferior:** predicative; cf. *mortuus prōcubuit, immōtī adstābant*, etc.
3–4 **fauce improbā ... incitātus:** See p. 13 above.
13 **iniūstā nece:** Discuss with the class the best way of translating the ablative here.

The questions printed in the students' textbook in this Stage vary in type from author to author; some are easy comprehension questions, to aid as well as test understanding, while others are more probing, to encourage literary exploration after students have established the surface meaning. Those on Phaedrus are fairly straightforward; if you wish to give extra help, simplify them further, e.g.:

What two animals are mentioned?
What had they done? Had they each come to a different stream? Why had they come?
What was the wolf doing? etc.

Agreement of separated noun and adjective is indicated from time to time in this and subsequent Stages by underlining, as in lines 5–6. As the students gain experience in reading poetry, this use of underlining is steadily reduced as the Stages advance, though it continues to be used in cases of unusual difficulty.

After using question 6 to establish Phaedrus' moral ("Might is right," "Jungle law," "Any excuse will do," etc.), ask the class whether it is an accurate comment on human nature.

Suggestions for Consolidation: present participle (6); 2nd person singular present deponent (7); perfect passive participle in nominative (2, 4, 9) and accusative (13; cf. Stage 41, p. 122, line 3).

Vocabulary Check: *īdem* (1); *longē* (3); *incitō* (4); *quārē* (5); *queror* (7).

Stage Commentaries

Catullus I (from *Poem* 39)

Commentaries: Fordyce, Quinn

If you introduce the new vocabulary before students read the poem (see p. 14 above), pronounce and discuss the new words, don't just look at them. For example, link *candidus* with *candidātus*, *ōrātor* with *ōrāre*; explore the connection between the definitions of *urbānus* in lines 8 and 10, and compare them with the meaning of *rūsticus*; add other examples of impersonal passives (e.g. *curritur*, *clāmātur*, *venītur*) to *lūgētur* and *ventum est*.

Notes

2–4 **sī ... ille:** The prisoner's friends gather around him in court, to give both moral and vocal support. The picture on p. 143 shows the scene, with the pleader appealing to the audience's emotions in a *miserātiō*, while the defendant's wife and family add to the pathos. Encourage the class to identify Egnatius in the picture.
4 **ad:** The meaning ("at") may have been forgotten, but is included in the wording of students' question 2.
5 **orba cum flet:** *cum* postponed from the "normal" position. The students' textbook sometimes gives help with such postponements in this and subsequent Stages, either by underlining words on either side of the postponed word or by including a note in the vocabulary. Also encourage the students to read the phrase or sentence straight through before translating.
7 **morbum:** predicative accusative. Encourage such translations as "this is a disease he has."
9 **monendum est tē:** unusual and difficult variation on *monendus es*.

If you need to simplify the questions in the students' textbook, do it as follows:

What does Egnatius possess? And because he possesses them, what does he do?
Where does Catullus imagine Egnatius has arrived (refer students to the picture if necessary)? What is going on there? What does Egnatius do?
What activity does Catullus then imagine is taking place? Where? Who is present? What is she doing? etc.

Question 2 can be further extended; encourage the class to pick out and comment on such words as *piī* and *ūnicum*, which stress the mournfulness of the occasion and therefore the inappropriateness of Egnatius' behavior.

Some students may reply to questions like number 3 by saying "for emphasis"; if so, encourage them to say what is being emphasized and why. Note that the repetitions of *renīdet* nearly all occur at the same point of the line, highlighting the maddeningly predictable repetition of Egnatius' smirk.

Ask the students "How does Catullus stop the list of names in lines 10–11 from becoming monotonous?". When the students have grasped the function of the adjectives, invite them to work out modern analogies ("If you were from the Big Apple, Beantown, Montréal, the Ozarks" etc.), provided they can do this without injuring the regional sensitivities of individuals in the class.

If you ask the students, "How do we know what Catullus wrote?" their replies usually reveal that they naturally but wrongly believe that Catullus' autograph manuscript survives, and they are amazed to learn that the oldest surviving manuscripts of Catullus were written fourteen centuries after the poet's death. Mention the variant readings in line 11, *pinguis* (from a grammarian's quotation) and *parcus* (reading in manuscripts): which reading appeals more to the students? The purpose of such discussion is not to train the students to be textual critics but to introduce the idea that the words of Roman writers are not known as certainties but have to be reconstructed by the labors of scholars. On the copying of an author's work, cf. the Unit 4 students' textbook, Stage 39, p. 88; and see Tingay and Badcock 153–55, and Dilke, *Ancient Romans* 165–67.

The implication that Egnatius' methods of dental hygiene are in some way unpleasant is conveyed in lines 10–12, and question 6 should bring this out. At your discretion, you might then study with students the final lines of the poem, written up on the blackboard, in which the details of Egnatius' habit are revealed with cheerful coarseness:

nunc Celtibēr es: Celtibēriā in terrā
quod quisque mīnxit, hōc sibi solet māne
dentem atque russam dēfricāre gingīvam
ut, quō iste vester expolītior dēns est,
hōc tē amplius bibisse praedicet lōtī.

Suggestions for Consolidation: ablative of comparison (14)

Vocabulary Check: *ut* + indicative (8).

Catullus II (*Poem* 101)

Commentaries: Fordyce, Quinn

Stage Commentaries

Notes

2 **ad:** meaning "at" or "for" (cf. "Catullus" I, p. 32, line 4), recurs in line 8.
īnferiās: an offering to the *dī mānēs*, consisting of wine, milk, honey, and flowers, illustrated in the students' textbook.

6 **adēmpte:** The case often causes trouble. If students translate as "You have been taken away," point out that there is no *es*.

7–9 **haec ... accipe ... mānantia:** This is where the students will probably need the most help. With the help of the footnote in the text, guide the class to take *haec* as the object of *accipe*, qualified by *mānantia*.

9 **mānantia:** The idea may seem bizarre and exaggerated to many students; help them see it as normal behavior in a first-century B.C. Roman context.

Students should try the questions in the students' textbook only after they have established the surface meaning of the poem. Help students with the first reading by composing simple questions like these:

What has happened to Catullus' brother? Did it happen in Rome? Near Rome?
Was Catullus there?
Where is Catullus now? What ceremony has he come for?
What is he going to do? What else (line 4)?

When students have a good grasp of the poem's meaning, ask them to outline the situation depicted there, supplying additional data as needed. Catullus' brother had died in the Troad, and Catullus, probably on route in 57 B.C. to the province of Bithynia, where he was on the governor's staff, paid a visit to the burial place of his brother's ashes, bringing the traditional offerings to the dead; he laments his brother and speaks the formal farewell *avē atque valē*. The ceremony has a special pathos, since it takes place far from home and Catullus is the only mourner. Students often misinterpret the visit as a funeral; lead them to a better analogy, e.g. a formal wreath-laying ceremony. Part of the observance (the speaking of *avē atque valē*) is incorporated into the poem, so that the poem both enacts Catullus' performance of the ritual and includes what could be taken as his spoken or unspoken thoughts as he performs it (see Quinn, *Latin Explorations* 80ff.).

Consider question 2 briefly in an early phase of the discussion, have it answered simply ("To visit his brother's grave"), and reconsider it more thoroughly later ("Has he come because he wants to? Or because he thinks he ought to? Does he think his visit will do himself or his brother any good? Does he 'believe' in the ritual?").

Question 4 may lead to awareness of the apparent contradiction of *intereā* (line 7) and *in perpetuum* (line 10). Even if this is resolved by following the commentators who interpret *intereā* as "in the circumstances, as things are," inconsistencies remain. If Catullus' brother can hear him from the spiritual realm, why does Catullus talk in line 10 of a final separation? If he doesn't believe in an afterlife, why does he speak to his brother and why does he bring the offerings and feature them so prominently in the poem?

Explore other points such as the meaning of *mūnere mortis* in line 3 (see Lyne, *Handbook* 56 for a valuable discussion of this and other points) and the significance of *indignē* in line 6 ("All men die; why is the death of Catullus' brother 'unfair'?").

The poem provides a good opportunity for studying assonance and alliteration. Read it aloud to the students and invite comment on its sound. From listening or looking, they are likely to pick up the high incidence of "m" (23 of the poem's 63 words contain "m," 13 in initial position) and may notice other instances of verbal patterning, e.g. with the letter "f." Do the students think this is coincidence or design? What is the effect? If they feel that the assonance and alliteration intensify the mournful dirge-like tone of the poem, do they think this is because the sound of "m" is peculiarly melancholy or because the assonance and alliteration, like salt in food, highlight an element already present? (See Wilkinson 25ff. for the view that usually sound is only expressive when it reinforces meaning.)

Balme and Warman 44–45 quote two translations of this poem for comparison.

The imperfect subjunctive deponent *adloquerer* (line 4) and the dative of disadvantage *mihī* (line 5) are handled by glosses, and there is no need to explore them further at this point. They are the subject of language notes in Stages 43 and 45 respectively.

Vocabulary Check: *gēns* (1); *cinis* (4); *auferō* (5); *mōs* (7).

Mārtiālis I (*Epigrams* IV.69)

The word order in line 3, and the case of *hāc lagōnā*, may cause trouble. Ask the students "What is said to have happened to Papylus? How?" Elicit the point of this epigram, if students do not see it, by asking "Does Martial at any point admit to believing the rumours about Papylus? What does the poem suggest about his real opinion?".

The relief on p. 153 of the students' textbook, showing slaves filling goblets from assorted jugs and jars, is from the third-century funerary Igel Monument, from near Trier, West Germany.

Suggestions for Consolidation: present, future, and imperfect indicative passive and deponent endings (3; cf. *quereris* in "Phaedrus," p. 140, line 7; *arbitror* in "Catullus" I, p. 142, line 8; *afflīgēbar, ūtar, verēris,*

Stage Commentaries

and *suspicor* in Stage 41 and the *-mur, -minī* endings in Stage 41, exercise 2; and for further practice, the LI Section of the students' textbook, "Review Grammar," p. 296, paragraph 2, and p. 303, paragraphs 2 and 3).

Vocabulary Check: *vel* (1); *negō* (2); *fīō* (3); *putō* (4).

Mārtiālis II (*Epigrams* VII.83)

For commentary, see Tennick 72. He notes the literal meaning of the Greek name Eutrapelus ("Dexterous," "Twinkle-Fingers"), and the use of rouge after shaving (*expingit*, line 2), then raises the question of Martial's target: is he satirizing the slowness and finickiness of Eutrapelus, or the hairiness of Lupercus (cf. *lupus*)?

Vocabulary Check: *dum* (1); *ōs* (1).

Mārtiālis III (*Epigrams* X.8)

Note the two different verbs meaning "marry": *dūcō* ("I take a wife") and *nūbō* ("I put on the marriage veil"), depending on whether the groom or bride is the subject; the distinction faithfully reflects a Roman attitude to marriage.

Vocabulary Check: *nūbō* (1); *cupiō* (1); *magis* (2).

Some Suggested Activities

"If Martial were alive today, for which television program do you think he would be a scriptwriter?"

Ask students to produce a written verse translation of one of the three Martial epigrams in this Stage. Free verse will probably be more effective than a rigid scheme with meter and rhyme. Make sure that students keep the shortness of the original and postpone the punch line or word until the end.

First Language Note (*Conditional Clauses*)

For further practice, examples of conditional clauses from the previous Stage can be picked out and retranslated. For example:

sī tū dīligenter excutiēs, inveniēs. (Stage 41, p. 114, line 11)
sī quid adversī..., poterunt. (Stage 41, p. 116, lines 8–9)

Stage 42

sī mīlitēs..., rēctē verēris... (Stage 41, p. 117, lines 6–7)
sī lēctī sunt,... pūniendī erunt. (Stage 41, p. 122, lines 5–8)
sī ad reī..., renīdet ille; sī ad piī...renīdet ille. (Stage 42, "Catullus" I, p. 142, lines 2–6)

When you lead the class through the examples in paragraph 4, practice both ways of translating *nisi*.

Paragraph 5 makes a deliberately brief mention of subjunctive conditional sentences, of which only two examples have occurred so far. Concentrate on the correspondence between the use of the subjunctive in the Latin sentence and the translation "would" or "should" in the English, and do not at this point analyze the use of the different tenses. Ask the students "Does the first example in paragraph 5 imply that 'you' *are* a city-dweller?" "Does the second example in paragraph 5 imply that 'she' *is* older?", etc., to establish that in each of these sentences the condition is an "impossible" one, incapable of being fulfilled. Such conditionals are often called "unfulfilled" or "contrary-to-fact" (see Unit 4 students' textbook, LI Section, "Reference Grammar," p. 332, paragraph X.1). The commonest type of subjunctive conditional sentence, involving the pluperfect subjunctive in both main clause and conditional clause, is the subject of a language note in Stage 46.

For an entertaining ghost story in which Latin lessons and conditional clauses play a prominent part, see "A School Story" in James 7–15.

Ovidius *(Ars Amatoria* I.469–78)

Commentary: Hollis

Notes

4 **equī:** delayed subject. Remind the students of the importance of reading the line straight through, and use comprehension questions such as "What are the next animals to be mentioned? What does Ovid say about them?"
6 **assiduā...humō:** Stress the need to make the sense clear in translation, and encourage students to reject "continual ground" in favor of "continual contact with the ground," etc.
9 **perstā modo:** The parenthesis separates the object from the verb. Phrase and intone carefully while reading aloud.

Use the questions in the students' textbook after they have read and translated the passage, and understand the surface meaning. Invite them to summarize Ovid's advice as briefly as possible (Can they boil it down to three words?) or to cite any proverbs or anecdotes which convey the same advice as Ovid ("If at first you don't succeed..."). Ask them "Which is the key word in Ovid's argument?" (point out lines 3, 4, and

Stage Commentaries

10 if necessary) and "Find a word in lines 5-6, not necessarily a noun, which conveys the same ideas as the key word."

The final part of question 1 may provoke the class to contrast the logic (or lack of it) in Ovid's argument with its psychological effectiveness. To say "Other people have succeeded; therefore so will you" is strictly a *non sequitur*, but may still be a good way of raising morale.

Ovid also has a literary reason for his use of *exempla* in these lines: such *exempla* are a typical feature of didactic poetry, which Ovid is here parodying. The point could be demonstrated by reading the class a translation of some earnest didactic poetry, e.g. Lucretius I.311ff., quoted by Balme and Warman 34-35, and asking students to compare it with Ovid. Ovid and Lucretius both use *exempla* (sometimes the same ones) to make their point, but the tone and theme of Lucretius are serious, whereas Ovid's tongue is firmly in his cheek. Similarly in lines 9-10, referred to in question 2 in the students' textbook, Penelope, the archetypal example of a faithful wife, is mischievously used by Ovid to exemplify a supremely difficult challenge for a would-be seducer. It is not hard to see why the *Ars Amatoria* might have been a contributory cause of Ovid's exile. While Augustus was embarking on a program of moral reform, Ovid was burlesquing the highly respectable genre of didactic poetry, which usually dealt with such edifying themes as agriculture and astronomy, and transferring its characteristic mixture of maxims, mythological allusion, and scientific observation to the world of seduction and intrigue.

Ask the students, if you are feeling adventurous, whether they agree with Ovid's implicit generalization about women, that they can always be won if the men try long enough.

The picture in the students' textbook (p. 148), from a fifteenth-century manuscript of Ovid, actually accompanies the *Metamorphoses*. Do your students believe it is equally (or more) suitable as an illustration for the *Ars*?

Suggestions for Consolidation: ablative of comparison (two examples in line 7, cf. "Catullus" I, p. 142, line 14); future participle (2).

Vocabulary Check: *spērō* (2); *patior* (4); *magis* (7); *dūrus* (7,8); *mollis* (7, 8).

Vergilius (*Aeneid* III.192-206)

Commentaries: Williams (large commentary on *Aeneid* III, shorter notes in his commentary on *Aeneid* I-VI), Page.

Stage 42

The following is one possible sequence of operations for reading this passage:

1 Add further comment to the introduction in the students' textbook, explaining that Troy has been destroyed by the Greeks, and the Trojans are in search of a new home.
2 Explore with your students the facing vocabulary.
3 Read the passage aloud.
4 Let students answer the "A" questions orally or in writing.
5 Let students, with your guidance, work out the translation together, and put the translations of the more difficult phrases on the blackboard for subsequent reference.
6 Explore further, using some of the "B" questions.
7 Read the text aloud a second time, or let a student volunteer do so.

When exploring the long facing vocabulary, point out that one reason for its length is the use of some familiar words with new meanings. Discuss examples with the class. Explore the connection between the two translations of *volvere*, as well as the link between the translations of *caecus*, and their connection with the literal meaning (cf. "blind corner").

Notes

1 **nec...ūllae:** The translation is difficult at first, but straightforward when you have established the sense by comprehension questions.
5 **magna:** predicative ("the seas were running high," Day Lewis); cf. *servus mortuus prōcubuit, lupus superior stābat*, etc.
10 **negat:** cf. *rūmor tam bona vīna negat* ("Mārtiālis" I, p. 145, line 2).
   caelō: unfamiliar use of ablative; use context to establish meaning. (Local ablative will be discussed in a language note in Stage 47, when the students have met more examples of it.)
11 **Palinūrus:** postponed subject may cause difficulty, though the footnote in the students' textbook should help. If necessary, give further help by asking "What does Palinurus do in line 10?"
15 **vīsa:** (sc. *est*) governs *sē attollere* in line 14, *aperīre* and *volvere* in line 15. Again, use the context as a guide to the meaning. Vergil's description should touch a chord of recognition in any student who has approached land from the sea, and watched it first appear as a smudge on the horizon, then reveal hills, cliffs, and other geographical features, and finally houses and people (cf. question A10).

Use questions A4 and B2 to explore Vergil's evocative description of the sea in lines 4 (*inhorruit*) and 5 (*ventī volvunt mare*); invite volunteers from the class to draw on the blackboard their idea of the sea's appearance, as described in each of these lines. Encourage students to pick out the

Stage Commentaries

various elements in the scene suggested by *inhorruit*, such as the shivering surface of the ocean, the sound of a choppy sea, and the white caps of the waves discernible among the *tenebrae*. Do they believe that Vergil also suggests a responsive shudder in the sailors?

Ask students "What aspect of the storm does Vergil emphasize most strongly? The violence of the wind? Rain? Darkness? The roughness of the sea?" Ask them to pick out some of the words and phrases by which the darkness is emphasized.

For helpful suggestions for other possible questions, see Tingay, *Comprehendite* 83.

Divide the class up into small groups for discussion of questions B3 and B5, as suggested on p. 107 above. Students often begin by assessing the literal accuracy of the rival translations; concern for accuracy is of course not a bad thing, but encourage them to see that there are also other points at issue in translating poetry. If B5 is too vague, rephrase it in more specific terms on the lines of B3. The compactness of Latin emerges from a comparison of the number of words used in lines 12–13 by Vergil and his translators: for Vergil's 12 words, Dryden has 13, Jackson Knight 24, Day Lewis 20, Mandelbaum 16, Fitzgerald 15 (notice the return in the more recent translators to the conciseness of Dryden). Has Dryden left anything out? Have Jackson Knight, Day Lewis, Mandelbaum, and Fitzgerald added anything? Is Vergil more to the point than his translators, and does this make his lines more effective, or less? Question B5 could also lead to discussion of the meaning of *incertōs* (line 12) and the way the translators have handled it. Does it mean (as Page says) that the Trojans couldn't tell whether it was day or night, or (as Williams says) that throughout they were in a state of uncertainty and bewilderment about everything, not just about the time.

The picture is from a fourth-century A.D. mosaic discovered at Low Ham, Somerset, England, and shows the Trojan ships landing at Carthage. On the right, Achates lands with a necklace as a gift for Dido; the reason for his curious position, apparently on his back, is that he also belongs in the adjacent mosaic picture, which was at right angles to this one.

Suggestions for Consolidation: 1st person plural passive endings (6,9); expressions of time (12–13,14); variation of nominative-accusative-verb word order (1,5,7).

Vocabulary Check: *undique* (2); *aequor* (6); *auferō* (8); *cursus* (9); *negō* (10); *meminī* (11); *errō* (13); *sīdus* (13); *procul* (15).

Stage 42

Second Language Note (*Poetic Word Order*)

Encourage the students to read each line of verse through at least twice, noting the more easily identifiable case-endings as they read, then to check the other case-endings if necessary before attempting a translation. The various examples provide useful incidental practice in recognizing cases (especially nominative, accusative, and ablative) of both nouns and adjectives.

It is desirable for the students to notice some of the effects created by the verbal patterning in these lines of verse, and not attribute the word order to clumsiness or perversity on the poet's part. For instance, note the close collocation of two contrasted adjectives in the first example in paragraph 2, and ask students to spot for themselves the similar effect in paragraph 4, example 2. Point out to students, too, that it is often the two adjectives which are placed early in the line, while the two nouns, which generally carry more of the emphasis, are held back to the end, as in paragraph 2, example 1, where the line is rounded off by the juxtaposition of the two beasts, killer and killed.

The English poem in paragraph 3 is by Dorothy Parker. Note that Parker falsified the first three assertions by making a patently false assertion about herself at the end. Did Parker choose "Marie of Roumania" (as opposed, say, to "Mary of England") because she was a well-known contemporary queen (she visited New York City with twenty-six steamer trunks of clothes), or because of the metathesis ("reversal") of "m" and "r" in the two parts of her name and the opportunity for a rhyme with "extemporanea"? For comment on the similarity between the patterns created by rhyme in English verse and those created by noun and adjective phrases in Latin, see p. 65 above.

Drills

Exercise 1 Type: vocabulary
Grammatical point being practiced: meanings of *ēmittere, petere,* and *referre*

Some of the examples in this exercise have more than one possible answer. Provide similar practice with other verbs, e.g. *agere* (see Unit 4 students' textbook, "Complete Vocabulary," p. 357).

Exercise 2 Type: completion
Missing item: verb
Test of accuracy: morphology
Grammatical point being practiced: 1st, 2nd, and 3rd

Stage Commentaries

persons singular and plural, future passive of 3rd and 4th conjugation verbs

Direct the students if necessary to the tables in the Language Information Section, "Review Grammar," p. 296.

Exercise 3   Type: transformation
            Grammatical point being practiced: indirect statement with present passive and future active infinitives, introduced in Stage 38

The Background Material

The time chart pulls together and supplements various pieces of chronological information scattered through previous Units, and puts the five poets of Stage 42 in their historical context. (A similar chart, with a larger number of authors but without the list of historical events, appears in Stage 46.) It is sufficiently brief, if you wish, for students to copy the dates and events into their notebooks. They can add information to their notebook charts from time to time as their knowledge of Roman literary history increases.

Ask students what other historical events or names of Roman authors they can recall; their dates (exact or approximate) can then be related to the information in the time chart. If you wish to list the names of first-century emperors on the blackboard, they are probably easier for students to assimilate if they are presented in three groups: Julio-Claudians; emperors of the A.D. 69 civil war; Flavians.

Explore the connections between the dates of the poets and the historical information presented in the chart. "Of the five poets listed here," you might ask, "which one lived entirely in the Republican period? Which poet lived under the largest number of emperors?" Consider the problems faced by Martial and his contemporaries during the more autocratic phase of Domitian's rule, and recall the sycophancy of some of Martial's writing from Stage 36, e.g. "Marcus Valerius Mārtiālis" II, p. 20, lines 11–14. If someone asks the question, "Who had more extensive experience of living through civil war, Vergil or Ovid?", encourage students to develop a comparison between Vergil's commitment to the Augustan régime and Ovid's more detached or subversive attitude, which led eventually to his punishment.

Vocabulary Checklist

While discussing *caecus*, refer to its occurrences in "Vergilius," p. 150, lines 9 and 12. Compare the pair of cognates *caecus–caecitās* with *vīlis–vīlitās*, which were met in the previous Checklist. For *reperiō–repertor*, cf. *vincō–victor*, *scrībō–scrīptor*, etc., including harder examples such as *augeō–auctor*.

Suggestions for Further Work

Present the class with Xeroxed copies of an extract from George Orwell's *Animal Farm*; William Golding's *Lord of the Flies*; Samuel Coleridge's epigram, "Swans sing before they die – 'twere no bad thing / Did certain persons die before they sing"; Sir John Suckling's "Song," beginning "Why so pale and wan fond lover?" (a close parallel to Ovid); extracts from Sir Alfred Tennyson's *In Memoriam* (or W. H. Auden's *In Memory of W. B. Yeats*); or John Milton's *Paradise Lost*. (You can, of course, easily substitute alternative examples; for instance, there are many examples of didactic verse in Brett's or Matthiessen's anthologies or of epigrams in Harmon's anthology.) Without telling the class which is which, indicate that each example belongs to the same type or family as one of the Latin poems in Stage 42, and ask students to match the genre of each English example with that of a Latin poem or extract.

STAGE 43: ŪNIVIRA

BRIEF OUTLINE
Reading passages   Petronius, *Satyrica* 111–12 (adapted)
                          extracts from *I.L.S.* 8393 (*laudātiō Tūriae*)
                          (adapted)
Background material   divorce and remarriage
Language notes   imperfect subjunctive: passive and deponent
                          genitive and ablative of gerund
                          position of verb of speaking, asking, etc. with
                              indirect statement and question

DIGEST
There are two selections in this Stage. The first is about a widow who falls in love with another man despite her vows not to, and the second is a eulogy by a husband of a deceased, extremely beloved wife.

The two reading passages present two sharply contrasting treatments of the themes of love, marriage, fidelity, and bereavement. The first – taken from Petronius' satirical novel – is fictitious, cynical, and lightweight; the second – based on an inscription – is historical, tender, affectionate, and serious.

Stage Commentaries

NARRATIVE POINTS

B.C. and A.D. Date	Setting	Characters Introduced	Story Line
Various	Ephesus; Rome	Widow of Ephesus; Vespillo and Turia	Selections about marriage and widowhood: story about widow, based on the one in Petronius' *Satyrica*; speech by Vespillo, praising his dead wife Turia

GRAMMATICAL POINTS

imperfect subjunctive: passive and deponent
    e.g. *ita nōta erat propter pudīcitiam ut ab omnibus fēminīs illīus locī laudārētur.*
gerund in the genitive and ablative
    e.g. *diffīdēns fēcunditātī tuae et dolēns orbitāte meā, nē ego, tenendō tē in mātrimōniō, spem habendī līberōs dēpōnerem, dīvortium prōpōnere ausa es.*

SENTENCE PATTERNS

increased incidence of variation in word order of the verb of speaking, asking, etc., introducing indirect discourse
    e.g. *mātrōnae quid accidisset exposuit.*
increased incidence of clustering of participles of different forms
    e.g. *sepulcrum ingressus, vīsāque mātrōnā pulcherrimā, attonitus cōnstitit.*
mālō + INF + *quam* + INF
    e.g. *mālō mortuum impendere quam vīvum occīdere.*

Title Picture

This affectionate husband and wife date from the Republican period and are now in the Museo Vaticano.

mātrōna Ephesia I (Petronius, *Satyrica* 111–12)

Supplement the introduction in the students' textbook with a brief comment on Petronius, e.g. by reading Tacitus' colorful obituary of him in *Annals* XVI.18–19 (attractively translated by Balme, *Millionaire's Dinner Party* 8). Explain also that the *Satyrica* is a huge episodic narrative of the travels and escapades of a disreputable hero and his hangers-on, parodying romantic fiction and adventure stories and greatly influencing later writers from Cervantes in *Don Quixote* to James Joyce in *Ulysses* (for the episodic structure, cf. television soap operas); the present episode is a story-within-a-story, narrated by one of the hero's friends to the captain of the ship on which he and his companions are traveling.

Stage 43

There are some trickily long sentences in the passage (see Notes below), but other sections are sufficiently easy to be handled by phrase-by-phrase translation in the way described on p. 13 above.

Notes

3–5   **nōn modo ... prōsecūta est:** Remind the class of the importance of reading the clause straight through to the end before attempting a translation.

5   **sepulcrō:** It is of some relevance to the story that a tomb in Roman times could be large and relatively comfortable; cf. the illustration in the students' textbook, p. 160.

11–12   **cīvibus affirmantibus:** an ablative absolute independent from the rest of the sentence. Translate literally at first, and then ask students for idiomatic versions.

14   **prōvinciae:** Asia.

15–19   **proxima ... fieret:** Read the whole of this long sentence aloud to the students, then ask comprehension questions on it, before (or instead of) having it translated. Able students may be able to understand much of the sense while listening, with their books closed, to you reading aloud. But give the students some prior help with key vocabulary (see p. 14 above).

16–17   **nē corpora ... dētraherentur:** The humiliation of public exposure and non-burial (or delayed burial) of the corpse was an important element in crucifixion. As an example of non-burial of an offender, some students may know of the Antigone myth; see also the narrative in the Gospels (e.g. Mark 15.42–46) for Joseph of Arimathea's special request to the Roman governor for the crucified body of Jesus.

29   **eīsdem blanditiīs:** Explain the form and meaning of *eīsdem*, and the relationship of *eīsdem blanditiīs* to *quibus* in line 30. Ask comprehension questions such as "What did the soldier begin to do? How?"

Some Suggested Questions

Why was the matron praised by all the women of Ephesus?
How did she behave at her husband's funeral? (For the flamboyance and uninhibited nature of ancient mourning, cf. Stage 42, p. 142, lines 4–5 and p. 144, line 9. For a full account of the ritual, see Toynbee 43–55, Paoli 128–32, and C.S.C.P. *The Roman World Handbook 2*, 123 and 126, and for a picture of a funeral procession, the Amiternum relief shown in (e.g.) C.S.C.P. *The Roman World* 5b, Paoli 124, Tingay and Badcock 84, Balme, *Millionaire's Dinner Party* 20–21, and described in detail by Toynbee, 46–47.)
What orders did she give to her slaves?
Whose appeals did she reject? What had she decided to do?

Stage Commentaries

How long did she go without food? What did the people say about her?
Why was the soldier near the tomb at night?
What attracted him to the tomb? What attracted him to the widow?
What arguments did he use to get the widow to eat? What did he mean
by *inānī* (line 23)? What do you think of his arguments?
How did he persuade the widow to agree to his next request?

Suggestions for Consolidation: locative (1; see Unit 4 students'
textbook, LI Section, "Review Grammar," p. 314); substantival
participle (18,22,23; see also "Review Grammar," p. 315, and p. 204
below). Review more basic points, such as time phrases (7,11, etc.;
accusative and ablative usages are contrasted in the "Review
Grammar," pp. 312–13), participles (3,4, etc.; for example, ask the
students whether *cōnfecta* agrees with *inediā* in line 26) and various uses of
ut (2,3,4,5). Adopt a "question-per-line" approach, e.g.:

What is the antecedent of *quae* in line 1?
Why is *laudārētur* (2) subjunctive?
What case is *marītō mortuō* (3)? etc.

Vocabulary Check: *quīdam* (1,16); *propter* (1); *mōs* (4); *īdem* (5,29); *ūnā*
(6); *coepit* (7,23,30); *cōnstituō* (9); *vērus* (12); *praestō* (13); *interim* (14); *lūgeō*
(15); *ēligō* (16); *gemitus* (18); *cognōscō* (19); *fīō* (19); *cōnsistō* (20); *iaceō*
(33). Pay special attention to disentangling *cōnsistō* from *cōnstituō*.

mātrōna Ephesia II (*Satyrica* 112)

Notes

6–7 **mātrōnae ... exposuit:** Use the captioned line drawing in the
students' textbook to help with the word order. The postponement of a
verb of speaking or asking, so that it follows an indirect statement or
question, is discussed in a language note later in the Stage.

8–9 **potius sē ... esse:** indirect speech continued from previous sentence.
Cf. *omnibus ... pereundum esse* in "mātrōna Ephesia" I, p. 162, line 24.

14–15 **illī quae ... crucī:** Use question 6 in the students' textbook, expanded
if necessary, to help the class with the postponed antecedent.

Question 8 usually leads to lively discussion. Quote the comment of the
sea captain to whom the story is related, that if the commander of the
soldiers had been an honorable man he would have put the dead man
back in the tomb and nailed the woman to the cross. Ask the class,
"What else could the woman have done? Should she have allowed her
new lover to go ahead and kill himself?"

Question 9 may provoke a variety of answers: the neat way in which the corpse of the woman's first love becomes the means of saving the life of her second; the complete reversal of the woman's attitude during the course of the story; the interwoven themes of love and death, with the former ultimately triumphant. Adverse comment is, of course, permissible; students should be free to say, if they wish, that the story has been overrated. Older students will enjoy pursuing the question "Is this story a sexist joke?" Relevant here are the irony of *nōn minus misericors quam pudīca* (lines 10–11) and the identity of the story's narrator (the homosexual Eumolpus) in its original context in the *Satyrica*. (If students give a positive answer to question 8, argue that Eumolpus' sexist gibe misfires.)

Details of other versions of the story are given in Sedgwick (141). The poetic diction of Christopher Fry's play on the subject, *A Phoenix Too Frequent*, may make it difficult for some high-school or even college students. But everyone may enjoy reading the closing pages, beginning with the re-entry of the soldier Tegeus after he has discovered the theft of the body from the cross. (Fry's play, unlike the present adaptation, follows Petronius in including a third character, the kindly maidservant who encourages her mistress.)

Suggestions for Consolidation: perfect passive participle in accusative (3; see also Appendix D); ablative of time (1,11).

Vocabulary Check: *ūnā* (1); *auferō* (4); *supplicium* (6); *vereor* (6); *accidō* (7); *negō* (7); *īdem* (11); *mālō* (12); *ūtor*+ablative (16).

First Language Note (*Imperfect Subjunctive Passive*)

If (as is usually the case) these endings have caused no trouble when students met them in "mātrōna Ephesia," point out that they have already seen several examples of the imperfect subjunctive passive and translated them successfully, probably without realizing that they were meeting anything new.

Many of the suggestions made in connection with the present subjunctive passive (pp. 93–94 above) are equally applicable here. Refer students to the verbs in Part Four of their Language Information Section, "Complete Vocabulary," pp. 354–97, and ask them to use the infinitive forms there listed, e.g. *laudāre*, *redūcere*, and *tangere*, to deduce the subjunctive for "they were being praised," "we were being led back," "I was being touched," etc.

After studying their LI Section, "Review Grammar," p. 305, some students will be able to make appropriate comments on the deponent verbs with little or no prompting: e.g. that as usual the forms are passive but the meanings active, and that if the endings *-r*, *-ris*, etc. are removed, a present active infinitive form invariably appears.

Tūria I (*I.L.S.* 8393, I.3–8, IIa.2–5, II.5–7)

The passages in the students' textbook are based on the inscription traditionally known as the *laudātiō Tūriae* (*I.L.S.* 8393, *C.I.L.* VI.1527, 31670 and 37053). The bulk of this inscription is on two stone slabs which were originally tightly juxtaposed and may have formed an integral part of the tomb of the woman commemorated by the inscription; possibly it was carved *in situ*, with the stonecutter crouching or lying on the ground to complete his work. Other smaller fragments of the inscription have also been discovered, one of which (dated circa 8–2 B.C.) is shown in the photograph on p. 175 of the students' textbook (see pp. 124–25 below for a transcription and translation of this fragment). For more information on this fragment and a photograph of both it and another in the Museo Nazionale, Rome, see Gordon 103–104 and plate 17.

The inscription itself is the record of a spoken *ōrātiō*, delivered by the husband of the dead woman. The version in the students' textbook is a free adaptation, loosely based on *I.L.S.* 8393, but making large omissions and including some material from other sources. It was long believed that the speaker of the *ōrātiō* was the Quintus Lucretius whose adventures, together with those of his wife Turia, are the subject of lively accounts in Appian, *Civil Wars* IV.44 and Valerius Maximus VI.72, and who was further identified with the Lucretius Vespillo who was consul in 19 B.C. These identifications, however, have now been generally rejected, most recently by Horsfall, who points out that the speech in *I.L.S.* 8393 shows an absence of political involvement and family pride, as well as evidence of some deficiencies in the speaker's rhetorical education, so that the speaker is most unlikely to be an ex-consul. The use of "Vespillo" and "Turia" in the students' textbook is purely for the convenience of having names which students can use.

Lewis and Reinhold I.484–87 and Lefkowitz and Fant 208–11 contain translations of the bulk of the inscription. There is an engaging (if somewhat rose-tinted) account of it in Warde Fowler 159–67, and there are helpful discussions in Balsdon, *Roman World* 204–205 and Lefkowitz's *Greece and Rome* article (31–47, especially 42–44). Horsfall's article, to which these notes are much indebted, is not easily accessible but contains the fullest and most recent discussion.

The text, even in its adapted form, contains some difficult parts. Be ready to help if students become bogged down (see p. 13 above).

Stage 43

Notes

1–2	**utrōque parente ... occīsīs:** perhaps by their slaves.
3	**mors ... mānsit:** Remind students that Turia at this time might still have been in her teens or early twenties. She was forbidden to speak in court because of her sex, but was still able to play a leading role in the proceedings – a good illustration of the point that a woman's power and position in classical times did not totally depend on her legal status.
4–5	**efflāgitandō ... investīgandō ... ulcīscendō:** the first appearance in the students' textbook of the ablative form of the gerund. The first example is translated in the facing vocabulary, and students should have little difficulty in working out the other two examples by analogy.
5–6	**sī adfuissem ... potuissem:** conditional sentence with pluperfect subjunctive; the apodosis is translated in the facing vocabulary. Do not discuss it further with students at this point; it will be the subject of a language note in Stage 46.
13–14	**inter cameram ... cēlātum:** This detail comes not from the inscription but from Valerius Maximus VI.7.2; it illustrates the troubles to which the proscribed and their families were put. Students may enjoy spotting Vespillo in the picture on p. 167 of the textbook.
14–15	**tanta ... cōnārēris:** The 2nd person singular form of the imperfect subjunctive of a deponent verb is likely to cause students some hesitation; the picture may provide a helpful reminder of the context.

Some Suggested Questions

What disaster happened to Turia on the night before her wedding? (If the students need more help, ask a series of simpler questions, e.g. "What did Turia suddenly become? When? How? Where did it happen?" etc., and similarly with the questions which follow.)
Why was Vespillo unable to help her in avenging her parents?
What two qualities did Turia display? What compliment does Vespillo pay to her efforts?
When Vespillo fled for his life, what practical help did Turia provide (a) at the time (b) regularly thereafter?
When Vespillo was declared a "public enemy," how did his friend react? What was Turia's advice? Where did she hide Vespillo? Why does Vespillo say that she was acting *nōn sine magnō perīculō* (line 15)?
The most suitable topic for exploration in this passage will probably be the historical background. Read some of the following material to the class, or have students themselves make reports on it:

(a) the proscription edict (Appian, *Civil Wars* IV.8–11, quoted by Lewis and Reinhold I.301–303);

Stage Commentaries

(b) the adventures of some of the proscribed (e.g. from Appian, *Civil Wars* IV.37–51);
(c) the humiliating treatment of "Turia" by the triumvir Lepidus, and her eventual success in seeking an amnesty for her proscribed husband (from a section of *I.L.S.* 8393 not included in the students' textbook, but given in Lewis and Reinhold I.486, Lefkowitz and Fant 210).

Suggestions for Consolidation: predicative dative (7); dative pronoun and participle at head of clause (7,9); perfect passive participle in accusative (8,14; see also Appendix D below); 1st and 2nd persons singular, perfect passive and deponent (1,12); purpose clause with relative pronoun (8).

Vocabulary Check: *fīō* (1); *uterque* (1); *maneō* (3); *officium* (3); *adsum* (5); *amplius* (5); *auxiliō est* (7); *praebeō* (10); *vītō* (11); *patior* (12); *cēlō* (14).

Tūria II (*I.L.S.* 8393, II.25–27, 31–36, 40–47)

Most students will again need help from time to time with the passage.

Notes

3   **precibus ... fortūna fāvisset:** The word order may catch the unwary.
3–4   **fāvisset ... cupīvissēmus:** conditional sentence with pluperfect subjunctive (see note on p. 117 above, on "Tūria" I, lines 5–6).
4   **annīs ... lābentibus:** If students are bewildered, ask for a literal translation first and then encourage a more idiomatic one.
6–8   **diffīdēns ... īnfēlīx:** After you have read this aloud, ask "What was Turia pessimistic about? What saddened her? What fears did she have about Vespillo?" etc.
10–11 **tē ipsam ... esse:** indirect statement continued from previous sentence. Ask the class "Who will find the wife whom Vespillo supposedly deserves? Is this Vespillo's own statement or is he reporting Turia's words? How can you tell? How will Turia regard the children of the new marriage?"
12   **quibus verbīs audītīs:** cf. *quibus verbīs dictīs*, "mātrōna Ephesia" II, p. 162, line 13.
       incēnsus sum: cf. *servātus sum*, "Tūria" I, p. 167, line 12. The question "What were Vespillo's feelings?" will bring out the point that Vespillo not only rejected Turia's suggestion, but was appalled by it.

The main point for discussion is likely to be Turia's proposal and Vespillo's reaction to it. What do the students feel about the contrasting

Stage 43

attitudes of Turia and Vespillo? What might the reaction of their Roman contemporaries have been (use this question as either an introduction or a follow-up to the background material)? Might the men, paradoxically, have tended to agree with Turia, and the women with Vespillo? In particular, would men have disagreed with Vespillo's undervaluing of *necessitās habendī līberōs* in lines 13–14? (If so, why does Vespillo say in line 15 that divorce would have been a *dēdecus* to him?)

Explore some other points of detail:

What does *vacuam* (line 9) mean? (Ask questions like this often, however obvious the answer may seem to you. The students are likely to see the point if you ask them to consider it, but if you do not draw their attention to it, they may not think about it.)

What does Turia mean by *dignam* (line 10)? What other qualities besides fertility might she look for in her successor?

What are Vespillo's four arguments against his wife's proposal? What does he mean by *fidem fallere*, and by *certa* and *dubiīs*, in line 14? Why does he break off in lines 14–15 with *quid plūra*? Does he feel that further details are irrelevant, or undignified?

Which word in lines 15–16 contrasts with *meō*, and which with *dolōre*? Antitheses like these support the view that, in spite of the occasional clumsiness, this *laudātiō* is not a totally artless piece of writing.

Suggestions for Consolidation: possessive dative (13).

Vocabulary Check: *fruor* + ablative (2); *magis ac magis* (2); *līberī* (2); *teneō* (7); *fīō* (8); *audeō* (8); *dignus* (10); *quaerō* (10); *adeō* (12); *vix* (12); *maneō* (15); *cēdō* (15).

Tūria III (*I.L.S.* 8393, I.28–30, II.54, 58–60, 69)

Notes

1 **contigit nōbīs:** If students find this hard, remind them of its occurrence in "Tūria" II, p. 168, line 1. Students may recall the *dī mānēs* from their mention on tombstones in Unit 3, Stage 28.

Some Suggested Questions

How long did the marriage last? What aspect of the marriage does Vespillo pick out for special comment? (Some alert students may spot the contradiction between Vespillo's phrase *sine ūllā discordiā* (1) and his previous account of the quarrel with Turia over her suggestion of a divorce.)

Why had Vespillo not expected his wife to die before him? (Note that

Stage Commentaries

the commonest reason in Roman times for a wife to predecease an older husband, death in childbirth, does not apply in this instance.) What encourages Vespillo to struggle against his grief? What is his consolation? What is his final prayer?
Invite students to comment on the qualities for which Vespillo praises Turia; are some of them a little unexpected? Are they the same qualities as the ones a modern husband might praise in his wife? (Study some of the original Latin words: *pudīcitia, obsequium, cōmitās, facilitās, assiduitās lānificiīs, religiō sine superstitiōne, ōrnātus nōn cōnspiciendus, cultus modicus.*)

The drawing on p. 165 shows "a virtuous woman spinning," based on a mosaic from North Africa. The woman is holding a distaff with her left hand and pulling out and twisting the thread with her right.

Suggestions for Consolidation: possessive dative (6; see also "Tūria" II, p. 168, line 13, and for further examples, the Unit 4 students' textbook, LI Section, "Review Grammar," p. 311, paragraph 4e, and p. 203 below).

Vocabulary Check: *dolor* (3,5); *aliquandō* (4); *ēripiō* (5); *adhūc* (6); *patior* (7).

Second Language Note (*Genitive and Ablative of Gerund*)

Reassure your students by telling them that they have now met all forms of the gerund in common use, since it has no nominative and no plural, and the dative is rare.

1 *servus meus numquam artēs legendī et scrībendī didicit.*
2 *Vespillō, diū latendō, inimīcōs fefellit.*
3 *tantus erat strepitus ut amīcus noster nūllam occāsiōnem dormiendī habēret.*
4 *cōnsul, bellum callidissimē gerendō, hostēs tandem reppulit.*
5 *tacēte, puerī! nihil querendō efficitis.*
6 *omnēs mīlitēs studiō pugnandī ardēbant.*

Drills

Exercise 1   Type: vocabulary
              Grammatical point being practiced: synonyms
Students may confuse *fīdus* and *fidēs*. You may supplement this drill with words from the "Synonym Searches" at the end of Stages 41–43.

Exercise 2   Type: completion
Missing item: verb
Test of accuracy: sense and morphology
Grammatical point being practiced: future tense
Incidental practice: conditional clauses, introduced in Stage 42

Exercise 3   Type: translation from English, using restricted pool of Latin words
Grammatical points being practiced (the relevant page of the Language Information Section, "Review Grammar," is given in parentheses): 1st person plural imperfect passive (296); fearing clauses (318, paragraph 8); ablative absolute (313, paragraph 6h); 4th declension (284); ablative of time (312, paragraph 6d); present infinitive (301); perfect indicative (304) and present indicative (303) of deponent verbs; *id quod* (292, paragraph 9).

Third Language Note (*Position of Verb of Speaking, Asking, etc. with Indirect Statement and Question*)

The main point to stress is the need to read the sentence straight through before translating. The so-called rule, "First find the verb" is usually less helpful than an instruction to *notice* the verb of speaking, asking, etc. while reading through the sentence.

The tense of the verbs of speaking, etc. in paragraph 3 varies between present and past. Be on the lookout for any signs of insecurity in either recognizing or coping with these tenses, and provide further examples if needed. Incorrect translation of paragraph 3, sentence 6, may indicate that students need additional practice.

Note that sometimes an English translation is more effective if the Latin word order is kept:

quārē Imperātor Agricolam revocāverit, numquam sciēmus.
(Why the emperor recalled Agricola, we will never know.)

rēgem rēctē occīsum esse, nēmō negābit.
(That the king was justifiably killed, no one will deny.)

For further examples, refer students back to *mīles, quī mātrōnam esse ... animadverterat* ("mātrōna Ephesia" I, p. 162, line 28) and *mātrōnae quid accidisset exposuit* ("mātrōna Ephesia" II, p. 162, lines 6–7, with illustration).

Stage Commentaries

The Background Material

On divorce and remarriage generally, Balsdon *Roman World* 209–23 is invaluable. There is a full account of the legal aspects in Corbett 218–51 and a concise summary in Hammond and Scullard, s.v. *Marriage, Law of*, paragraph 8. Crook 105–106 is useful, and Carcopino 109–15 is lively and readable, if somewhat rhetorical and over-ready to take everything Martial and Juvenal say at face value. Williams quotes Aulus Gellius' account of the Carvilius divorce in full (*Tradition and Originality* 372), and discusses Vergil's use of Roman marriage concepts, including the *ūnivira* ideal and the *de facto* nature of Roman marriage, in *Tradition and Originality* 374–87 (73–77 in abridged version).

The Juvenal quotation in the students' textbook is from *Satires* VI.225ff. "They marry to divorce, divorce to marry" is Seneca, *De Beneficiis* III.16.2. The Zois and Antipater divorce agreement is given in full in Lewis and Reinhold II.407–408; it is apparent from the complete text that the marriage lasted less than a year.

The most interesting way to approach the topic is probably to look at particular instances of divorce in Roman times, especially involving individuals mentioned elsewhere in the Course or otherwise known to the students. In some cases, students can find out the details themselves, with the aid of references supplied by you, and report their findings back to the class. For example:

The tempestuous marriage of Quintus Cicero and Pomponia (from which an incident was described in the Unit 4 students' textbook, p. 71) not surprisingly ended in divorce in 45 B.C. Quintus contemplated remarriage, but decided against it, remarking that life offered no happiness greater than a single bed (Cicero, *Ad Atticum* XIV.13.5).

The marriage of Quintus Cicero's more famous brother Marcus to Terentia lasted for thirty years, but eventually broke up. Of the twenty-four surviving letters he wrote to her, the earlier ones (especially those written from exile) are affectionate, but the tone grows distinctly cooler as the marriage deteriorates; in the end, believing she was swindling him, he divorced her. Being then in acute difficulties over the repayment of her dowry, he married the young and wealthy Publilia, only for this marriage, too, to collapse in a few months, leaving Cicero's financial problems unmitigated.

When P. Clodius, a young man of colorful reputation, was discovered disguised as a girl in the house of Julius Caesar during a religious rite from which men were excluded, people claimed he was having an affair with Caesar's wife Pompeia. Caesar thereupon divorced her, but declared he did not believe the accusation himself, and on being asked "In that case, why the divorce?" made his infamous remark that Caesar's wife must be above suspicion. (Mention of Clodius in this incident may help prepare the way for the appearance of his sister Clodia in the background material of Stage 45.)

The five marriages of Pompey (two terminated by death, two by divorce, and the last by his own death) illustrate not only the exploitation of marriage and divorce by Roman *nōbilēs* for political reasons but also the fact (exemplified in Pompey's marriage to Caesar's daughter Julia) that a marriage arranged out of political calculation can still be characterized by strong mutual affection.

If the inscription *C.I.L.* V.5279 refers to the father of Pliny the Younger (a disputed attribution), the marriage of Pliny's parents ended in divorce, and his father went off to live with a concubine called Lutulla, by whom he had two sons.

Lewis and Reinhold I.508–509 quote from Valerius Maximus' collection of instances in Republican times where a husband divorced his wife for trivial or eccentric reasons, such as visiting the games without his knowledge or going out with her head uncovered. Perhaps few of the anecdotes are authentic, but they illustrate the Romans' belief that in Rome's earlier days, male dominance had emphatically been the norm in marriage.

Generally, the law was more insistent on formalities and public proceedings for ending a marriage *cum manū* than a marriage *sine manū*. (Augustus made a short-lived attempt to extend the formalities to *sine manū* marriage, for example, by requiring a declaration of divorce before witnesses.) If the wife had been married *cum manū*, her husband, if he wished to divorce her, had to take the necessary legal steps to transfer her to the *manus* of somebody else, either a member of her own family or an appointed guardian. Whether the marriage was *cum manū* or *sine manū*, the return of part or all of the dowry to the woman's family was crucial, to help her to secure a second marriage. Students may note that the dowry of Zois, in the divorce document quoted in the textbook (p. 175), was relatively paltry; if she had been a member of a powerful dynasty of Roman *nōbilēs*, the dowry would have been much more substantial.

Seneca, *De Matrimonio* 72–77, quoted by Balsdon, *Roman World* 208, records several anecdotes illustrating Roman admiration of *ūnivirae*. But the social and economic pressures for marriage (and remarriage) meant there was a sizeable gap between preaching and practice. Rudd 42–47, in an interesting discussion of Dido's actions in *Aeneid* IV, suggests that

Stage Commentaries

by the time of Augustus, *ūnivirātus* enjoyed a sentimental esteem as a pleasant if rather old-fashioned ideal, but this respect for *ūnivirātus* had little significant effect on people's behavior, nor were people likely to blame a widow if she remarried. Augustus himself had no doubts about the matter. His marriage legislation imposed financial penalties on childless widows between the ages of twenty and fifty if they failed to remarry within a year of their husband's death, and he made frequent use of divorce and remarriage in his own family when the political occasion required; for example, his daughter Julia was married first to Marcellus, then on Marcellus' death to Agrippa, then on Agrippa's death to Tiberius, who had himself been forced to divorce his existing wife in order to marry Julia.

Some Suggested Activities

Encourage students to decipher as many letters as they can from the first five lines in the photograph of the fragment of the inscription shown in their textbook, p. 175. Ask them to copy out on a sheet of paper as many letters as they can, leaving space for those they cannot decipher. Make sure they copy the letters exactly as they appear in the inscription, including flourishes, interpuncts (instead of spaces between words), tall "I"s (for "i"s with macron), and "V"s (= consonantal "u"s) for "U"s (= vocalic "u"s). (Sometimes they will have difficulty distinguishing among "I"s, "H"s, "T"s, and "E"s. Provide them with a good magnifying glass.) When the students are totally stymied, distribute the following transliteration as a handout and let them use it to complete their transcripts:

[DĪS MĀNIBVS ... U]XŌRIS
[AMPLISSIMA SVBSI]DIA FVGAE MEAE PRAESTITISTĪ;
ŌRNĀMENTĪS / [TVĪS IV̄VISTĪ MĒ], CVM OMNE AVRVM
MARGARĪTAQUE CORPORĪ / [TVŌ DĒTRACTA
TRĀD]IDISTĪ MIHI ET SVBINDE FAMILIĀ, NVMMĪS,
FRV̄CTIBVS, / [CALLIDĒ DĒCEPTĪS A]DVERSĀRIŌRVM
CVSTŌDIBVS, APSENTIAM MEAM LOCVPLĒTĀSTĪ. /

Notes: Letters in square brackets [] are missing on the stone, and have been supplied by scholars; CORPORĪ: for this use of the dative, see students' textbook, "Review Grammar," p. 311, 4d; -D- in A]DVERSĀRIŌRUM, is a damaged letter (note interpunct between AD and VERSĀRIŌRUM which is usually inscribed between words, not syllables, as here, within words); APSENTIAM = ABSENTIAM; LOCVPLĒTĀSTĪ = LOCVPLĒTĀVISTĪ.

Stage 43

To the sacred memory of [my] wife.
You furnished most ample means [?] for my escape; with your [?]
jewels you aided me [?] when you took off all the gold and pearls
from your person and handed them [?] over to me; and promptly
with slaves, money, [and] provisions, having cleverly deceived [?] the
enemies' guards, you enriched my absence...
(Gordon 103)

Ask students to answer the following questions about their transcripts;
you may need to help them with some of the answers, particularly the
difference between the sound "p" and the voiced "b" for the last one:

What do you notice about the size of the letters in successive lines of the
  inscription? Do you do the same sometimes? Why?
How did the inscriber mark breaks between words? Is there an
  exception to this practice? What is it?
How did the inscriber mark breaks between the two sentences in the
  first four lines (between PRAESTITISTĪ and ŌRNĀMENTĪS)? Is
  this the modern way of showing breaks between sentences?
How did the inscriber mark long "i"s, that is, "i"s with implied long
  marks?
How did the inscriber write "u"s? Did he make them different from
  "v"s?
Which word was evidently pronounced by the composer of the
  inscription and/or the inscriber differently from what modern Latin
  dictionaries state? Are the two variant letters in this word very
  different in sound? Why?

Suggestions for Discussion

1 Why did the Romans like to think that divorce was not introduced
  into Rome until the 3rd century B.C., whereas in fact it had already
  existed for two centuries by that date? (This could lead to discussion
  of the Romans' tendency to idealize their early past as a moral
  Golden Age (cf. the myth of the Four Ages in Ovid, *Metamorphoses*
  I.89–150); do other societies similarly idealize the past?)
2 Why is there no masculine equivalent for *ūnivira*?

Vocabulary Checklist

Check students' understanding of the difference between *magistrātus* and
English "magistrate." With *ulcīscī–ultiō–ultor* compare *scrībere–scrīptiō–
scrīptor, dēfendere–dēfēnsiō–dēfēnsor, coniūrāre–coniūrātiō–coniūrātor*, etc.

Stage Commentaries

Suggestions for Further Work

For examples of funerary inscriptions which students could study, discuss, and compare with "Turia" (especially Section III), see Lewis and Reinhold I.489, II.283–86, and the inscriptions in C.S.C.P. *The Roman World*, e.g. numbers 1,2,5,7,9,11,14,16.

STAGE 44: DAEDALUS ET ĪCARUS

BRIEF OUTLINE
Reading passages   Ovid, *Metamorphoses* VIII.183–235
Background material   Icarus in art
Language notes   historical present
                        omission of word from one of two clauses
                        3rd person plural perfect in *-ēre*

DIGEST
This mythical story from Ovid's *Metamorphoses* describes the ill-fated escape of Daedalus the engineer and his son Icarus from the island of Crete. It has a clear narrative structure, blends humor with pathos, and can appeal powerfully to the imagination. (It is a favorite with teenagers who are having problems with their parents!) It also presents the students with a more substantial piece of poetry than those in Stages 36, 39, and 42, and prepares the way for the increased complexities of the poetry in Stages 45 and 47. The illustrations and background material use the Icarus episode to exemplify the power of classical myth to inspire later artists and writers.

GRAMMATICAL POINTS
historical present
    e.g. *dīxit et ignōtās animum dīmittit in artēs.*
increased incidence of *-ēre* for *-ērunt*
    e.g. *inter opus monitūsque genae maduēre senīlēs.*
increased incidence of economy of expression by omission of words
    e.g. *et movet ipse suās et nātī respicit ālās.*

SENTENCE PATTERN
framing/separation in verse word order
    e.g. *mōtāque pependit in aurā.*

Part I (*Metamorphoses* VIII.183–89, 191–92)

(The obscure and probably corrupt line 190 has been omitted.)
Hollis' commentary will be helpful throughout this Stage.

Explain the title of Ovid's poem, *Metamorphoses* ("changes of shape"), to the students. Add that Ovid uses ingenious digressions and transitions to

Stage 44

include several stories which do *not* contain a metamorphosis (like the present episode of Daedalus and Icarus, unless one regards it as a tale of metamorphosis from man to bird). Tell the students some of the earlier parts of the story, such as Pasiphaë's infatuation with the bull, the birth of the Minotaur (and perhaps his killing by Theseus), and Daedalus' construction of the Labyrinth. The king's refusal to allow Daedalus to leave was a punishment for facilitating Pasiphaë's union with the bull. Use the map in the students' textbook, p. 180, to establish some basic data: that Crete is an island, that Daedalus' hometown was Athens, etc.

Notes

1–2 **longum ... exilium:** In dealing with these and other split phrases, help the class by carefully phrasing while you read aloud, and by periodically reminding the students that they must read each phrase or sentence straight through to the end. See also "Suggestions for Consolidation" below.

3–4 **clausus erat pelagō ... undās obstruat:** Not only is Crete an island, but Minos also has many ships at his command.

6 **dīxit et ...:** Encourage the class to avoid literal translations in favor of "So he spoke, and..." or "When he had said this, he...," etc.

8–9 **clīvō ... avēnīs:** The range of ablative uses is a feature of Latin poetry with which students need to become familiar; this familiarization is usually slow and gradual. Do not draw up lists of different ablative usages, as this merely discourages students by opening up an apparently infinite field of possibilities. Instead, encourage them to use the context as a guide to the required meaning, and discuss the variety of uses when the students have encountered many more examples; some comment appears in a language note in Stage 47.

At first, maintain a brisk pace and concentrate on establishing the narrative, postponing detailed exploration of the text until students have become more used to Ovid and his language. Focus on Daedalus' wish to escape, his reasons for choosing to escape by air, and the making of the wings.

Use comprehension questions to highlight the precision of Ovid's account in lines 7–9. "What was the first thing Daedalus did with the feathers? In what order did he arrange them? What appearance would they have had to an onlooker?" Help the class to visualize the arrangement of feathers in order to interpret the difficult phrase *ut clīvō crēvisse putēs* ("the feathers seem to have grown naturally (*crēvisse*) in order of ascending length (*clīvō*)" (Hollis)). If they are puzzled, use the simile which follows for clarification, ask "What exactly is the point of similarity between the wings and the Pan-pipes?" and invite volunteers to draw both wings and pipes on the blackboard.

Stage Commentaries

Suggestions for Consolidation: Throughout this Stage, there are opportunities to practice split phrases, in which an adjective is separated from the noun it describes and noun + adjective phrases are juxtaposed or intertwined with each other, as described in Language Notes in Stages 36, 39, and 42 (see above on lines 1–2). When the students have read and discussed the passage, pick out examples of split phrases (e.g. those in lines 1–2, 6, 8–9, and 9, some of which are underlined to help the students) for the students to study, read aloud, or retranslate, identifying the case and sometimes noting the effect achieved by the phrase (e.g. the highlighting of the key word *ignōtās* in line 6).

Vocabulary Check: *intereā* (1); *pelagus* (3); *unda* (3); *animus* (6); *pōnō* (7).

Part II (*Metamorphoses* VIII.193–202)

Notes

1   **adligat:** to be understood with *mediās*; both ablatives qualify both accusatives.

4   **ignārus:** used in a way unfamiliar to students, to introduce indirect statement. Use question 2 to establish the sense, or ask the class to identify the case of *sē* and form of *tractāre*.

5–8   **ōre ... opus:** Several comprehension questions may be necessary before the students attempt a translation. Develop and expand the first part of question 3: "What were the two things Icarus did? Which feathers was he trying to catch? What was he doing to the wax?" etc.

9   **lībrāvit:** Students are usually slow to see that this governs *corpus*. Ask "What did he balance?" and if they say "the wings," tell them to take a second look at line 10.

Elaborate now, on the blackboard or overhead transparency, the diagram mentioned above in connection with Part I. Ask a student to mark in the wax and thread at appropriate points. Ask the class, on *parvō curvāmine* in line 2, "What was bent, the wings' edge or their surface?"

    Ovid's description of Icarus playing is noteworthy not only for its homely and sympathetic realism, but also because the characterization of Icarus prepares us for the eventual tragedy, and lends it plausibility; there is pathos, too, for those who know (as presumably all Ovid's original listeners knew) that Icarus is doomed. Question 2 might be expanded by a further question, "Does Icarus understand at all what is going on?", to bring out the significance of line 4 ("If he only knew what he was fooling with, he would stop fooling at once!"). Elicit the fact that Icarus is too young to be expected to behave responsibly – and is therefore all the more of a risk on the journey – by asking "Does Ovid

Stage 44

suggest that Icarus is doing all this because he is a naughty boy?" or "Why doesn't Daedalus rebuke his son?" The students may be able to pick out such phrases as *ōre renīdentī* (line 5) and *lūsūs ... suō* (line 7), which make it clear that to Icarus his father's activity is simply a new and agreeable game.

Question 4 attempts to establish that Daedalus, having constructed the wings, is making a trial run. Ask the class to describe his action in detail, and help them to feel the vividness and tension of Ovid's narrative. The moment when Daedalus puts his whole weight on the wings (*lībrāvit in ālās*, line 9), the steady beating of the air *mōtā*, line 10), and the hovering (*pependit*, line 10), are all described concisely and effectively.

The picture in the students' textbook, p. 183, shows Michael Ayrton's bronze, *Daedalus winged*. Ask the class to describe the bronze, helping them if necessary with such questions as "What moment in the story do you think the bronze illustrates?" "Suggest a reason for the posture in which Daedalus is standing." "Do Ayrton's wings differ from Ovid's Latin description?"

Suggestions for Consolidation: perfect passive participle in accusative (2; see also Appendix D); split phrases (3,4,5, etc.; see "Suggestions for Consolidation" on Part I, p. 19 above).

Vocabulary Check: *cēra* (1,6); *compōnō* (2); *vērus* (3); *opus* (8); *āla* (9); *pendeō* (10).

Part III (*Metamorphoses* VIII.203–209)

Notes

1 **et:** postponed. Compare the use of *-que*.
1–2 **"mediō ... moneō":** The interweaving of direct speech and narrative, and the displacement of *ut*, may cause difficulty. Read the sentence straight through to *moneō* and then ask "What did Daedalus say?"
2 **"moneō":** placed after the indirect command which it governs. Perhaps try a simpler example, with the subject expressed, e.g. *centuriō mīlitibus ut pugnārent imperāvit*, or *senex puerōs ut festīnārent monuit*.
5 **"iubeō":** See previous note.
  "strictumque Ōriōnis ēnsem": Explain (or ask an astronomically-minded student to explain) to the class that Orion with his sword is a prominent constellation in the south, useful to navigators.
6 **"mē duce":** Remind students of parallel examples (*Eleazārō duce, mē auctōre*, etc.) from previous Units.

Stage Commentaries

Some Suggested Questions

What advice did Daedalus give to Icarus?
What were the dangers of going too low or too high?
How would Icarus know which way to go?
What else was Daedalus doing while giving this advice?
Which word in line 7 highlights the idea of danger?
Why is Daedalus' advice so detailed, and why does he repeat himself (*mediō ... līmite* in line 1; *inter utrumque* in line 4)? Is he just a fussy old man? Is he shrewdly aware of the importance of repetition when giving instructions? Is he desperately trying to explain a highly risky situation to someone too young to understand it? Is the point being emphasized because Ovid wants to prepare the reader (or listener) for the story's eventual climax?

Suggestions for Consolidation: gerund (6); split phrases (1,5,7)

Vocabulary Check: *penna* (3); *uterque* (4); *nec* (4); *aut* (5); *āla* (7).

First Language Note (*Historical Present*)

The class could pick out additional examples of the historical present from the opening lines of Part II (p. 182) and the end of Part III (p. 184), noting that it can be used alongside perfect or imperfect tenses (as in the example in paragraph 1, and the lines referred to in paragraph 4). Point out that the historical present occurs in English as well as Latin, though less frequently. Often it is colloquial ("I was standing on the corner when all of a sudden this car draws up and three men jump out," etc.).

Part IV (*Metamorphoses* VIII.210–20)

Notes

4	**comitīque timet:** first occurrence of *timeō* used with the dative. Draw students' attention to the context, and to the case of *comitī*.
5	**quae:** appears unusually late in its clause. Phrase carefully while reading aloud.
7	**ālās:** object of both *movet* and *respicit*. Put *movet ipse suās ālās* on the blackboard or overhead transparency for translation, then add *et nātī respicit ālās*, and finally remove the first *ālās* as superfluous. Sentences like these are discussed in the next language note.
8–11	**hōs...deōs:** a complex sentence. After students have studied the facing

Stage 44

vocabulary, and you have read the lines aloud, ask them questions about the scene described by Ovid. Such questions help to establish the surface meaning and also add to the students' appreciation of the poetry. For example:

Teacher: Who are the three people mentioned here? ... What are they doing? ... What does Ovid say about the fisherman? ... *Why* was the rod quivering? ... (*Students:* He's catching a heavy fish ... he's surprised at the sight of the aeronauts.) ... What about the other two people? What are they doing? ... Does *innīxus* refer to the shepherd, the plowman, or both? ... Why are they leaning on the staff and plow-handle? ... (*Students:* ... to get a better view of Daedalus and Icarus ... they've just stopped to take a breather.) Does the next line help you to decide? ... (*Students: vīdit* comes after the description of the two men, so the shepherd must have been leaning on his staff already, when Daedalus and Icarus came into view.) Does that help to explain the fishing-rod? ... (*Students:* ... he was catching a fish; that's why the line was quivering – and then as he hauled the fish out of the water, his gaze happened to move up and he saw the aeronauts.)

Such an approach is in fact exploring the precision and pictorial quality of Ovid's description without ever using such terms explicitly. It is probably a better approach than "How skillfully does Ovid describe the scene?" and certainly better than "Notice how good Ovid is at visual description."

10–11 **quīque ... deōs:** relative clause placed before main clause and antecedent. Question A4 may be helpful here.

Lead the students, while they are looking for points of similarity between the aeronauts and the birds (in answer to question B2), from the more obvious points ("Both pairs are flying" and "Both pairs are parent-and-child") to the physical resemblances in the situation ("The older leads the way, looking back continually at the younger, weaker one – *teneram* – and showing him how to fly") and the similarity of emotion (*comitīque timet*, line 4, applicable both to Daedalus and to the mother-bird). Abler students may be able to spot not only the similarities but also a significant difference: the situation of the bird and nestling is a natural one, whereas that of Daedalus and Icarus is not.

Students will readily find *oscula ... nōn iterum repetenda* (lines 2–3) and *damnōsās* (line 6) when they are searching for overtones of disaster in answer to question B3. Guide them to the ominous implications of *crēdidit esse deōs* in line 11 (in the world of classical mythology, it is ill-advised for mortals to usurp the attributes of gods).

Draw the students' attention to the fact that the Pompeian wall-painting reproduced on p. 185 is a composite picture, showing two different phases of the story. Icarus is depicted twice, once in the top

131

Stage Commentaries

right-hand corner falling out of the sky and again as a corpse in the center at the bottom. This is clearer in slide IV.1. Do the students think it would have been better to have painted *two* pictures, on adjacent panels of the wall, or is something gained by showing both phases within a single picture? Encourage the class to describe the painting in their own words, perhaps noting how the painter has built up a context for Icarus' death: not just sky and sea but a walled town on an island, men in boats (perhaps they have just retrieved the corpse?) and a sacred pillar in the foreground by the spectators.

Suggestions for Consolidation: 4th declension nouns (1,2); split phrases (1,2,2–3,4–5,6,8).

Vocabulary Check: *opus* (1); *gena* (1); *penna* (3); *comes* (4); *hortor* (6); *āla* (7); *aliquis* (8); *aethēr* (10).

Part V (*Metamorphoses* VIII.220–35)

Discuss question A1 in the students' textbook as soon as students have read lines 1–3. Ovid locates the scene of the catastrophe fairly precisely, partly to conform to the requirements of the myth and partly to spell out the circumstances of the tragedy ("So much had been safely accomplished, and so much had still to be done, when disaster struck"). Some students may ask why Daedalus and Icarus, after flying steadily towards Athens, have swerved unexpectedly eastwards. The closing lines of the section will reveal an explanation. Ask the class why Ovid adds *Iūnōnia* (line 1) and *fēcunda ... melle* (line 3). (On the use of adjectives to add variety to a string of names, see p. 101 above.)

Use simple comprehension and grammatical questions to help students with lines 4–9. For example:

Which verb tells you Icarus' feelings in line 4? Which adjective describes his flight?
What did he do to his leader? Does "left him behind" mean that he passed him, or something more?

Tingay, *Comprehendite* 79 is a useful source of ideas for further questions.

Lines 10–11 are the hardest lines in this section, partly because of the intertwining of nouns and adjectives, and partly because Ovid is combining two points; the description of Icarus, shouting until his cries are stifled in the water, merges into the explanation for the name of the Icarian sea. Expand on question A4 by asking "Was Icarus already

Stage 44

dead when he hit the water? How do you know?" followed by "Where did Icarus fall? What was the name of the sea?" Further study of the map should now clear up the puzzle about the aeronauts' route which was left unresolved at lines 1–3, and the role of myth in explanations of place-names should become clear.

Consider one or two of the following questions:

"Why does Ovid describe Daedalus in line 5 as *ducem* rather than *patrem* (which he in fact wrote in his earlier version of this story, *Ars Amatoria* II.84)?" Possible answers might include the alliteration with *dēseruit* (used, as often by Ovid, to mark a key moment in a story), and the use of *ducem* to indicate the role which rightly belonged to Daedalus (cf. *mē duce*, Part III, p. 184, line 6).

"What is the point of *odōrātās* in line 7?" ("Proleptic – the smell of the wax is brought out as it melts in the sun" (Hollis).) If you ask "Has Ovid suggested earlier that the wax was easily softened?", students may be able to find *mollībat* in Part II, p. 182, line 7. Discussion of the tense of *tābuerant* (line 8) may help to bring out the rapidity with which Ovid's narrative moves at this point.

"In what sense were Icarus' arms bare (*nūdōs*, line 8)? Does *quatit* refer to his attempts to stay airborne or is he trying to attract attention?"

"How can the same word (*rēmigiō*, line 9) mean both wings and oars? What is the point of similarity?" On metaphor generally, see p. 127 above. Hollis compares the movement of a bank of oars beating the water to the movement of wings beating the air. There may also be irony in Ovid's choice of "oars" as a metaphor for wings; oars (and a boat) are very much what Icarus needs.

"How appropriate is the repetition of *dīxit* (lines 12–13) and the change to *dīcēbat* (line 14)?"

"Is Icarus' behavior here consistent with what we have been told about him previously?" Students generally decide that Icarus' irresponsible adventurousness here fits well with his playfulness in Part II; but they also often feel that there has been a shift in Ovid's presentation of him, from child to young man.

Before students attempt to answer question B3, have them re-read all five Parts rapidly. Take the lead and do most of the translation for them, but require regular contributions from the class. The question "Should either of the characters be blamed for the accident?" might be answered by referring to the indications of Icarus' impetuosity in Part V, pp. 188–89, lines 4–5, or to Daedalus' self-recrimination, p. 189, line 15, and the hints in Part IV, p. 186, lines 1–2, that he foresaw the tragedy. Ovid himself, though showing plenty of sympathy for Daedalus' and Icarus' feelings, nevertheless adopts the conventional attitude of the

Stage Commentaries

ancient world to "tampering with nature" (cf. *ignōtās* in Part I, p. 181, line 6, and Part III, p. 184, line 7; *nātūram ... novat* in Part I, p. 181, line 7, etc.).

Ask the students whether they sympathize with one character more than the other. Some may see Icarus as a rash fool; others may find Daedalus' cautious attitude irritating, no less so when justified by the event. Some may see the characters as "types" – the Cautious Father and Impetuous Son. You might ask, "Why does the younger man reject the fruits of his father's greater experience? Is this far-fetched or is it like real life? Would it be better if youth *always* listened to the cautious advice of older generations?" etc.

The question on p. 188, "Describe what you see in this picture," is particularly useful with the painting by Allegrini there reproduced and could also be used with other illustrations in this Stage. Students are very familiar with looking at pictures, on television and elsewhere, and are often quicker than adults at spotting visual details. On Allegrini's painting, ask them "Does the picture help to explain why Icarus came to grief but Daedalus escaped?" "Are the two spectators on the promontory behaving differently from the others?" "In what ways does this painting differ from the Pompeian wall-painting (p. 185)? For example, which painting gives more sense of spaciousness?"

Vocabulary Check: *coepī* (4); *ūllus* (9); *excipiō* (11); *īnfēlīx* (12); *unda* (14).

Second Language Note (*Omission of Word from One of Two Clauses*)

If necessary, use simpler examples of this point in the Unit 2 students' textbook, LI Section, "Review Grammar," p. 189, and on p. 35 above. Stress the importance of reading the sentence through to the very end before attempting a translation. If the class find paragraph 5 difficult, expand on examples 3–8 in the same way as examples 1 and 2. Put the expanded version on the blackboard or overhead transparency in stages; for example, in example 3 write *nōs in urbe habitāmus*, then add *vōs prope mare habitātis*, and finally remove *habitāmus* (cf. note on Part IV, line 7, p. 130 above). When the students have gotten the point, ask them to work out an expanded version for themselves, inserting the word that has to be "supplied" from one clause to another. Encourage them to compare the relative effectiveness of the "shorter" and "longer" versions of each example; they are usually quick to see that the "shorter" version, though harder to translate, sounds neater and more forceful.

Further examples:

1 *culpam mīlitēs in servōs, servī in mīlitēs trānsferre poterunt.* (Stage 41, p. 116, lines 8–9)
2 *Fortūna multīs dat nimis, satis nūllī.* (Martial)
3 *dum caelum stēllās, dum vehit amnis aquās.* (Tibullus)

Drills

Exercise 1   Type: vocabulary
              Grammatical point being practiced: meanings of *solvere*

Exercise 2   Type: completion
              Missing item: adjective
              Test of accuracy: sense and morphology
              Grammatical point being practiced: agreement of noun and adjective

Allow competent and ambitious students to complete some or all of the sentences with adjectives of their own choice, not taken from the pool printed in the textbook.

longus (in pool) is sometimes confused with *longior* (LI Section, "Review Grammar," p. 288).

Exercise 3   Type: transformation
              Grammatical points being practiced: 1st and 2nd persons singular and plural, present, future, and imperfect passive, introduced in Stages 35 and 39; ablative singular and plural

The exercises in the students' LI Section, "Review Grammar," pp. 296–97, paragraphs 2 and 3, may be helpful as either an introduction or a follow-up to this exercise. Students tend to have difficulty with the meaning of *moritūrus*, and consequently the tense of *sepelient*, in sentence 3a.

Exercise 4   Type: completion
              Missing item: infinitive phrase
              Test of accuracy: sense and morphology
              Grammatical point being practiced: indirect statement

For further practice, see students' LI Section, pp. 319–20, paragraphs 1 and 3.

Third Language Note *(3rd Person Plural Perfect in -ēre)*

The most convenient way of practicing this ending is to concentrate on the point which is most likely to bother students – the possibility of confusion between this form and the infinitive. Select a number of verbs

Stage Commentaries

from the Unit 4 students' textbook, Part Four, "Complete Vocabulary," pp. 354–97, of the LI Section, and ask the class to pick out the infinitive of each verb and then to give the verb's 3rd person plural perfect form in *-ēre* (easily deducible from the 1st person perfect form, listed immediately after the infinitive). Compare the two forms, and their respective translations. This exercise can also provide students with useful incidental practice in verbs whose perfect stem is hard to recognize; for example, the class might study pairs like *agnōscere* and *agnōvēre*, *scindere* and *scidēre*. Finally, drill a mixture of assorted infinitives and 3rd person plural perfect *-ēre* forms (e.g. *exercēre*, *iussēre*, *servāvēre*, etc.).

For a brief account of the use made of the *-ēre* perfect form by Roman writers, see R. D. Williams (large commentary) on Vergil, *Aeneid* V.580.

The Background Material

Stress the date of the vase-painting in the students' textbook, p. 184, to make the point that the myth was not invented by Ovid but was already a very old story when Ovid wrote.

When students are discussing Ayrton's bronze statue, p. 183, tell them that Ayrton's work was dominated for ten years by the Daedalus myth. His interest, however, had been aroused not by Ovid, but by Vergil's account in *Aeneid* VI.14ff. Another of Ayrton's works on the Icarus theme is shown in slide IV.3.

When students are considering Bruegel's painting, p. 197, encourage them to comment on the behavior of the bystanders (who ignore Icarus' fall completely, unlike the spectators in the Pompeian and Allegrini paintings) and the extreme lack of emphasis on Icarus himself (the students may take a while to find him). Why do they think Bruegel called his painting *The Fall of Icarus* and then paid so little attention to Icarus himself? Judging from the picture, do the triumphs and tragedies of manned flight matter less than the everyday business of real life? Is the German proverb "No plow stops just because a man dies" relevant? Is this also the point of Auden's poem? Or are Auden and Bruegel suggesting that people just want to get on with their own lives, rather than become involved in other people's tragedies? In which painting is Icarus' fate sadder – the Pompeian wall-painting, where he is surrounded by people grieving about his death, or the Bruegel painting, where nobody wants to know? Morford, in a helpful discussion, points out that Bruegel is strongly influenced by Vergil (*Georgic* I) as well as by Ovid.

Suggestions for Discussion

1 Of the various treatments of Icarus in art, which did you most like or dislike, and why? (Emphasize to the class that there was never any "standard" version of the myth; each artist, including Ovid and Auden, handled the myth in the way which most appealed to him, choosing details which he wanted to use, rejecting others and inventing further ideas of his own.)
2 Suggest reasons why this story has appealed to so many artists and been retold so often. (Students should, between them, be able to suggest several possibilities: that the story is visually dramatic, for example, or that the characters are easy to relate to or sympathize with, or that the story arouses strong childhood memories. Mention that, for similar reasons, many other stories in the *Metamorphoses* have strongly influenced later art and literature. Tell various other such stories, or better yet, name some of the best known (e.g. Daphne, Phaëthon (a myth with a moral similar to that of Icarus), Pygmalion, Baucis and Philemon) and let a student who knows one of them tell it in summary form.

If your students are not acquainted with Ovid or the myths of the *Metamorphoses*, assign readings, as homework for younger students, among the wonderfully retold versions of Thomas Bulfinch in Bulfinch and Holme 43–105, 114–227, 234–243. (Bulfinch is something of an American classic himself; he flourished during the nineteenth-century "American Renaissance" of literature in New England, and first published his retold versions of myth in 1855 under the title *The Age of Fable*. The modern abridgement by Bryan Holme is still very readable, beautifully illustrated, and widely available as a Penguin paperback.) As homework for older students, assign selections in English from the best of the several translations of the *Metamorphoses*, i.e. by Horace Gregory (see Bibliography, p. 255), or if this is unavailable, from translations by other writers.

Vocabulary Checklist

Compare the pair of cognates *vincīre–vinculum* with *vehere–vehiculum*, *spectāre–spectāculum*, *mīrārī–mīrāculum*, etc.

Suggestions for Further Work

Consider Ovid's text from the point of view of a director making a film of the episode. Which moments might s/he treat by long-range shots, and which by close-ups? How could s/he realize the similes in Parts I and IV effectively on the screen?

Ask your students to write their own scripts, describing their choice of

Stage Commentaries

successive shots with notes and/or sketches, and adding ideas of their own for such things as musical accompaniment, "zoom" shots, fade-outs, and fade-ins, and special visual effects. They often show considerable expertise on technical points, and sometimes spend long hours producing a script which is meticulously written, sophisticated, and (in spite of occasional gimmickry) very effective.

STAGE 45: LESBIA

BRIEF OUTLINE

Reading passages	Catullus, *Poems* 51, 5, 3, 70, 72, 85, 8, 11
Background material	Clodia (Cicero, *Pro Caelio* 30–32, 49, 59–60 in translation)
Language notes	jussive subjunctive
	relative clauses with antecedent deferred or omitted
	dative of disadvantage

DIGEST

Seven of these poems by Catullus focus on his relationship with Lesbia, and one (given partly in translation), on his friendship with Furius and Aurelius, though the latter poem also refers to Lesbia without naming her. The subject matter generally appeals to adolescent readers, and much of the poetry is syntactically straightforward. Roman numerals indicate the numbers assigned to these poems within Stage 45; arabic numerals indicate the standard numbering system used in (e.g.) the Oxford Classical Text edition.

Read the poems as a sequence: first encounter of Catullus and Lesbia – mutual love – Catullus' suspicions – his conflicting feelings – the end of the affair. Such a sequence will facilitate the students' first reading, but avoids a number of controversial questions. During or after their reading of these poems, the students might consider what we know (or do not know) about the order in which the poems were written, and their relationship (if any) with events in Catullus' life.

GRAMMATICAL POINTS

jussive subjunctive, positive and negative, 1st, 2nd (less frequently), and 3rd persons
  e.g. *vīvāmus, mea Lesbia, atque amēmus.*
  miser Catulle, dēsinās ineptīre.
conditionals: present subjunctive
  e.g. *nūllī sē dīcit mulier mea nūbere mālle*
      quam mihi, nōn sī sē Iuppiter ipse petat.
dative of disadvantage
  e.g. *tam bellum mihi passerem abstulistis.*
quod in apposition to whole preceding sentence
  e.g. *dulce rīdentem, miserō quod omnēs*
      ēripit sēnsūs mihi.
genitive of value
  e.g. *rūmōrēs...*
      omnēs ūnius aestimēmus assis!

SENTENCE PATTERNS
increased incidence of ellipsis (including complexity of a parenthesis)
e.g. *nam mellītus erat suamque nōrat
ipsam tam bene quam puella mātrem...*

*ille mī pār esse deō vidētur
ille, sī fās est, superāre dīvōs...*

continuation of features of word order in verse: for example, a-b-b-a order of nouns and adjectives
e.g. *rūmōrēsque senum sevēriōrum
omnēs ūnius aestimēmus assis!*

relative clause preceding the main clause
e.g. *...sed mulier cupidō quod dīcit amantī,
in ventō et rapidā scrībere oportet aquā.*

Title Picture

Based on a first-century painting of a girl decanting perfumes, from the Villa Farnesina on the right bank of the Tiber, and now in the Museo delle Terme, Rome.

I "ille mī pār esse..." (*Poem* 51)

The commentaries of Fordyce and Quinn will be helpful throughout this Stage; so will Wiseman 130–82. References to other books and articles are given below from time to time in connection with individual poems. On the present poem, see Lyne, *Handbook* 25ff. and G. Williams, *Tradition and Originality* 251ff. (55ff. in abridged version); Williams also discusses several other poems in this Stage.

Notes

1   **ille:** Encourage your students to leave this initially as an unexplained "he"; then, when they have reached line 3, indicate that *quī ... audit* supplies the explanation.

2   **superāre:** When students have realized that the line is incomplete as it stands, a reminder about line 1 will probably enable them to see that *vidētur* is the word to be supplied.

5   **quod:** postponed. Comprehension questions, such as "What does this do to Catullus?", may help.

5–6 **miserō ... mihi:** Encourage students to discard initial literal translations, e.g. "miserable me," in favor of more idiomatic versions, e.g. "me in my misery."

Stage Commentaries

7   **aspexī:** "Have set eyes on" may prepare the students better than "set eyes on" for the present tenses which follow.
9   **sed:** postponed to second word. Note how the students are coping with this feature, which they have now met several times, and give help if necessary.
9–10   **tenuis ... flamma:** separated. Encourage the students to read straight through to *dēmānat* before they translate.
15   **et ... et:** Students tend to go wrong when they assume that the first *et* links *ōtium* with *rēgēs*. A simpler example may help, e.g. *dominus et servōs et ancillās laudāvit*.

Begin the discussion by asking "Who do you think *ille* is? Is he a real person? Which word in the first stanza indicates that *ille*, whether real or imaginary, enjoys a permanent relationship with Lesbia?" Also consider two points of interpretation: "Is *sī fās est* (line 2) short for *sī fās est dīcere* or for *sī fās est dīvōs superāre?*"; "To what does *quod* (line 5) refer? The attractive laughter? The sight of Lesbia? The sight of Lesbia in the presence of another man?"

Amplify the second part of question 1 by asking "Why can Catullus not enjoy what the other man enjoys?", which might lead to a discussion of the other man's status (husband, established lover, etc.). Discussion of question 2 (e.g. argument over whether *tenuis flamma* and *sonitus* are examples of "loss of sense") will help to clarify Catullus' picture in lines 7–12. Add further questions: "Is Catullus' description convincing? If it's not physically true, does it nevertheless give us a clear idea of his feelings?" Rudd and Foster, in a helpful discussion in Greig 42–48, suggest the question "Do these lines describe painful or pleasurable feelings?"

For opposed views on the status of the fourth stanza, referred to in question 3, see Fordyce *ad loc.* and Lyne, *Handbook* 27–29. Encourage the airing of both points of view; that this is a coherent poem, in which Catullus feels he is being carried away by emotion, and writes a final stanza of warning to himself on the traditional theme of *ōtium* as a cause of *amor*, decadence, and disaster (see, e.g. Balme and Warman 106–107 for documentation of this theme); or that the contradictions between the address to Lesbia and the self-address to Catullus, and between the passion of lines 1–12 and the moralizing of 13–16, indicate that we have here not one poem but two, attached to each other in the manuscripts because of their identical meter.

At this point in the discussion, reveal that the poem is substantially a translation of a Greek poem by Sappho of Lesbos. (The class might consider whether the case for accepting lines 13–16 as part of the poem is weakened by the fact that they correspond to nothing in the original Sappho.) Wilkinson, quoted by Quinn, *Catullus* 241, suggests that the

Stage 45

poem leaves Lesbia free to take it either as an exercise in translation or as a declaration by Catullus. Catullus' decision to translate a Sappho lyric as well as his choice of "Lesbia" as a pseudonym can both be taken to imply that Clodia is appreciative of lyric poetry and that she is beautiful, like the women of Lesbos whom Sappho wrote about. Mention, too, that "Lesbia" and "Clōdia" are metrically interchangeable, and so Catullus would have been able to substitute the real name for the pseudonym when he read his poems aloud to her.

Vocabulary Check: *pār* (1); *identidem* (3); *ēripiō* (6); *aspiciō* (7); *ōs* (8); *ōtium* (13ff.); *molestus* (13); *et ... et* (15).

II "vīvāmus, mea Lesbia..." (*Poem 5*)

Bramble's discussion in Greig 18–22 usefully complements Quinn and Fordyce.

Notes

1–3   **vīvāmus ... assis:** Perhaps best handled by a series of comprehension questions. "Who is Catullus addressing? What does he say they should do? What else?", etc. Question 1 in the text should enable students to cope with the separation of *rūmōrēs* from *omnēs* in lines 2–3.

5   **nōbīs:** The most convenient translation may be the literal one, "for us."

6   **ūna:** perhaps surprisingly, often causes trouble. Ask the students "How many nights?"

10   **fēcerīmus:** Guide the students to idiomatic translations, "we have had," "we have exchanged," etc.

11–13   **nē sciāmus ... bāsiōrum:** On first reading, do not get over-involved while explaining these lines. Establish the main point, "for fear that we, or anyone else, should know the number," then explore the lines in more detail later; see below.

Combine a second reading with exploration. Get the class to work out the translation of lines 1–6, and then to attempt an answer to question 2. Follow translation of lines 7–9 with question 3, giving help if the students are slow to see that human mortality is being used by Catullus as a proposition to Lesbia: "Life is short, let us enjoy it while we can." Similarly, follow translation of lines 10–13 with exploration of question 4, to which the class can find a variety of answers: that it is not very romantic to be stingy with one's love; that an infinity of kisses is better than a finite number; that to know and state the precise amount of one's good luck is dangerous, since it invites Fortuna to sweep it away. Then discuss the shift at the end of the poem. Not only are Catullus and

Stage Commentaries

Lesbia not to know the number, but neither is anybody else, partly because Catullus and Lesbia would be objects of envy (*invidēre*, line 12) and partly because of the primitive belief that to have exact knowledge of personal details about other people gives power over them, enabling an ill-wisher to cast the evil eye on them (another meaning of *invidēre*).

Also consider one or two of the following questions:

"Since there is only one sun, why is *sōlēs* (line 4) plural?"

"What does *lūx* (line 5) refer to?"

"Which words in lines 5–6 contrast sharply with each other? What do you notice about the way Catullus positioned *lūx* and *nox*?" (Or the point could be explored the other way around by asking "How does Catullus emphasize the contrast between *lūx* and *nox*?")

"Study Catullus' use of numbers in this poem; how do they help him to emphasize what he is saying to Lesbia?" Make sure that the students notice the juxtaposition of *ūnius* with *omnēs* in line 3, and the contrast between *ūna* in line 6 and the vast and ever-increasing numbers in lines 7–10, also the regular pattern in those lines, contrasting with the idea of disruption in line 11.

"How did the ancient world keep count? Why would it be easy for Catullus to upset the reckoning (line 11) with a single movement?" For details of the abacus, see *Omnibus* 5, p. 4, and the drawing in the Unit 2 students' textbook, p. 3 top.

"Does the *malus* in line 12 remind you of anyone Catullus has mentioned earlier in the poem?" The second reference to a critical or jealous observer, in lines 2 and 12, strengthens the unity of the poem, as does the recurring "numbers" motif.

"How does the situation described in this poem differ from that of the previous one (*"ille mī pār esse..."*)?" For evidence that Catullus is now no longer a tongue-tied outsider, as in the previous poem, students may be able to point both to the confident tone behind his proposition and to the suggestion in lines 2–3 that his relationship with Lesbia may now be a subject of public gossip.

Balme and Warman 40–42 have an interesting trio of translations of lines 1–6 for comparison. A musical setting of the poem, composed by a student for voice and guitar accompaniment, appears in *Omnibus* 10, p. 16.

The marble lovers shown in the photograph on p. 203 and from the Capitoline Museum are thought to be a Roman copy of a late Hellenistic work of the 2nd or 1st century B.C. They are usually interpreted as Cupid and Psyche. In some versions of the pair the figures have wings.

Vocabulary Check: *vīvō* (1); *brevis* (5); *sciō* (11,13); *malus* (12).

First Language Note (*Jussive Subjunctive*)

Further examples:

1 *castra hostium oppugnēmus; aut occīdāmus aut occīdāmur.*
2 *amēmus patriam, pāreāmus senātuī.* (Cicero)
3 *nē haesitet amīcus vester.*
4 *vīllam ingrediāmur; nē diūtius in hortō morēmur.*

With your help, the class might work together to produce a translation of Cato's instructions on the overseer:

5 *haec erunt vīlicī officia: aliēnō manum abstineat; sua servet dīligenter; vīlicus nē sit ambulātor* ("be always wandering off"); *sobrius sit semper.*

The jussive subjunctive provides a convenient opportunity for students to practice the difference between present indicative and present subjunctive forms in each conjugation by translating paired examples such as *recitāmus–recitēmus, trahāmus–trahimus*, etc. Indicate the conjugation to which each verb belongs, or let students find this out for themselves by consulting Part Four, "Complete Vocabulary," in their LI Section.

Invite comments on the tone of the two examples in paragraph 3; for example, do the students believe that the jussive is gentler or ruder than the imperative as a way of ordering people around?

III "lūgēte ō Venerēs..." (*Poem 3*)

Lyne, *Handbook* 6–9 and Balme in Greig 6–12 have useful comments on the poem.

Read the entire poem aloud, and go over the vocabulary with students. Ask the following questions:

Who are addressed in line 1? What are they asked to do?
Who else are to mourn? Why?
How is it described?
How fond of the bird was Lesbia? (Students may need help with *illa* in line 5, unemphatic "she"). Why? How well did it know her?
How can we tell from line 8 that it was very tame?
What actions of the sparrow are described in lines 9–10? (If the students have trouble with *modo... modo*, remind them of the boy Icarus in Stage 44 (p. 182, lines 5–6), *modo* chasing feathers, *modo* playing with the wax.)
Translate *it* in line 11. Explain in your own words where the sparrow is going, then translate Catullus' description of its journey (line 11) and

Stage Commentaries

destination (line 12). (Students may need further help. They often say "deny a return to anyone"; point out the case of *quemquam* and form of *redīre*.)

Whom does Catullus curse in lines 13–14? What does he say about them? What in particular have they done?

Whom does he address at the end of line 16? What does he call it?

What has been the effect of the sparrow's death on Lesbia? (Remind the class to read lines 17–18 straight through to the end, to help them find the delayed subject of *rubent*.)

The class might then read the poem through again on their own, before proceeding to translation, a second reading aloud, or further exploration. Question 2 may provoke more than one answer: the Venuses and Cupids, as deities of love, may be invoked because Lesbia loved the sparrow and/or because Catullus loves Lesbia. If students know about birds, mention the attempts of ornithologists to identify the bird from the clues in lines 8–10. It is unlikely to be a sparrow, since sparrows are virtually impossible to tame. Fordyce 87–88 has a full discussion of the rival candidates, favoring the Italian blue rock-thrush, *monticola solitarius*, of which there is a good picture in Bruun and Singer 255. But "sparrow" has, over the centuries, become the traditional translation for the most famous pet bird in European literature.

A good topic for discussion, to which question 5 might lead, is Catullus' attitude to the bird's death. Is the poem a genuine lament? Does Catullus share Lesbia's grief? Is he trying to cheer her up? Is it a love poem disguised as a lament? Students are often good at picking out the affectionate phrases of pathos in lines 6, 9–10, etc., and contrasting them with the mock solemnity of the addresses in lines 1 and 2, the mock-heroic or bathetic line 11 (in which the onomatopoeic *quī nunc it per iter* reinforces the somewhat absurd picture of the sparrow hopping down the dark road to Hades), and the (mock?) indignation against Hades and the sparrow in lines 13 and 15–16, all of which might suggest that Catullus' laments are not to be taken very seriously. The change of mood between lines 10 and 11, referred to in question 5, is taken by some students as a move from pathos to farce, by others as a move from lightness to seriousness (cf. lines 12 and 14); the point is worth debating. Questions 3 and 5 sometimes evoke from students the suggestion that Catullus is obliquely reproaching Lesbia for being too absorbed in the bird's death and for being unresponsive to Catullus; for this view, cf. Lyne, *Handbook*, especially 8–9. (Do the students take *miselle* in line 16 as tender or harsh?)

Discuss the assonance of the repeated "l"s and "m"s in this poem (cf. the comments on "Catullus" II, p. 103 above). Discuss, too, the phrase *plūs ... oculīs suīs* in line 5: is this just a poetic cliché, or does Catullus say anything later in the poem to give the phrase special appropriateness? Students are also often intrigued and amused by the old theory that *passer* is an obscene *double entendre* for *mentula*.

For a reproduction of a medieval manuscript of Catullus, showing the first five lines of this poem, see *Omnibus* 9, p. 19, and for interesting sets of comprehension and exploratory questions, see Tingay, *Comprehendite* 67 and Balme and Warman 19.

Suggestions for Consolidation: *negō* (12; practice both translations); ablative of the gerund (18); diminutives (16,18); ablative of comparison (5; see also the Unit 4 students' textbook, LI Section, "Review Grammar," p. 312, 6f, and p. 203 below). Translate *male sit* (13) literally and link it with the note on the jussive subjunctive in the students' textbook, p. 204.

Vocabulary Check: *lūgeō* (1); *plūs* (5); *modo ... modo* (9); *iter* (11); *illūc* (12); *unde* (12); *malus* (13); *fleō* (18).

IV "nūllī sē dīcit..." (*Poem* 70)

Notes

1 **nūllī ... mālle:** The placing of the dative at the front of the sentence and the embedding of *dīcit mulier mea* inside the indirect statement usually causes problems. Use comprehension questions to help: "Who is speaking? Who is she speaking about? What does she say about herself?", etc.
3 **mulier ... amantī:** Even with the help provided in the vocabulary, the word order is still likely to be difficult. Ask "Who is the woman in line 3 talking to?", and for the use of *quod*, compare a more familiar example such as *(id) quod dīcis falsum est*.
4 **scrībere oportet:** In the absence of an accusative, the Latin is ambiguous. It can mean both "she (i.e. the woman) should write" and "one (anyone) should write." Perhaps a passive translation ("ought to be written") best preserves the ambiguity; it is in any case the translation most likely to occur to the class.

The class might consider the real or imaginary situation envisaged in lines 1–2. Is the remark of *mulier mea* Lesbia's response to a serious proposal of marriage from Catullus? Is it a protestation of innocence in the face of Catullus' suspicions that she has other lovers beside himself? *nūbere* can be used of casual and temporary relationships as well as marriage (none of Jupiter's consorts, for example, was formally married to him except Juno); which meaning(s) does the word have in the present context? Students could also discuss the appropriateness of the

Stage Commentaries

mention of Jupiter in line 2. His supreme status and desirability as king of the gods are obviously relevant; so, too, are his erotic adventures. Is the statement weakened by being put in the form of a (possibly trite) proverb, or is it appropriate to the hyperbole of lovers' talk? Is there a modern equivalent?

In answering question 2, students are sometimes attracted by the translation "That's what *she* says" for the first *dīcit* in line 3; but this anticipates a skepticism which appears only later in the line.

Expand on question 4 during discussion. Does the image of wind and water mean that women's words are unreliable, unworthy to be permanently recorded in writing like the words of a marriage contract? What is the point of the reference to *cupidus amāns* in line 3? Does Catullus mean that it would be unreasonable to hold a woman to a statement which she's been badgered into making by her demanding lover?

For further comments and suggested questions, see Lyne, *Handbook* 13–15 and Balme, *Intellegenda* 71.

The seduction scene shown on p. 201 has some extraneous features of interest which could be pointed out to students: the man reclining on his left arm in the customary manner, his drinking horn (rhyton), the very elegant table. Students may enjoy speculating about what is on the table or in the box which the slave-girl is bringing. What is the woman wearing over her hair?

Vocabulary Check: *nūbō* (1); *mālō* (1; mention its derivation from *magis volō*, and practice various forms of *volō*, *nōlō*, and *mālō*); *petō* (2); *oportet* (4).

V "dīcēbās quondam..." (*Poem* 72)

Notes

1–2 **dīcēbās ... Iovem:** Students should be able to recognize the statement attributed to Lesbia here as closely similar to the one quoted in the previous poem.
4   **ut:** postponed. *ut vulgus* in the previous line should help.
5   **impēnsius:** Students may need a simpler example of the comparative adverb, perhaps with *quam*, e.g. *Marcus celerius quam Sextus cucurrit*.
7   **quod:** not difficult to understand, but encourage the class to expand their translations to "It is because..." or similar.
     amantem: substantival. Cf. *amantī* in line 3 of the previous poem.

Question 2 could lead to discussion both of the simile's meaning and of its effectiveness. A father's love for his sons (with the spelling *gnātōs* adding an archaic flavor and increasing the emphasis by alliteration with *generōs*) is contrasted with the erotic feelings of a man for his mistress; the contrast is heightened by the addition of *generōs*. Has Catullus succeeded in conveying the idea of a love which is warm, intense, and true, but to which sexuality is irrelevant? Or are Quinn and Lyne (*Handbook* 15–19, *Latin Love Poets* 39–41) right to consider the simile as a brave failure? Do the students find the description of Catullus' feelings in 3–4 convincing? Is it inconsistent with lines 5–12 of "*ille mī pār esse...*" (p. 92)?

The middle sections of question 3 might lead to a consideration of the metaphor *ūror*: "What does Catullus mean by 'being on fire'? What aspect of love is emphasized by *ūror*?", etc.

The structure of the poem is exceptionally clear. It abounds in pairs of contrasted words and phrases. Encourage the class to pick some of them out. *quondam* (line 1) is first reinforced by *tum* (line 3), then contrasted with *nunc* (line 5). *ut vulgus amīcam* (line 3) corresponds with *pater ut gnātōs*, etc. (line 4). *impēnsius ūror* (line 5) expresses Catullus' increased passion, *multō ... es vīlior et levior* (line 6), his increased distaste and contempt. In the final couplet, which describes the double result of Lesbia's infidelity and thus explains lines 5–6, *magis* contrasts with *minus*, and *amāre* with *bene velle*.

Vocabulary Check: *quondam* (1); *dīligō* (3); *tantum* (3); *cognōscō* (5); *vīlis* (6); *tālis* (7); *cōgō* (8); *minus* (8).

Second Language Note (*Relative Clauses with Antecedent Deferred or Omitted*)

It is often useful for the class to go through the additional examples in paragraphs 1 and 2, picking out the antecedents, and also to practice translating *id quod* both literally ("that which") and idiomatically ("what"). Encourage idiomatic translations of *(is) quī* and *(eī) quī* ("the man who," "people who," etc.).

For additional examples of *is quī*, and relative clauses in which the antecedent is deferred or omitted, see the Unit 4 students' textbook, LI Section, "Review Grammar," pp. 292–93, paragraph 9, and p. 201 below.

Note how the students manage with the jussive subjunctive in paragraph 3, example 4, and make up further examples if necessary.

VI "ōdī et amō..." (*Poem* 85)

Notes

1 **quārē:** The students have already met this word with its present meaning

Stage Commentaries

("why"); but, having just encountered it in the previous poem with a different meaning, they may need help.

2 **requīris:** main verb placed after indirect question. Cf. Language Note on p. 172 of the students' textbook.
fierī: impersonal passive. Encourage "happen" or similar translation.

A famous and much-praised couplet. After students have read and translated it, invite them to demonstrate how they think it should be read aloud. The poem contains fourteen words: how many are strongly emotional, and where are they placed?

The poem does not mention Lesbia, but is usually assumed to be "about" her; is this assumption reasonable? Is she the person addressed in line 1 (*requīris*)? Or is the addressee just an imaginary interlocutor, who enlivens the couplet by giving it the characteristics of a dialogue and providing a cue for Catullus to explain (or rather refuse to explain) his initial remark?

As in the previous poem, the students might note the extent to which Catullus' effect depends on antitheses: what examples can they find of pairs of contrasted or corresponding words? Students should be able to pick out *ōdī* and *amō*, *nescio* and *sentiō* easily enough. An interesting contrast is that of *faciam* and *fierī*; to Catullus, hating and loving are not things which he does but things which happen to him.

The suggested alternative answers to the question in the students' textbook are not intended to exhaust the possibilities.

VII "miser Catulle..." (*Poem 8*)

For detailed discussion, see Lyne (*Handbook* 20–25, Quinn, *Latin Love Poets* 47–51) and G. Williams (*Tradition and Originality* 460ff.; 91ff. in abridged version).

Notes

1–2 Note how the students manage with the jussive subjunctives *dēsinās* and *dūcās*, and the omitted antecedent in line 2, and if necessary, refer back to the language notes on pp. 204 and 209 of the students' textbook.
3 **candidī:** predicative. Cf. *servus mortuus prōcubuit*, etc., and for further examples if needed, see Appendix D.
5 **amāta:** The use of the participle to add a further point often causes difficulty here. It may be helpful to ask "Which word in line 4 is described by *amāta*? What does Catullus say in line 5 about the girl?"
9 **illa:** "she"; cf. line 5 of "lūgēte ō Venerēs," p. 205.
impotēns nōlī: Help the class to see that *nōlī* picks up *nōn volt* from earlier in the line, and that *impotēns* explains why Catullus is giving himself this advice.

10 **quae fugit:** For the positioning of the relative clause, and omission of the antecedent, cf. line 2.
17 **cuius esse dīcēris:** Compare a simpler example, e.g. *Lesbia mea esse dīcitur* "Lesbia is said to be mine."

Proceed with exploration and discussion along the following lines, with variations to suit the circumstances and taste of the students:

After students have translated lines 1–8, work through questions 1–2. ("Don't cry over spilled milk" is perhaps the most obvious answer to the second part of question 1, but others may occur to the class.) Then ask: do these lines refer to the past, present, or future? Why does Catullus call himself *miser*? Which of the first eight lines gives the strongest impression of Catullus' feelings about Lesbia? How is she described in that line? Which of them was the keener on the relationship? (There is room for argument here; line 4 suggests the harmony of their desires, but in line 7 he is eager while she merely acquiesces – unless the double negative *nec ... nōlēbat* is interpreted as a strong affirmative.) What is the point of substantially repeating line 3 at line 8? (One answer might be that the reminiscence in lines 4–7 expands and justifies the claim in line 3, making the repetition of it with *vērē* appropriate.)

Have lines 9–11 translated, and ask as before whether the reference is to past, present, or future; what is the effect of the first five words of line 9? Question 3 might be taken at this point. Which two lines in lines 1–8 do lines 9–11 correspond to? (Ask students "How do lines 1–2 *differ* in tone from 9–11?", and they may spot the change from the gentle urging of the subjunctives in 1–2 to the harsh imperatives of 9–11.) In which lines does Catullus emphasize that he must pull himself together and not weaken?

When students have translated lines 12–19, establish that the reference is now to the future. Whom has Catullus been addressing in lines 1–11? Whom does he address in lines 12ff.? How will he show the determination he refers to in line 12 (*obdūrat*)? Consider question 4 at this point. What question does Catullus repeatedly ask, in varying ways, in lines 16–18, and what answer does he imply to his own question? (Various possibilities might be suggested: "He doesn't know, but is curious to learn"; "Nobody"; "He realistically knows that there *will* be somebody, and that the 'somebody' won't be he.") Whom has he been addressing in lines 12–17? Why does he need to switch in line 19 to addressing himself?

Have students consider question 5 now, supplemented if necessary by such questions as "What feelings make it hard for him to be firm? What feelings help him? Have you met this mixture of feelings in any other of Catullus' poems?" Question 6 might also lead to a corollary: "What is

Stage Commentaries

Catullus' attitude to Lesbia in lines 15–18? Vindictive, compassionate, cynical, infatuated, or some or none of these?"

Balme and Warman 107–108 have questions comparing this poem with Michael Drayton's sonnet "Since there's no help, come let us kiss and part." *Omnibus* 2, pages 19 and 21, contains two translations of "miser Catulle..." by British students. Your students may like to discuss and compare them, and then perhaps attempt versions of their own, either of this poem or of another in this Stage.

Suggestions for Consolidation: future active, passive, and deponent (13–18); 3rd person plural perfect in *-ēre* (3,8).

Vocabulary Check: *fulgeō* (3,8); *quondam* (3); *quō* (4); *fīō* (6); *vīvō* (10); *at* (14,19); *doleō* (14); *videor* (16).

VIII "Fūrī et Aurēlī..." (*Poem* 11)

Lyne discusses this poem helpfully in *Handbook* 30–33 and in Greig 23–28.

Notes

18 **complexa:** Encourage students to move from the literal translation ("having embraced") to more idiomatic versions ("in her embrace," etc.)
24 **postquam:** Note how students manage with the postponement of this word, and give help with comprehension questions if necessary.

The following questions may help the class to establish the sense of the passage after the first reading aloud:

What is Lesbia to do? Who with?
What is she doing? How many?
Truly doing what? But repeatedly what?
What does Catullus say she is *not* to do?
When could she have counted on his love?
What has happened to his love? What is it compared to?
What has happened to the flower?

After students have translated the poem, discuss questions 1 and 2. Some students may believe that Furius and Aurelius are being compared favorably with Lesbia, as pals whom Catullus knows he can rely on; others may feel that the extravagant compliments of lines 1–16 are ironical, and that Furius and Aurelius are two of Lesbia's current lovers.

In studying Catullus' message to Lesbia, ask the class to find the pairs of contrasting words in lines 19–20 (*amāns ... rumpēns; nūllum ... omnium*).

While considering question 3, the students might note that *identidem* occurs both here and in "ille mī pār esse..." (p. 200, line 3) and that the stanzas of both poems consist of three short lines followed by a very short one. (They are in fact the only two surviving poems by Catullus in Sapphic meter, though Lyne argues against attaching significance to this.) *vīvat valeatque* (line 17) might conceivably be echoing *vīvāmus ... atque amēmus* (p. 202, line 1). Is this coincidence? Is Catullus recalling past expressions of love in order to strengthen his present expressions of rejection?

The simile in lines 21–24 may lead to the question: what are the points of similarity between Catullus' love and the flower? If his love is being compared to the flower, what (if anything) corresponds to the plow? Is it significant that a plow is inanimate ("The agent of destruction ... does not intend or know what it has done" – Lyne, *Handbook* 33), and that the flower is at the edge of the meadow, killed quite accidentally?

The contrast of mood between lines 17–20 and 21–24 is variously interpreted. Many commentators take 17–20 as bitter, heartfelt abuse, replaced by a gentler tone in 21–24 which accommodates the tender simile; Lyne, however, reads 17–20 as lively but not too serious ribaldry, and 21–24 as a more earnest, urgent message.

Question 4 invites the class to consider whether lines 17–24 should be taken at face value. Some students (and scholars) read the text as a final dismissal of Lesbia (or even as the rejection of an offer of reconciliation made by Lesbia through Furius and Aurelius as intermediaries). Others believe that Catullus "protests too much," and is using words of dismissal to make a veiled appeal to Lesbia to resume their relationship. Others again see in this poem a recurrence of the *ōdī-et-amō* theme. Lyne, warning against a too ready assumption that the poem marks the final breakdown of the relationship, points out that the lovers have a notorious habit of saying good-bye more than once.

At this point, the class should consider the order in which the poems of Stage 45 have been arranged. Would it have been a more convincing sequence if the poems had been printed in their manuscript order (III-II-VII-VIII-I-IV-V-VI)? This could in turn raise the vexed but intriguing question of the relationship (if any) between Catullus' poetry and the events in his life. Do the poems provide us with any reason for believing that Lesbia existed and that Catullus had a love affair with her? If students are tempted to read the text as a transcript of historical reality, on the grounds that it is "sincere" or "convincing," point out that much convincing love poetry has been written in the context of

Stage Commentaries

wholly imaginary relationships (e.g. *Romeo and Juliet*). If, on the other hand, students take up a position of complete skepticism, and argue that we know nothing whatever about the historical Catullus and the historical Lesbia, say that the picture emerging from the poems is at any rate coherent and internally consistent, and that there is at least a little external evidence to support it. For example, some scholars (though not all) believe that "Lesbia" can be identified with a historical woman, known to us from other sources. Refer students here to the background material.

Suggestions for Consolidation: jussive subjunctive (17,21); present participles (19,20,23).

Vocabulary Check: *vīvō* (17); *simul* (18); *teneō* (18); *vērē* (19); *identidem* (19); *praetereō* (23); *tangō* (24); *arātrum* (24).

Drills

Exercise 1 Type: vocabulary
            Grammatical point being practiced: antonyms

Exercise 2 Type: transformation
            Grammatical point being practiced: present subjunctive active and passive, introduced in Stages 36 and 41
            Incidental practice: indirect question

Exercise 3 Type: completion
            Missing item: gerund
            Test of accuracy: sense
            Grammatical point being practiced: accusative, genitive, and ablative of gerund, introduced in Stages 41 and 43

For further practice, see the Unit 4 students' textbook, LI Section, "Review Grammar," p. 324, paragraph 1.

Third Language Note (*Dative of Disadvantage*)

This grammatical point sometimes bothers students. They believe that "advantage" and "disadvantage" are natural opposites, and that it is illogical of Latin to use the same case for both. Encourage them to look not just at the dative, but at the sentence as a whole, for example by comparing the example in paragraph 1 with the first example in paragraph 2. Each sentence contains a nominative (*pater, Fortūna*) indicating the person or agency who did the action, an accusative (*dōnum, frātrem*) indicating the person or thing to whom the action was done, and also a dative (*nōbīs, mihi*) indicating another person or persons involved in the action. Whether they gain or lose by this involvement may affect the way the sentence is translated; but it does not affect the relationship of *nōbīs* and *mihi* to the other words in the sentence.

Examples of the dative of disadvantage met earlier in Stages 41–45:

1 *fortūna mihī tētē abstulit ipsum* (Stage 42, p. 144, line 5)
2 *miser indignē frāter adēmpte mihī* (Stage 42, p. 144, line 6)
3 *fortūna mihi nōn omnia ēripuit* (Stage 43, p. 169, line 5)
4 *quod omnēs / ēripit sēnsūs mihi* (Stage 45, p. 200, lines 5–6)
5 *tam bellum mihi passerem abstulistis* (Stage 45, p. 205, line 15).

The Background Material

Wiseman 15–53 provides an illuminating and immensely readable account of Clodia Metelli. Her identification with Lesbia is discussed by, among others, Austin 148–50 (who regards the identification as "probable"), Fordyce xiv–xviii ("not unlikely"), and Quinn, *Catullus* xvi–xviii ("extremely probable"). Wiseman rejects the identification, and is at pains to separate his account of Catullus and Lesbia (130–82) from what he says about Clodia Metelli.

One purpose of this section of background material is to introduce the students, however cursorily, to Roman oratory and Cicero, since they are unrepresented elsewhere in Stages 41–48. If the class contains effective and confident readers, ask each one to read aloud one of the quoted paragraphs to the rest of the class. Students should have no difficulty in picking up Cicero's allusions to the rumors about Clodia's incest and the murder of Metellus (fourth line of the translation on p. 217 of the students' textbook, and last paragraph on p. 217). Mention the ambiguity of *amīca* ("friend" in line 8, p. 217); the word can have either a respectable or disreputable meaning.

The class might also look at translations of one or two Catullus poems which are or might be connected with Clodia, Cicero, and Caelius Rufus. In *Poem* 77 Catullus addresses a Rufus with great bitterness, accusing him of breach of friendship and perhaps of stealing his mistress from him; in *Poem* 58 he addresses a Caelius, lamenting the promiscuity and degradation of Lesbia; in *Poem* 49 he addresses Cicero in complimentary (or mock-complimentary) terms, thanking him effusively for an unspecified favor (believed by some to be the delivery of the *Pro Caelio*; Quinn and Fordyce are both skeptical).

Stage Commentaries

Interpretations of the fourth-century mosaic from Sicily shown on p. 216, in which the girls are obviously displaying their charms, vary considerably and include a water ballet and an athletic contest, either real or parodied. According to the latter interpretation, the mosaic (detail) shows a competitor for the long jump (holding weights) and a discus thrower.

Suggestions for Discussion

1 How fair do Cicero's remarks seem to you? How relevant? Do they give you an unfavorable impression of Roman justice?
2 Is Cicero's description of Clodia consistent with the picture of Lesbia presented by Catullus?
3 Does it "matter" who Lesbia is? Does it make the poems more enjoyable? More interesting?

Vocabulary Checklist

Encourage the class to recall the links between *candidus* and *candidātus* and between *ōtium* and *negōtium*. With the cognates *culpa–culpāre*, compare *cēna–cēnāre, cūra–cūrāre, lacrima–lacrimāre, mora–morārī, mina–minārī*, and *pugna–pugnāre*. To the compounds of *rumpere* add *interrumpere, perrumpere*, and *prōrumpere*, and note how the meaning of *corrumpere* shifted to become metaphorical. With *tegō* compare *tēctum*, which the students have already met in the sense of "roof" and are about to meet in the sense of "building."

Suggestions for Further Work

1 If the students have enjoyed this Stage, ask them to pick a favorite poem from the selection and write ten lines about it, saying why it appealed to them.
2 The class may enjoy listening to some of Carl Orff's *Carmina Catulli*, which include "ille mī pār esse...," "vīvāmus, mea Lesbia...," "lūgēte, ō Venerēs...," "ōdī et amō...," "miser Catulle...," and (in *Carmina Catulli* II) "multās per gentēs..." from Stage 42. How well do they think Orff's melodies and rhythms capture the mood of Catullus?
3 Present the class with copies of two or more translations of one of the poems in this selection for comparative study and discussion.
4 Older students would enjoy reading and reporting on two excellent historical novels, by American authors, about Catullus and his milieu: Thornton Wilder's classic *The Ides of March*, first published in 1948

Stage 46

and frequently reprinted, and Benita Kane Jaro's more recent *The Key* (New York: Dodd, Mead and Company, 1988), which is enhanced with idiomatic translations of many of Catullus' poems, including some in this Stage.

STAGE 46: CLĀDĒS

BRIEF OUTLINE

Reading passages	Pliny, *Letters* VI.20.2–20 (adapted)
Background material	time chart (authors)
Language notes	pluperfect subjunctive passive
	conditional clauses with pluperfect subjunctive
	omission of forms of *esse*

DIGEST

Adapted letter from Pliny the Younger to Tacitus, describing his and his mother Plinia's escape from the violence of Mt. Vesuvius erupting. Pliny's description of the eruption is extremely vivid, and is still quoted by modern vulcanologists as a classic account of a volcanic catastrophe.

GRAMMATICAL POINTS

pluperfect subjunctive: passive and deponent
   e.g. *vix cōnsēderāmus, cum dēscendit nox dēnsissima, quasi omnia lūmina in conclāvī clausō exstīncta essent.*
conditionals: pluperfect subjunctive
   e.g. *nam sī diūtius morātī essēmus, sine dubiō periissēmus.*
subjunctive of alleged cause with *quod*
   e.g. *pāret invīta, castīgatque sē, quod mē morētur.*
historical infinitive
   e.g. *tum māter mē ōrāre hortārī iubēre ut quōquō modō fugerem.*
increased incidence of omission of forms of *esse*
   e.g. *iam hōra diēī prīma; sed adhūc dubia lūx.*

SENTENCE PATTERNS

increased complexity of subordinate clauses in indirect discourse: conditional clauses in indirect statement
   e.g. *affirmāvit mē, quod iuvenis essem, ad salūtem pervenīre posse; sē quae et annīs et corpore gravārētur, libenter moritūram esse, sī mihi causa mortis nōn fuisset.*
increased complexity in use of conditional clauses
   e.g. *ego respondī mē nōlle incolumem esse nisi illa quoque effūgisset.*

Title Picture

An eighteenth-century engraving of the eruption of Mt. Vesuvius in 1754.

Stage Commentaries

tremōrēs (*Letters* VI.20.2–8)

The commentaries of Sherwin-White and Levens will be useful throughout this Stage.

Introduce this letter by reading part of a translation of its companion-piece (VI.16, on the death of the elder Pliny; cf. also Unit 4 students' textbook, "Supplementary Reading," pp. 340–42), e.g. paragraphs 4–10, from the first sighting of the volcanic cloud to the departure of Pliny the Elder on his rescue mission. Use the map on p. 223 of the students' textbook to establish the positions of Misenum (base of the western Italian fleet, of which Pliny the Elder was commander), Vesuvius, Pompeii, Herculaneum, Naples, and Stabiae (where Pliny the Elder perished).

Notes

3–4   **tremor terrae ... solitus:** The students may recall the earthquake which shook Pompeii severely in A.D. 62. Its effects are illustrated on p. 224 of the students' textbook.
4   **Campāniae:** A reminder may be necessary that this was the name of the district, not of a particular town.
7   **āreā domūs ... dīvidēbat:** "The house [of Pliny the Elder] is within the town of Misenum, and is built by the shore" (Sherwin-White). Only a narrow courtyard separates sea from house, and so when the buildings begin to shake (lines 13–14) the danger to those in the courtyard is very great.
8–9   **librum ... legere coepī:** Supply some details, omitted from this adapted version for the sake of simplicity, if there is time: the book Pliny demanded was a volume of Livy, and following his uncle's usual practice (*Letters* III.5.10), he made notes and extracts from it as he read.
13   **hōra diēī prīma:** The day is 25 August and the hour about 6 a.m. At such a time and date, one would normally expect bright sunshine in Campania, which adds point to Pliny's next remark.
14   **fugere:** i.e. outside of the town, well away from any collapsing buildings. "They pass along the neck of land to the north of the town [see map], till they reach the ground rising up to the hill beyond Baiae, whence they look down [cf. "tremōrēs" II, p. 224, line 15] to the promontory and to the island of Capri beyond" (Sherwin-White).

The main focus of the attention in this section might be the causes and circumstances of the flight of Pliny and his mother; use the map in the students' textbook (p. 223), and the notes where appropriate, to establish a clear picture in the students' minds of the topography. Leave detailed discussion of Pliny's behavior until after the students have read the next section, but invite the class to comment on his sang-froid, as displayed in lines 8–13. Levens 152–53 quotes an amusing eighteenth-century criticism of Pliny, written in the form of an imaginary rebuke from his uncle, and continues: "there is certainly something irritating in Pliny's complacent account of his own imperturbability. At the same time it must be admitted that in finding an occupation to steady his nerves he was acting very sensibly."

Some Suggested Questions

How did Pliny spend the rest of the day after his uncle's departure?
What signs of trouble had been noticed during the previous few days? Why did this cause less panic than might have been expected? How did the situation change during the night?
What did Pliny's mother do when the tremors became violent? What was Pliny himself doing, and with what purpose in mind? What did he and his mother do then?
How did Pliny try to calm his mother's fears? Who was his uncle's friend angry with, and why? What was Pliny's reaction to the friend's rebuke?
Why did Pliny and his mother finally decide to leave? How far did they go before stopping?

For other possible questions, see Tingay, *Comprehendite* 47 to which the present version is indebted for two adaptations of Pliny's original (*ipse* in line 6 for Pliny's *invicem*, and *dubia lūx* in line 13 for *dubius et quasi languidus diēs*).

Suggestions for Consolidation: word order of *irrūpit cubiculum meum māter* and *advenit amīcus* (5–6,9; for further examples, see Appendix D); historical present (9–11, 16–17); *ad* with gerundive (6) and gerund (16); present passive infinitive (5); ablative absolute (1, 13–14).

Vocabulary Check: *proficīscor* (1); *ideō* (1); *quia* (4); *videor* (5); *poscō* (8); *ōtium* (9); *quīdam* (9); *etiam* (10); *adhūc* (13); *cōnstituō* (15); *cōnsistō* (16); *patior* (17).

tremōrēs II (*Letters* VI.20.8–12)

Notes

1   **vehicula:** The original plan was to escape from the town on foot, then take to the carriages if it became necessary to flee further. In the event, the plan of using carriages is abandoned, and when Pliny and his mother resume their flight (lines 20–21), they proceed on foot.

Stage Commentaries

3 **mare in sē resorbērī:** perhaps because of disturbance of the seabed.
5 **ab alterō latere:** i.e. landwards, as opposed to the sea scene just described.
6 **nūbēs ātra:** the cloud of ash and smoke in which Pliny the Elder choked to death at Stabiae (cf. Unit 4 students' textbook, "Supplementary Reading," p. 342, lines 22–31). Pompeii and Herculaneum suffered especially severely from this cloud, owing to the strength and direction of the wind (see map on p. 223 of students' textbook).
7 **fulguribus:** Lightning is in fact often generated during a volcanic eruption. It is shown clearly in Turner's painting *Vesuvius in Eruption* (reproduced in Unit 1 students' textbook, p. 193).
8 **vehementius:** Cf. *impēnsius*, Stage 45, p, 207, line 5.
15 **Capreās, Misēnī prōmunturium:** Refer students again to the map in their textbook, p. 223.
16 **ōrāre hortārī iubēre:** handled in the facing vocabulary. Historical infinitives are the subject of a language note in Stage 48.
18 **corpore:** Evidently she was somewhat on the stout side, like her brother (Pliny, *Letters* VI.16.13; cf. Unit 4 students' textbook, "Supplementary Reading," p. 340, line 10).

Allow students to answer question 2 with a drawing. This can and should be as rigorous and demanding a task as a verbal description. Since the object is to test comprehension, students' intentions are more important than their draughtsmanship.

The main focus for discussion might be the behavior of Pliny, his mother, and the friend. Encourage variety of opinion in response to question 6. Pliny and his mother could be regarded as courageous or foolish, the friend as cowardly or sensible ("We can hardly blame [him] for losing his temper; young Pliny's insufferable priggishness must have been getting on his nerves for some time" – Levens 154). There is obvious educational value in encouraging students to look critically at the way material is presented in historical sources such as the present text. For example, Pliny's emphasis in lines 13–14 on the speed and direction of the friend's departure invites the reader to condemn the friend for being self-centered; but the information given by Pliny himself could support a more favorable interpretation: that the friend, having lingered as long as possible to try to dissuade Pliny and his mother from risking their lives in vain, gives up in despair and rushes off at top speed, perhaps to a situation where he can be of more use. The extracts from Tacitus in Stage 48 will provide further opportunities for critical study of this kind.

Such discussion can lead to further questions. Does Pliny's behavior differ in any way from that of his mother, or are they both presented in very similar terms? Do the students find the account of their behavior credible? Is it to be dismissed as melodramatic self-glorification or are such details as *cōgō* and *pāret invīta* (21) convincing? Were Pliny and his

Stage 46

mother right to postpone flight for so long? It is easy to criticize Pliny for not fleeing earlier, but how many people would in fact run away from a dangerous situation if a mother was left behind to an uncertain fate?

The questions in Tingay, *Comprehendite* 47 (especially the final one, which asks students to pick out details and phrases which help them to visualize the event) will continue to be a useful source of ideas.

The text contains four examples of a subordinate clause in indirect statement (lines 9–10,17,18,21). If you wish to practice the point further, you will find examples in the Unit 4 students' textbook, LI Section, "Review Grammar," p. 327, and p. 209 below.

The picture on p. 224 of the students' textbook, showing the effects of the Pompeian earthquake in A.D. 62, is from the relief carved on the *lararium* of the banker Caecilius Iucundus, whom students will probably recall from Unit 1. This section shows the Vesuvius Gate collapsing and narrowly missing two mules pulling a cart. For further carvings from this relief, see Filmstrip (and slide) I.6 and C.S.C.P. *The Roman World*, Unit II, Book 6, 6–7.

Suggestions for Consolidation: participle in agreement with unexpressed subject (12,20); present passive infinitive (1,3; cf. "tremōrēs" I, p. 222, line 5); indirect statement with main verb postponed (3; see also Unit 4 students' textbook, LI Section, "Review Grammar," pp. 319–21, and p. 206 below); 2nd person plural of present tense of deponent verb (10; practice this further with a "substitution exercise," e.g. by contrasting *cūnctāminī* with *cūnctābiminī* and *cūnctābāminī*, then with *cūnctantur, cūnctor, cūnctāmur, cūnctāris*, etc.).

Vocabulary Check: *īdem* (3); *lītus* (4); *et ... et* (7,18); *vehementer* (8); *hortor* (8,16); *moror* (12,21); *convertō* (12); *cōgō* (21); *pāreō* (21).

First Language Note (*Pluperfect Subjunctive Passive*)

Encourage your students to volunteer their own comments on the way this tense is formed and the way it differs from the pluperfect indicative passive. Ask them to practice the morphology by converting assorted forms of the pluperfect indicative passive into the corresponding subjunctive forms after *cum*, e.g. by turning *laudātī erāmus, ductus erās, monita erat*, into *cum laudātī essēmus, cum ductus essēs, cum monita esset*, adding the translation in each case. For further practice, they could work out the Latin for (e.g.) "when I had been greeted," "when you (pl.) had been forced," "when they had been spoken," etc., with the aid of the

Stage Commentaries

information given under *salūtō, cōgō, loquor,* etc. in Part Four, "Complete Vocabulary," of the students' textbook.

One or two of the examples in the language note would more usually be expressed in Latin by means of a participial phrase. Compare *cum omnēs servī dīmissī essent* in paragraph 2 with *omnibus servīs dīmissīs*, and *cum multās gemmās adeptī essēmus* in paragraph 4 with *multās gemmās adeptī*.

tenebrae (*Letters* VI.20.13–16, 18–20)

Notes

5   **nox dēnsissima:** not a real night, but daytime darkness. Students may recall a comparable scene from the Vergil passage in Stage 42, p. 150.
11 **nusquam iam deōs ūllōs esse:** The rest of Pliny's sentence (omitted from the students' textbook because of grammatical complexity) makes it clear that the crowd thought they were witnessing the fulfillment of the popular belief that the world would end in a fiery blaze. People thought that the end of the world would be preceded by the death or departure of the gods.
15–16 **opertī atque etiam oblīsī pondere:** Compare the fate of Pompeii.
18 **diēs rediit:** still 25 August, since the *nox* of lines 5ff. was "darkness by day."
20 **noctem:** 25–26 August.
22 **cognoscerēmus ... esset:** His body was in fact found on the same day, 26 August (*Letters* VI.16.20; cf. Unit 4 students' textbook, "Supplementary Reading," p. 342, lines 31–34), but Pliny and his mother may have had to wait some time for news to reach them at Misenum from Stabiae.

Some Suggested Questions

Why did Pliny and his mother turn aside in their flight? What happened as soon as they had sat down?

What sounds did they hear?

Why were they not reassured when light reappeared in line 12?

What new danger threatened them in lines 14–16? What preventive measures did they take?

When the sun finally appeared in line 18, why were they amazed by what they saw?

Why were they unwilling to leave Misenum again, even though the tremors persisted?

Discussion of this section might concentrate on Pliny's narrative

Stage 46

technique, especially in lines 1–11, through such questions as the following:

How effective is the simile in lines 2–3? In what way(s) did the thick black cloud resemble a river?

Does *vix ... cum* (line 5) merely indicate the time when the two events happened? Or does it emphasize that Pliny and his mother had a narrow escape?

Does the comparison in lines 5–6 help you to imagine the darkness? (In the full text, Pliny contrasts the darkness of a closed unlighted room with the less intense darkness of a moonless or cloudy night.)

In each of the two clauses *vōcibus ... requīrēbant* and *vōcibus ... nōscitābant*, do the voices belong to the searchers or to the people they are looking for? How detailed a picture does Pliny convey by these four words? Describe the scene in your own words.

Can you find other examples of sentences in which a key word is repeated, in either the same case or a different one? How effective is the paradox *metū mortis mortem precābantur* (9–10)? Is it just a flashy attempt to achieve an impressive phrase, or is it possible that people might indeed, in the agony of suspense, have prayed for what they feared? (Cf. a similar paradox, *et apud illum [avunculum Plīnium] ... ratiō ratiōnem, apud aliōs timōrem timor vīcit*, in Unit 4 students' textbook, "Supplementary Reading," p. 342, lines 19–20.)

Compare the three similes in the passage (lines 2–3, 5–6, 19). Which is the most effective?

Lines 1–11 are very suitable for students to read aloud (after a little practice) to the rest of the class, aiming less at melodrama than at an intelligently phrased reading which emphasizes the sense of the words. Round off the story by reading from a translation of Pliny VI.6; if paragraphs 4–10 were read before, paragraphs 11–20 (taking the story down to the discovery of Pliny the Elder's corpse) could be read now.

Remind your students of their previous encounter with Pliny from Stage 41. Do they detect any similarities of character between 17-year-old Pliny amidst the eruption, and middle-aged Pliny governing Bithynia?

The photograph in the students' textbook of plaster casts of corpses from Pompeii (p. 227) should serve as a reminder that many victims were less successful than Pliny and his mother in avoiding the catastrophic effects of the eruption. Students may be able to recall, from their earlier reading about Pompeii, the way in which archaeologists make such casts (see Unit 1, Stage 12, p. 199, for details).

Stage Commentaries

Suggestions for Consolidation: jussive subjunctive (3; see also Unit 4 students' textbook, LI Section, "Review Grammar," p. 318, and p. 205 below); 1st person plural of passive (4; cf. *patimur*, "tremōrēs" I, p. 222, line 17, and *cōnārēmur*, "tremōrēs" II, p. 223, line 8); purpose clauses with *nē* (3–4); possessive dative (21; see also Unit 4 students' textbook, LI Section, "Review Grammar," p. 311); omission of first of two verbs (9,12); conditional sentence with *nisi* (14–15); *attonitī* predicative (18; for further examples, see Appendix B); 4th declension (7,9,10,20); genitive of gerund (21; cf. *praecepta volandī*, Stage 44, p. 184, line 6).

Vocabulary Check: *quasi* (2,5); *effundō* (3); *lūmen* (6); *adsum* (6); *requīrō* (8); *cāsus* (9); *lūgeō* (9); *procul* (13); *identidem* (14); *fulgeō* (18); *mūtō* (19); *abeō* (21); *cognōscō* (22).

Second Language Note (*Conditional Clauses with Pluperfect Subjunctive*)

For further practice, pick out and retranslate examples of conditionals with the pluperfect subjunctive already met in the reading material. For example:

ego ipse ... efficere potuissem. (Stage 43, p. 166, lines 5–6)
sī precibus ... ultrā cupīvissēmus? (Stage 43, p. 168, lines 3–4)
sī diūtius ... periissēmus. (Stage 46, p. 222, lines 15–16)
sī adfuissēs ... fēminārum (Stage 46, p. 226, lines 6–7)
nisi identidem ... pondere essēmus. (Stage 46, p. 226, lines 14–16)

Ask the students "Does the first example in paragraph 1 imply that the young man *did* look around?" "Does the first example in paragraph 2 imply that the sailors *did* remain in port?", etc., to establish that in each of these sentences the condition was an "impossible" one, incapable of being fulfilled. Such conditionals are often called "unfulfilled" or "contrary-to-fact" (see Unit 4 students' textbook, LI Section, "Reference Grammar," p. 332, paragraph X.1).

Drills

Exercise 1 Type: transformation
Grammatical point being practiced: singular and plural of nouns and adjectives

If students have difficulty with the absence of an expressed subject in sentence 7, or the ablative of comparison in sentence 8, discussion and further practice may be appropriate. Explanation and practice are also sometimes required in connection with *tuī* and *meīs* in sentences 2 and 8;

Stage 46

some students try to change them to forms of *vester* and *noster*, or are misled by the idea of "possession" into attempting to turn *meīs* into the genitive.

Exercise 2 Type: translation from English, based on "tremōrēs" I,
          p. 222, lines 1–12
          Grammatical points being practiced: various forms of verb and noun

Translation from English into Latin has occurred in the Course so far only in the form of suggested substitution drills ("If *parābant* means 'they were preparing,' what's the Latin for 'we were preparing'?", etc.) or guided composition such as Stage 43, exercise 3. The present exercise is somewhat more advanced (but note that all the vocabulary and much of the morphology is given in the original passage). The students could do some or all of the sentences working together as a class, with one student writing up the Latin translation on the blackboard or overhead transparency. Alternatively, students might work in groups; each group could then grade another group's work. If you make up further sentences on similar lines using this or other passages in Stages 41–48, be cautious and do not require students to execute too many changes from the original text.

Exercise 3 Type: substitution
          Grammatical point being practiced: connecting relative, introduced in Unit 3

This is the last and most difficult of a series of substitution exercises involving *is* (Stage 24, exercise 2) and *quī* (Stage 35, exercise 3; Stage 40, exercise 3). The difficulty can be very much lessened if you first elicit from the class that the case of the relative pronoun will always be the same as the case of the noun it is replacing.

This Stage would be a suitable point to begin consolidation work based on the Unit 4 students' textbook, LI Section, "Review Grammar," pp. 284–328.

Third Language Note (*Omission of Forms of* esse)

Demonstrate to the class that this grammatical point, far from being an eccentric peculiarity of Latin, is already very familiar to them in English, e.g. in colloquialisms ("No problem," "Pity you didn't say so"), school reports ("Much improved"), written messages ("Supper in oven"), newspaper headlines ("Two climbers missing"), and among store clerks ("Total five ten [$5.10], please"). Encourage students to suggest further examples.

The Background Material

The information presented in the time chart has been deliberately kept brief. Experience shows that multiplicity of detail often leads students to forget or mix up more important points. After they have studied the chart, an effective way of testing and reinforcing their grasp of the information is to list authors and works in two columns on the blackboard or overhead transparency, in scrambled order, e.g.:

Ovid	epigrams
Pliny	*Aeneid*
Vergil	speeches
Tacitus	the "Lesbia" poems
Martial	*Letters*
Cicero	*Annals*
Catullus	*Metamorphoses*
	etc.

With their textbooks closed, students then have to match each author with the correct work.

Encourage students to contribute further information about any of these authors from their own knowledge, and to recall (from the Stage 42 time chart or elsewhere) any ways in which the various authors are connected either with each other or with some particular event or imperial reign. For example, remind students of the possible link between Catullus and Cicero, through Clodia and Caelius Rufus (in Stage 45, background material). Also remind them that both these authors were writing during the last year of the Republic, and were also contemporaries of Julius Caesar, who featured prominently in the Stage 42 time chart and whose exploits in Britain and Gaul were referred to by Catullus in his poem "Fūrī et Aurēlī..." (Unit 4 students' textbook, pp. 211–12) and in the background material of the Unit 2 students' textbook, Stage 14, p. 36. Vergil and Ovid, on the other hand, lived in the era of the civil war and the establishment of the principate by Augustus; the class may recall from the background material of Stage 39 that Augustus punished Ovid and was Vergil's patron. Similarly, remind the class of the links between Petronius and Nero, Pliny and Tacitus (who received Pliny's letter about the eruption of Vesuvius on which the Latin passages in this Stage are based), Pliny and Trajan (Stage 41), Tacitus and Agricola (Unit 3, Stage 26), and Martial and Domitian (Stage 36). Discussion of this sort can be very helpful in drawing together a number of rather scattered threads and giving the students as coherent a picture as possible of the chronology of the various authors and their historical context. Give special emphasis to Vergil and

Stage 47

Tacitus, from whose work the final selections in the Course, in Stages 47 and 48, are taken.

Vocabulary Checklist

The different forms of *sternō* may require comment from you and special attention from the students; with *strātus* compare "prostrate." With the cognates *iūdex–iūdicāre* compare *rēx–regere*, *dux–dūcere*, and *lūx–lūcēre*; with *iūdicāre–iūdicium* compare *aedificāre–aedificium*, *imperāre–imperium*, *bene + facere–beneficium*, *studēre–studium*, *gaudēre–gaudium*, *taedet–taedium*, and *coniungere–coniugium*.

Suggestions for Further Work

1 Ask the class to write a summary, in not more than (e.g.) 150 or 200 words, of the events described in the Latin passages in this Stage (an extremely difficult exercise, but very good for testing comprehension).
2 Read Samuel Pepys' eye-witness description of the great fire of London (*Diary* 2, September 1666) and ask the class to compare it with Pliny's account of the Vesuvius eruption. What similarities and differences do they notice in (a) subject matter and (b) manner of telling the story?
3 This Stage provides a convenient opportunity to recall, from Unit 1, details of the destruction and excavation of Pompeii. To prompt the students' memory, show them a selection of frames from Filmstrip 1 (or slides from the first edition of Unit I) or the superb National Geographic Video, *In the Shadow of Vesuvius* (1987), which contains – among other interesting scenes such as a simulation of the swift destruction of Herculaneum – documentary footage of the 1944 eruption of Mt. Vesuvius. Ask the class to provide identifications of the slides and to comment on the video as appropriate. Students are often pleased to discover how much they can remember from the early Stages of the Course.

STAGE 47: LŪDĪ

BRIEF OUTLINE

Reading passages	(from) Vergil, *Aeneid* V.114–243 (part Latin, part translation)
Background material	Homer's chariot race (*Iliad* XXIII.358–441, 499–533, in translation)
Language notes	ablative meaning "in" or "from" without preposition
	plural for singular

Stage Commentaries

DIGEST

This passage is Vergil's description of a boat race off the coast of Sicily which was part of Aeneas' funeral games in honor of his father Anchises. The narrative, with its vivid incidents and sympathetically observed characters, is a virtually self-contained episode, leading up gradually to a natural climax in the moment of victory. The story is told partly in the original and partly in translation, with occasional abridgement, so that students will have as complete a view as possible of the episode while simultaneously being able to manage with the Latin. A translation of Homer's chariot race is included as background material for comparison with Vergil's boat race so that students can see for themselves how Vergil (like other Roman poets) made creative use of Greek predecessors.

GRAMMATICAL POINTS

poetic plural for singular
 e.g. "*vīna liquentia fundam.*"
ablative without preposition, signifying "in" or "from"
 e.g. *inde ubi clāra dedit sonitum tuba, fīnibus omnēs
  (haud mora) prōsiluēre suīs.*

SENTENCE PATTERNS

framing and interlacing in verse word order continues
 e.g. *est procul in pelagō saxum spūmantia contrā
  lītora, quod tumidīs summersum tunditur ōlim
  flūctibus, hībernī condunt ubi sīdera Cōrī...*
increased incidence of postponement of sentence elements: subordinate conjunction, apposition
 e.g. (see example above)
   *hīc viridem Aenēās frondentī ex īlice mētam
   cōnstituit signum nautīs pater...*

---

certāmen I (*Aeneid* V.114–23, in translation, abridged)

The commentaries of R. D. Williams (large commentary on *Aeneid* V, shorter notes in his commentary on *Aeneid* I–VI), and of Page, will be helpful throughout this Stage.

Begin by asking students to recall the reason for the Trojans' wanderings, and their quest for a new home. (If they are unacquainted with the story of the *Aeneid*, assign, as reading, the entire book of Frenkel, *Aeneas: Virgil's Epic Retold for Young Readers* (see Bibliography, p. 255) or for older students, Bulfinch and Holme 285–304.) Then read aloud (or have a student read) the translated passage.

 The ships are of different sizes, but have equal numbers of rowers. Each ship is named after a monster, which would be represented by the ship's figurehead; Pristis (possibly a sawfish) is unlikely to be known to students, but they may have come across Scylla (Bulfinch and Holme 87), centaurs (Bulfinch and Holme 151–52), or the fire-breathing Chimaera (Bulfinch and Holme 144–47) in mythology or English literature classes. Write the names of the four captains and their ships (perhaps with the addition of Gyas' helmsman Menoetes) in two columns in a corner of the blackboard or on an overhead transparency. Periodically refer to this during the reading. Also, use additional diagrams, on the blackboard or on successive overhead transparencies, in which you mark the progressive positions of the four ships.

Review some words which occur in this Stage, but which the students have met previously and may have forgotten (many of them appeared in Unit 2, Stage 15, "lūdī fūnebrēs," pp. 51–53), e.g. *aequor, aethēr, lītus, pelagus, saxum, sīdus, unda, cursus, mēta, pondus, rēmus*, etc. When reviewing these words, help the students by supplying a context; thus, not "What does *mēta* mean?" or "What are *rēmī*?" but "The ships had to race to a *mēta* and back; what was a *mēta*?" or "What were the *rēmī* which the sailors used?" Write the Latin words, perhaps with their English translations, on the blackboard or overhead transparency throughout the review period.

certāmen II (*Aeneid* V.124–27, 129–31, 139–41, 151–58)

Vergil presents the learner with special problems as well as special rewards, and even when students can easily understand his words, he can be an exceptionally difficult poet for them to translate. Begin, therefore, by going over the new vocabulary (see p. 14 above) and then ask a big cluster of comprehension questions. Assign some of the questions printed in the students' textbook, e.g. on the present passage and on "victor" II, as homework; then, on the next day, explore the passage and go over the answers in the homework before proceeding to a shared, oral translation in class. Since Vergil provides particularly rich opportunities for discussing the nuances of translation, sometimes pick a short passage, as here, for shared, oral translation, and have a student write the final version on the blackboard.

Notes

2 **summersum tunditur:** Encourage students to translate the participle and verb with two finite verbs ("is submerged and battered," etc.).

6 **signum:** predicative. The first two parts of question 2 may help.

6–7 **unde revertī scīrent:** The purpose clause dependent on *unde*, and the infinitive dependent on *scīrent*, are likely to cause trouble. Use comprehension questions to establish the sense before eliciting a

Stage Commentaries

> translation. Williams has: "so that they should know where to make the turn for home."

7 **ubi:** postponed. Compare the previous example in line 3, which is explained in the glossary.

12 **Gyās:** If the long postponement of the subject causes difficulty, try a simpler example, e.g. *appāruit in līmine nūntius*; but also encourage comment on the effect produced by the word order (see p. 109 above).

15 **priōrem:** not the overall lead, but a lead in the struggle for third place.

16 **victam:** perfect passive participle in accusative. For further examples, see Appendix D.

18 **longā ... vada salsa carīnā:** If you encourage your students to listen carefully while you read the line aloud, they will find it easier to disentangle the two noun + adjective phrases.

Begin the discussion with Vergil's description of the rock. He pictures it in both calm and stormy weather, and each description involves both sound and appearance. Ask the students what use Vergil makes of contrasting words or phrases to emphasize the difference between the two descriptions. Which words or phrases in line 4 correspond to *tumidīs ... flūctibus* (lines 2–3), *tunditur* (line 2), and *summersum* (line 2)? (The picture in the students' textbook may be helpful here.)

Emphasize to the students that the course the contestants are to follow is a double one, out to the rock, around it, and back again, in the manner of a chariot race. Ask them what the purpose of the oak branch is.

Students might try their wits on one puzzle mentioned by Williams: why is Cloanthus said (in lines 13–14) to be held back by the weight of his ship, whereas earlier it was Gyas whose ship was mentioned as especially massive (line 4, English)? Compare the gloss on *iūnctīs* (line 15) with the word's literal translation: what does the literal meaning suggest about the appearance of the two prows? Finally, the students might consider the questions "Which lines are most easily visualized? At what points can we hear as well as see the action?".

Suggestions for Consolidation: 3rd person plural perfect in *-ēre* (9; at this point, study examples in the Unit 4 students' textbook, LI Section, "Review Grammar," p. 296; more examples will be met in this Stage and more again in Stage 48); split phrases (3,5,7, etc.; for further examples, see Appendix D).

Vocabulary Check: *procul* (1); *pelagus* (1); *lītus* (2); *sīdus* (3); *revertor* (6); *aethēr* (9); *unda* (11); *cōnsequor* (13); *rēmus* (13); *pondus* (13); *praetereō* (16); *ūnā* (17).

Gyās et Cloanthus I (*Aeneid* V.159–71 in translation)

When the students have read the passage, make sure they have a clear grasp of the situation, especially the point of Gyas' instructions in line 5 and the reason why Cloanthus is able to pass him. A diagram on the blackboard or overhead transparency is helpful at this point (note that the boats go around the rock counterclockwise). Compare the need for careful judgment at the turn, going neither too close nor too wide, with the tactics necessary in chariot racing.

What impression of Gyas' character do the students have from this passage?

Gyās et Cloanthus II (*Aeneid* V.172–73, 175–82)

The questions in the students' textbook are intended for their use *after* they have read the passage and established the surface meaning. Give plenty of help on the first reading, for example by simple comprehension questions ("What feeling blazed up? Where?" etc.).

Notes

1   **iuvenī:** Students are likely at first to translate as "of the young man"; accept this translation, but return to the word when the students have read the entire passage and discuss the case further.
    ossibus: The context will probably suggest an appropriate translation ("in the bones," etc.); local ablatives are discussed in the next language note.
4   **rēctor ... magister:** both words predicative. Question 2 may help.
6   **ut:** postponed. Students often overlook it.
    fundō ... īmō: Note how the class manages with this noun + adjective phrase; if they are baffled, ask them whether there is an adjective describing *fundō* anywhere in the line.
9   **et ... et:** Compare a simpler example if necessary, e.g. *et rēgēs et urbēs* from Stage 45, p. 200, lines 15–16.
10   **pectore:** The context gives a strong clue to the meaning of the ablative; further examples will follow in the next language note.
    salsōs ... flūctūs: Bring this phrase to the students' attention, they will meet it again in the middle of a difficult sentence in "victor" II. For suggestions on handling the separation of noun and adjective, see above on *fundō ... īmō*, line 6.

Some Suggested Questions

Is "sadness" a good translation for *dolor* (line 1)? If not, can you suggest an improvement?
Can you recall another poem in which emotion was, as in line 1, felt in

Stage Commentaries

the bones or limbs? (If the students are reminded that in the previous poem the feeling was described as a *tenuis flamma*, this may help them recall Catullus' description from Stage 45 (p. 200, lines 9–10).)

Does *altā* (line 3) add anything important to your impression of the scene?

What translation would you suggest for *gravis* (line 6)? (Page has "heavily," Williams "in his sorry state." Make the point that this is a problem purely for the translator, not for the original readers or listeners; Vergil's immediate audience could have responded to several different associations of *gravis* simultaneously, without feeling any need to choose between them.)

Is the behavior of Gyas and Menoetes appropriate to their respective ages? If Gyas' action is grossly stupid, does *iuvenis* (line 1) imply an excuse for him?

Do you agree with Page's comment on the Trojans' mirth in lines 9–10, "Such merriment is natural, but we could spare the description of it in poetry"?

Use question 6 to bring out the point that Vergil presents the episode to us both through the eyes of the spectators (in the description of Menoetes' actions) and from his own point of view through "editorial" comments such as *gravis, iam senior*, etc.

Suggestions for Consolidation: verb + nominative word order (1,2; for further examples, see Appendix D); accusative + nominative + verb word order (9; see Appendix D); 3rd person plural perfect in *-ēre* (2,9; the class might note that *rīsēre* is used side by side with historical present *rīdent* in 10); split phrases (1,3, etc.).

Vocabulary Check: *cāreō* (2); *hortor* (5); *lītus* (5); *at* (6); *flūctus* (10).

Sergestus et Mnēstheus I (*Aeneid* V.183–200 in translation)

Vergil now switches from the struggle for first place to the battle between the third and fourth place boats. Remind the class of the description of the two prows at the end of "certāmen" II, and use a diagram to establish the positions of Sergestus and Mnestheus; Sergestus is in front, on the inside. Explain line 6: Mnestheus is striding up and down a central gangway.

The students might consider why Mnestheus mentions Hector and the crew's previous adventures in his pep talk (lines 8–11), and how the sentence might have ended which breaks off at "perhaps" (line 13); has Mnestheus accepted loss of first prize as inevitable, or does he still nourish a secret hope? Does he attract the reader's sympathy (Williams contrasts the tone of Mnestheus' speech with the previous arrogance and brutality of Gyas)?

Sergestus et Mnēstheus II (*Aeneid* V.201–204, 207–209)

First take the students through the new vocabulary and read the passage aloud to them, then ask the following questions and have the students answer them in writing and grade them in class:

What did chance do?
What was Sergestus doing in line 2? in line 3?
What happened to him?
What did the sailors do?
What did they bring out? What do you think their reason was?
What did they gather up? Where from?

When the students have answered and graded these questions, read the passage aloud again and then proceed to translation. The main points of difficulty will probably be the interlacing of the noun + adjective phrases in line 1, the postponement of *dum* in line 2, and the use of *īnfēlīx* to refer to Sergestus in line 4.

Establish that *honōrem* (line 1) refers to success in the race, and that *optātum* refers back to Mnestheus' words in Part I; then encourage your students to explain in their own words the situation described in lines 2–3. Sergestus is afraid that if he goes too wide, Mnestheus will cut in behind him and pass him on the inside (as Cloanthus did to Gyas earlier); he tries to forestall this by steering into the danger area (*spatiō ... inīquō*, line 3) close to the turn, but fouls his boat on the reef which projects outwards (*prōcurrentibus*, line 4) from the rock, mostly or wholly under water. Vergil attributes the crash to *ipse ... cāsus* (line 1); do the students believe that any word or phrase in lines 2 and 3 suggests a different cause?

Read line 4 aloud, and contrast it with a more dactylic line (like line 8 or 9 in "certāmen" II, p. 238); then ask the students if the sound of the line is in any way suited to the sense. They might also consider whether "Up jump the sailors" or "The sailors jump up" translates the start of line 5 more faithfully. Questions like this help students to see that a Latin author's variation of word order is not merely random or willful.

The meaning of *magnō clāmōre morantur* (line 5) is disputed. The vocabulary follows Williams in interpreting it as "hold the ship steady while shouting loudly." Most other commentators say "shout loudly at the delay." Which explanation do the students prefer? Which suits the

Stage Commentaries

situation better? The students might also consider the shouts; do they imagine these are shouts of panic? Anger? Despair at the crew's ruined prospects in the race?

The relief from an Attic inscription shown on p. 241 of the students' textbook gives names of the archons (magistrates) for the year A.D. 164–65. There were boat races, some between triremes, at various festivals in Athens, and this boat is probably a trireme tender, a small boat used for ferrying stores, oarsmen, etc. to and from the trireme. The number of oarsmen is determined by artistic rather than factual considerations.

Suggestions for Consolidation: *interior* predicative (3; see Appendix D).

Vocabulary Check: *optō* (1); *īnfēlīx* (4); *haereō* (4); *frangō* (7).

First Language Note (*Ablative Meaning "in" or "from" without Preposition*)

Students are sometimes discouraged by the apparently limitless range of possible meanings for the ablative, but reassured by a demonstration that the context normally makes the required meaning clear. Pick out a number of examples already met in Stages 41–47, in which the ablative means "in," "from," "with," "than," etc. After you have reminded your students of the context, ask them to identify the ablative and translate the sentence, noting how the appropriate translation of the ablative is determined by the rest of the sentence. Possible examples include:

> *quid magis est saxō dūrum?* (Stage 42, p. 149, line 7)
> *errāmus pelagō.* (Stage 42, p. 150, line 13)
> *flāvam ... pollice cēram mollībat.* (Stage 44, p. 182, lines 6–7)
> *quā tē regiōne requīram?* (Stage 44, p. 189, line 13)
> *quem plūs illa oculīs suīs amābat.* (Stage 45, p. 205, line 5)
> *sed obstinātā mente perfer, obdūrā.* (Stage 45, p. 210, line 11)
> *tranquillō silet.* (Stage 47, p. 237, line 4)
> *prīmīsque ēlābitur undīs.* (Stage 47, p. 238, line 11)
> *exarsit ... dolor ossibus ingēns.* (Stage 47, p. 240, line 1)
> *et salsōs rīdent revomentem pectore flūctūs.* (Stage 47, p. 240, line 10)

victor I (*Aeneid* V.210, 212, 220–24)

Your abler students can perhaps answer the comprehension questions in their textbook after the first reading. If the majority, however, cannot

Stage 47

answer them, precede or replace the questions with some like the following:

Which two adjectives in line 1 describe Mnestheus?
Which two verbs in line 2 tell you what he did?
Translate lines 1–2.
Find three present participles in lines 3–5 which describe what Sergestus is doing. Where is he struggling (lead students to *brevibus . . . vadīs*, line 4, as well as *in scopulō . . . altō*, line 3)?
Look again at lines 3–5: what does Mnestheus do to Sergestus?
Translate lines 3–5.
Whom and what does Mnestheus now overtake? How is he able to do this?
Translate lines 6–7.

The answer to question 3 in the students' textbook could lead to a brief summary of the earlier incident involving Gyas and Menoetes.

Single out one or two words for study and discussion. For example:

prōna (line 2). Williams points out that two meanings are involved: "downward," i.e. "shoreward" (cf. *dē* in *dēcurrit*, and contrast the English expression "the *high* seas"), and "easy" (because this is the homestretch, from the rock to the finish line, with no awkward turns or obstacles on route).

altō (line 3). The word might at first seem to contradict the earlier description of the rock in "certāmen" II (p. 237), where it was said to be so low that it became submerged in stormy weather; but, as Williams points out, even a jutting reef is high by comparison with the water around it (as Sergestus has found to his cost).

discentem (line 5). Why not *cōnantem*? What does *discentem* suggest about Sergestus' problem and his efforts to solve it? Is the phrase *frāctīs discentem currere rēmīs* a sympathetic one (Williams quotes Day Lewis, "taking a lesson in rowing with broken oars," saying it well expresses the mocking humor in English)?

currere (line 5). The students have met this verb many times as "run," in Stage 44 as "fly" (p. 184, line 1), and here as "sail." What do the three ideas all have in common? What does Vergil gain by using *currere* here rather than a "normal" word for "sail"?

Suggestions for Consolidation: split phrases (e.g. 2,3,5; see also Appendix D).

Vocabulary Check: *petō* (2); *pelagus* (2); *discō* (5); *inde* (6); *cēdō* (7).

victor II (*Aeneid* V.225–43)

Stage Commentaries

Notes

1 **iamque:** postponed. Note how the students manage, and give help if necessary.
2 **petit:** sc. *Mnēstheus*.
3 **sequentem:** substantival, or in agreement with unexpressed *eum* or *Mnēsthea*.
9 **Cloanthus:** nominative noun placed late in clause. Encourage the students to read the line straight through, and if necessary ask them which contestant took the initiative. They may need a reminder of the meaning of *nī* (met in line 6) and a quick reminder of the substance of line 8, in order to see how the long conditional clause of lines 9–10 fits into the sentence as a whole.
10 **-que ... -que:** cf. "Gyās et Cloanthus" II, p. 240, line 5.
11 **quibus:** possessive dative. Cf. *est mihi magna vīlla*, or *est mihi summum imperium*, etc.
12–13 **vōbīs ... reus:** a very tricky sentence. Ask your students to study it in pairs, with a warning about the interlaced noun + adjective phrases; if they still cannot disentangle the sentence, help them through it with comprehension questions. The students may recall the required meaning of *cōnstituō* if you remind them that Aeneas *viridem mētam ... cōnstituit* on the rock at the start of the race ("certāmen" II, p. 237, lines 5–6). Williams has a helpful note on *vōtī reus*, "bound by the obligation to pay what one has promised"; cf. the related phrase *vōtum solvere* which the class may have come across in dedicatory inscriptions, and which appeared in Stage 44, p. 191, exercise 1.
15 **dīxit:** cf. Stage 44, p. 181, line 6.
16–17 **Nēreidem ... Portūnus:** Students might like to identify the characters in the picture on p. 246.
17 **euntem:** cf. *sequentem* in line 3 above.
18 **citius:** Recall (with a reminder of context) *impēnsius* (Stage 45, p. 207, line 5) or *vehementius* (Stage 46, p. 223, line 8). Cf. also *melius*.
19 **portū ... altō:** Note how students manage with this phrase, after their recent language note on local ablatives (p. 243).

Questions A1–A4 should help the class to grasp the situation. Mnestheus is gaining on Cloanthus, but is running out of time in which to catch him; his spirited effort to come from behind and overtake the leader in a last-minute spurt wins the hearts of the spectators, who cheer him on enthusiastically. (Do students believe that Vergil's *cūnctī*, line 3, should be taken literally, or would Cloanthus continue to receive the cheers and encouragement of his own supporters?) Tension in Cloanthus' boat is acute; having led throughout the second half of the race, his crew feel an eleventh-hour defeat would be unbearable, and are straining desperately to hold off their challenger. Mnestheus' men, on the other hand, who were earlier struggling to avoid last place, now find themselves with an outside chance of outright victory. As line 7 makes clear, their success against Sergestus and Gyas has transformed their morale.

The answer to question A5 is disputable; most commentators take line 8 as meaning that the race would have ended in a dead heat, but Williams interprets it as "having (first) come up level, they would have (gone on and) won the prize"; which interpretation do your students prefer? As a follow-up to question A6, ask the class why Cloanthus chooses these particular deities, or why his promised offerings will be made on the shore and into the sea. Approach question A8 by asking students to read lines 17–18 aloud. Also ask the students whether they take *manū magnā ... impulit* literally or metaphorically; if it is metaphorical, what is happening literally? Question A9 might lead to the additional question: which is the more appropriate simile for Cloanthus' boat in line 19, the wind or the arrow?

Harris (*Sport* 128–32; see also his lecture in *Meminisse Iuvabit* 108–10) has an engaging commentary on the race, complete with a detailed diagram (though you and the students will probably prefer to work out a diagram for yourselves). Harris is very scathing about Vergil's climax, on the grounds that Cloanthus wins only by cheating – a view which may already have occurred to some sports-minded members of your class. Discuss the significance and appropriateness of Cloanthus' appeal to the gods. For example, can the intervention of Portunus be given a rationalized interpretation ("inspiration," "superhuman effort," "unexpected reserves of strength," etc.)?

Preface question B1 with a retrospective look at the whole race. The students might summarize the main events, or you might rapidly retranslate the entire episode, calling on students from time to time to supply the translation of individual words or phrases. Williams' view of the four captains is given on pp. xiv–xv of his edition of Book V, and in his note on lines 116f. in his edition of Books I–IV. (Other views are possible, of course. Some students might argue that the personalities of the four captains fail to make a lasting impression on the reader; Vergil himself seems to have forgotten the name of the winner by line 493 of Book V.)

When discussing question B2, encourage students to demonstrate how they think a particular line or passage ought to be read aloud. (They will find Cloanthus' prayer hard to read accurately because of its unusually large number of elisions; the teacher should not press students too hard on this.) Develop this into a full-scale reading of the whole Stage (see p. 64 above). Whether you should explain the scansion of the hexameter or not depends on the skill and interest of your students. If you do teach scansion, tell them to "linger" over syllables which contain long vowels or vowels succeeded by two consonants; go further, if time allows, and work out the scansion in feet, but do not over-emphasize meter to the exclusion of sense. Dissuade your students from trying to read every line in a single breath; indicate that the sense of the words often makes a pause in mid-line appropriate. They should try to think about meaning as much as possible while simultaneously thinking about scansion.

Suggestions for Consolidation: substantival participle (3,17); verb + nominative word order (3,15–16; see also Appendix D); accusative + nominative + verb word order (7; see also Appendix D); conditional sentence with *nisi* (*nī*) and pluperfect subjunctive (8); possessive dative (11; see also Unit 4 students' textbook, LI Section, "Review Grammar," p. 311, and p. 203 below); ablative of comparison (18; see also Unit 4 students' textbook, LI Section, "Review Grammar," p. 312, and p. 203 below).

Vocabulary Check: *petō* (2); *vīrēs* (2); *aethēr* (4); *quia* (7); *uterque* (9); *imperium* (11); *aequor* (11); *lītus* (12); *āra* (13); *flūctus* (14,15); *fundō* (14).

Second Language Note *(Plural for Singular)*

The quotations in paragraph 1 are from Ovid (Stage 44, p. 189, lines 10–11), Vergil (*Aeneid* II.255, IV.646), and William Vaughn Moody (*An Ode in Time of Hesitation*). The comparison with American poetry may help to make the point that the use of plural for singular is not an odd vagary peculiar to Roman authors, nor is it adopted merely for the sake of the meter (though metrical advantage is often one of its side-effects), but it is one of the ways in which poets may choose to express themselves differently from prose writers; other ways include the use of meter, or of a specialized vocabulary (*ēnsis* for *gladius*, "steed" for "horse," etc.). Quote English examples of the reverse practice, where the singular is used for the plural ("life on the ocean wave," "with downcast eye," "mariner for forty year," etc.).

Williams, on *Aeneid* V.98 (in his large commentary), has a very full and clear account of "poetic plurals," demonstrating their metrical convenience, distinguishing a number of ways in which their use developed, and recording some interesting objections by ancient critics (including Caesar).

Stage 47

Drills

Exercise 1 Type: transformation
Grammatical point being practiced: synonyms

Exercise 2 Type: completion
Missing item: verb
Test of accuracy: sense
Grammatical point being practiced: conditional clauses with pluperfect subjunctive, introduced in Stage 46

Exercise 3 Type: substitution
Grammatical point being practiced: deponent verbs
A wide range of morphology is practiced, including both present-stem and perfect-stem forms, and a subjunctive in sentence 6. Do one or two sentences orally in class before assigning the entire exercise as written work. Use one of the practice exercises on deponent verbs (in the Unit 4 students' textbook, LI Section, "Review Grammar," pp. 303–05) as either a lead-in or a follow-up to this exercise.

Exercise 4 Type: completion
Missing item: noun *or* verb *or* participle *or* adverb
Test of accuracy: sense and syntax, based on Stage 47 reading passages
Grammatical point being practiced: sentence structure

The Background Material

The lines translated are *Iliad* XXIII.358–60, 362–67, 369–441, 499–516, 523–27, 532–33. Take the trouble to sort out the identity of the chief characters, using the information in the students' textbook (including the Index, pp. 398–404) and perhaps listing the four contestants on the blackboard or overhead transparency. Students should read the passage through for themselves as homework; then read all or part of it aloud in class. Explain the phrase "single-foot horses" (horses with single, i.e. uncloven, hooves).

"The *Aeneid* is a poem wholly different in character from the Homeric poems. Yet it recalls them on every page and is constructed largely by the remoulding of Homeric materials" (Camps 75; see also ibid. 9–10). The gods are involved both in Homer's chariot race and in Vergil's boat race, but in very different ways. Portunus' helping hand, which enables Cloanthus to beat Mnestheus to the finish line, contrasts sharply with the energetic intervention of Homer's Athene, who not only picks up Diomedes' whip for him but wrecks his rival's chariot in a spectacular

Stage Commentaries

crash. Students may perhaps notice the further detail that whereas Athene's action is prompted simply by pity for Diomedes, Portunus' intervention is a response to a prayer.

Vergil's imaginative exploitation of Homer can also be illustrated, in microcosm, by a comparison between the incident at the "narrow place" in Homer's chariot race and Vergil's two incidents at the rock. In Vergil, the incidents happen at the turning-point; in Homer, the reader *expects* drama at the turn (especially after the long speech of Nestor, not included in the students' textbook, in which he gives Antilochos wordy advice about rounding the turning-point), but during the race the turn goes unmentioned and the actual drama takes place elsewhere. In Homer, Antilochos refuses to yield in the narrow place, and Menelaos has to drop back or be forced off the road; Vergil reshapes this event and splits it into two complementary incidents, in which first Gyas' helmsman allows himself to be passed while taking the turn too wide, and then Sergestus steers too close to the rock and runs aground.

Compare Antilochos' speech to his horses in 44–57 with Mnestheus' address to his crew in "Sergestus et Mnēstheus" I, p. 242. In each case, the speaker abandons hope of victory but is desperate to avoid the humiliation of last (or nearly last) place. The tone of the two speeches, however, is utterly different; Mnestheus' appeal is an engaging mixture of passion and humility, whereas Antilochos is all threat and bluster. The students will probably be able to find further parallels themselves between Vergil's boat race and Homer's chariot race, including some close similarities of verbal detail, e.g. between line 8 of "victor" II, p. 246, and lines 23, 104–105 of the *Iliad*. If the class have a chance to read (or listen to) a translation of the complete boat race episode (see "Suggestions for Further Work" below), they may spot an indirect allusion to Homer at the start of the race, where Vergil illustrates the speed of the boats with an extended simile drawn from chariot racing.

The gem shown on p. 253 is in the Museum of Fine Arts, Boston. The charioteer (in long dress) is turning the chariot. The Greek-vase fragment shown on p. 254 is in the National Museum, Athens. It depicts the funeral games in honor of Patroklos, and his name and the name of the painter (Sophilos) can be picked out in the inscription (written in "mirror writing"). The name of Achilles also appears on the right-hand edge. Students are usually intrigued to notice the four pairs of horses' forelegs; if they look carefully, they should also be able to distinguish the four heads. There is a more detailed description in Arias 285–86, illustration 39.

In addition to the illustration in the students' textbook, you can find further pictures of Greek chariot racing (some of which refer specifically to the *Iliad* XXIII race) in C.S.C.P. *Greek Foundation Course Folder V*

Stage 47

(orange card 10 and green card 20), Harris, *Sport* plates 62–67, Swaddling 67,69,70 and Drees plates 4,13a, 55 and V.

Suggestions for Discussion

Why do you think Vergil used material from Homer? Why did he not simply make up his own story in his own words? (Coleman 119–20, Camps 9–10, and Woodman and West *passim*, especially 195–200, all have helpful remarks; it is worth stressing that Vergil's readers and listeners were usually intimately familiar with the Homeric poems, so that part of their pleasure in Vergil would come from recognizing echoes of Homer and savoring Vergil's individual variations on Homeric themes and motifs.)

Vocabulary Checklist

There are some opportunities here to review grammatical points. From study of the nominative and genitive singular forms of *flūctus*, can your students deduce which declension it belongs to? What must the gender of *pondus* be, and what must be the form of its nominative and accusative plural? With *pondus–ponderōsus*, compare *pretium–pretiōsus*, *perīculum–perīculōsus*, *ōtium–ōtiōsus*, *aqua–aquōsus*, and *spatium–spatiōsus*.

Suggestions for Further Work

1 Read the complete boat-race episode (*Aeneid* V.114–253) in translation, including the presentation of prizes and the return of Sergestus, limping home in his crippled boat, as well as the elaborate similes (lines 144–47, 213–19) which were omitted from the students' textbook because of their grammatical complexity. (The two most recent translators of the *Aeneid* into English, Mandelbaum and Fitzgerald (see Bibliography), are both Americans, and paperbacks of their translations are readily available in North America.) If sufficient copies of the translation are available for students to refer to, they might study the similes in detail, deciding in each case what the points of resemblance are between the two things being compared.
2 The suggestion made on **pp. 137–38** above, that the class be asked to prepare a "shooting script" for videotaping the story they have just read, might be adopted here if not used already in connection with Daedalus and Icarus in Stage 44.
3 The class could invent another episode in the games, and write an account of it in prose or verse; it might be an event of their own choice or one specified by the teacher. As a variation on this, first

Stage Commentaries

read a translation of the boxing match in the Homeric games (*Iliad* XXIII.653–99), then ask the class to write their own boxing-match narrative, and finally, for comparison with both Homer and the students' versions, read them Vergil's account (*Aeneid* V.362–484) of the fight between Dares and Entellus.

4 Review the story of the boat games celebrated in Britain by King Cogidubnus on the anniversary of the Emperor Claudius' death (Unit 2, "lūdī fūnebrēs," pp. 51–53). Ask the students to find parallels between Vergil's account and that in Unit 2, beginning with the similarity between Sergestus and Belimicus.

STAGE 48: NERŌ ET AGRIPPĪNA

BRIEF OUTLINE

Reading passages	Tacitus, *Annals* XIV.3–9 (adapted)
Background material	the emperor
Language notes	direct and indirect deliberative questions
	historical infinitive
	perfect subjunctive passive

DIGEST

The reading material in this final Stage of the Course is taken from Tacitus' vivid and dramatic account of Nero's murder of Agrippina. Although the Latin has been adapted, sufficient flavor survives from the original to give students some impression of Tacitus' vigorous, colorful, and sometimes quirky style. The selected passages offer an opportunity for considering such questions as "Is it true? Should we believe this? Can we tell what really happened?" and for discussing the personality, behavior, and motives of the leading characters.

GRAMMATICAL POINTS

perfect subjunctive: passive and deponent
  e.g. *dīcite mihi quārē missī sītis.*
       num īnspexerit mātrem mortuam Nerō (ut multī affirmant) et fōrmam corporis eius admīrātus sit, incertum est.
indirect deliberative
  e.g. *ministrōs convocātōs cōnsuluit utrum venēnō an ferrō vel quā aliā vī ūterētur.*
separation of *id ... quod*
  e.g. *sī naufragiō Agrippīna perierit, quis adeō suspīciōsus erit ut scelerī id assignet quod ventī et flūctūs fēcerint?*
increasing complexity in use of conditionals
  e.g. *sōlum īnsidiārum remedium esse putāvit, sī nōn intellegere vidērētur.*

SENTENCE PATTERNS

asymmetry in sentence structure continues: for example, causal ablative + *quod* clause; relative clause of purpose + INF governed by the same verb

e.g. *nec dissolūtiō nāvis sequēbātur, turbātīs omnibus et quod plērīque nautae, sceleris ignārī, eōs impediēbant quī cōnsciī erant.*

mīsit igitur lībertum quī nūntiāret fīliō sē benignitāte deōrum et fortūnā eius ēvāsisse gravem cāsum; ōrāre ut Nerō ... vīsendī cūram differret.

increasing complexity in indirect discourse: ACC + INF and indirect command governed by same verb

e.g. *Acerrōnia autem, dum sē Agrippīnam esse imprūdenter clāmat utque subvenīrētur mātrī prīncipis, contīs et rēmīs cōnficitur.*

increasing variety in word order in sentences using indirect question

e.g. *quō modō vīs et caedēs cēlārētur nēmō excōgitāre poterat.*

num īnspexerit mātrem mortuam Nerō (ut multī affirmant) et fōrmam corporis eius admīrātus sit, incertum est.

increasing incidence of variety of word order within the accusative and infinitive construction

e.g. *... affirmāns iam iamque adfore mātrem ultiōnis avidam.*

increasing variety of word order within the ablative absolute

e.g. *interim vulgātō Agrippīnae perīculō, omnēs dēcurrere ad lītus.*

Title Picture

Obverse of an *aureus* from the first year of Nero's reign, A.D. 54; Agrippina shares equal, nose-to-nose (!) prominence with her son. The legend reads:

AGRIPP(INA) AVG(VSTA) DIVI CLAVD(II) NERONIS CAES(ARIS) MATER.

īnsidiae I (*Annals* XIV.3)

The commentaries of Woodcock and Furneaux will often be helpful during this Stage; Griffin (especially 23–49, 67–82), Warmington 43–48, and Woodcock 33–35 are very useful on the historical background.

Supplement the introduction in the students' text book (p. 258) with some additional historical information, though be careful not to confuse the students by overdoing the detail. Nero was the son of Agrippina by Cn. Domitius Ahenobarbus, who died in A.D. 40. Agrippina's ambition was to secure her son's accession to the principate and become the power behind the throne. She married the Emperor Claudius, ensured the adoption of Nero into Claudius' family above the natural heir Britannicus (son of Claudius and Messalina) and arranged Nero's marriage to Claudius' daughter Octavia. When Claudius seemed to be contemplating the reinstatement of Britannicus as his heir, he died under

Stage Commentaries

suspicious circumstances; it was generally assumed that Agrippina was responsible. With the help of Burrus, she arranged for Britannicus to be kept in the background while Nero was hailed as emperor.

By A.D. 59, when the events described in Stage 48 took place, a three-cornered struggle for power had developed between Nero, his mother, and the partnership of Burrus and Seneca (who for some time were effectively the rulers of the empire through their influence on Nero). One result of this struggle had been the poisoning of Britannicus, whom Agrippina had threatened to put in Nero's place as emperor. The situation was further complicated when Nero became infatuated with Poppaea. Both Nero and Poppaea were already married to others, but Poppaea's husband Otho was removed from the scene by being sent to Spain as governor of Lusitania. Nero's wife Octavia, however, was a more serious obstacle to Nero's plans. The marriage had originally been arranged by Agrippina, who was well aware that the divorce or murder of Octavia, followed by marriage between Nero and Poppaea, would be a clear sign that her own power and influence were on the wane. Burrus and Seneca watched the situation with concern, continuing to offer flattery, advice, and support to Nero in order to check the power of Agrippina, while trying not to give too much power to Nero himself.

Read relevant extracts from Tacitus, such as his accounts of the murders of Claudius (*Annals* XII.66–69) and Britannicus (XII.15–16), to the students in translation, for example in the versions of Grant (281–83, 290–91) or Tingay, *Empire* (68–69).

Notes

1 **vetustāte:** causal. Question 1 in the students' textbook might be expanded: "Why was Nero confident enough to attempt the murder?"
Poppaeae: For details of her role in the crisis, see above.

3–4 **utrum ... ūterētur:** indirect deliberative question. A few examples have occurred earlier in the Course, and both direct and indirect deliberatives are discussed in the next language note. The captioned drawing may help the students, especially if the teacher asks "What did Nero consult his advisers about?"
utrum ... an ... vel: Poison is contrasted with violence, which in turn is subdivided into (a) the sword (b) other violent methods. (For the combination *utrum ... an ... vel*, cf. Stage 41, p. 122, lines 4–5.)

6 **Britannicus:** see above.

7–8 **quō modō ... cēlārentur:** another indirect deliberative, this time preceding the main verb. Remind the students to read straight through to *poterat* before attempting a translation.

10 **Anicētus:** Nero's prefect of the fleet at Misenum (the same position which Pliny the Elder was holding later under the Emperor Titus when he was asphyxiated in the eruption of Mt. Vesuvius).

Stage 48

11 **nāvem ... compōnī:** Ask the students whether this is Tacitus' own comment or part of what Anicetus said (or elicit the same point by asking what is indicated by the fact that *nāvem* is accusative and *posse* infinitive).

11–12 **cuius pars ... solūta ... Agrippīnam ēiceret:** Comprehension questions may help: "What was to happen to the ship? What would this do to Agrippina?"

13 **capāx fortuitōrum:** Note how students manage with the omission of *est*.

Use question 2 in the students' textbook to establish that Nero does not ask his advisers *whether* his mother should be killed; he asks them *how*. Tacitus' account of the conferences creates a lurid impression of the current state of the imperial court: poison is ruled out because Agrippina has anticipated it and forearmed herself, and because after the killing of Britannicus, any sudden death will arouse suspicion; the sword is ruled out because there is no one Nero can trust, either to do the killing or to keep it secret. Question 5 highlights the key features of Anicetus' scheme: it will make the murder look like an accident, and state religion will be used to conceal the author of the crime. Help your students to appreciate the irony in Anicetus' speech by asking, "In what tone of voice would you read *fortuitōrum* (line 13)? In a deadpan style? With a sneer? With heavy emphasis, as if the word were placed in quotation marks? Might any other words in Anicetus' speech be read in a similar tone?" (Possible answers could include *naufragiō*, line 13, and *pietātem*, line 16.)

The coin on p. 260 is an *aureus* of Nero and Agrippina, minted at Rome in A.D. 55, with the legend:

NERO CLAVD(II) DIVI F(ILIVS) CAES(AR) AVG(VSTVS) GERM(ANICVS) IMP(ERATOR) TR(IBVNICIA) P(OTESTATE) CO(N)S(VL).

Agrippina, though still honored by inclusion on the coin, is less dominant than on the coin on p. 257; this time, she is placed behind Nero in the inferior position instead of facing him as before, and her titles are relegated to the reverse of the coin, whose legend is:

EX S(ENATUS) C(ONSVLTO) AGRIPP(INA) AVG(VSTA) DIVI CLAVD(II) NERONIS CAES(ARIS) MATER.

Further portraits of Nero and Agrippina are shown on slides V.31–33.

Suggestions for Consolidation: perfect passive participle in accusative (3; see also Appendix D); ablative of gerund (7,16 (twice); further examples of gerund in ablative and genitive occur later in this

Stage Commentaries

Stage; see also Unit 4 students' textbook, LI Section, "Review Grammar," p. 324); verb + nominative word order (4,8, etc.; see also Appendix D); fearing clause (3–9).

Vocabulary Check: *at* (1); *fīō* (1); *cōnstituō* (2); *vel* (3,16); *ūtor* (4); *inter* (4); *cāsus* (5); *cēlō* (8); *metuō* (8); *odiō est* (10); *ēiciō* (12); *adeō* (14).

īnsidiae II (*Annals* XIV.4)

Notes

2 **Bāiās:** for Baiae's reputation as a fashionable seaside resort, cf. the background material of Stage 45, p. 217, of the students' textbook.
   diem fēstum: The festival of the Quinquatrus was held in honor of Minerva from 19 to 23 March. It was celebrated by everybody whose employment was under the goddess' protection: schoolteachers and students, who had a school vacation; women (and children) in their role as spinners or weavers; and craftsmen, artists, poets, and painters.

3 **advenientī:** Position at front of sentence, and omission of *eī*, may cause trouble. An initial comprehension question such as "What did Nero do?" may help.

4 **manū et complexū:** Establish the literal translation first, then encourage students to suggest more idiomatic translations, such as "took her by the hand and embraced her," etc.

5 **stābat ... nāvis:** Pay attention to the emphatic word order here, especially if students are encouraged to reproduce it in translation ("Moored near the villa was a ship," etc.), as this will help bring out the point that this is "the" ship, i.e. the booby-trapped one.

10–11 **iuxtā Nerōnem ... collocāta:** Students may be able to recall the way in which reclining diners were grouped at a formal Roman meal; cf. Paoli 92–93, Balsdon, *Life* 35, and the Unit 1 students' textbook, Stage 2, pp. 30–31.

11–12 **modo ... modo:** If students are puzzled, remind them of contexts where they met *modo ... modo* previously, e.g. the young Icarus who played *modo* with feather, *modo* with wax (Stage 44, p. 182, lines 5–6), or the sparrow which hopped *modo hūc modo illūc* (Stage 45, p. 205, line 9).

13–14 **oculīs et pectorī haerēns:** It may be best to start with a literal version, then invite views on the question "What does Tacitus *mean* by this phrase?" before settling on a final translation. Woodcock has "hanging on her gaze and clinging to her breast."

Make the logic of lines 1ff. explicit to the class: by being on the coast Nero was already in the right place to put his plan into operation and the festival was a good excuse to persuade Agrippina to join him there.

Carefully clarify the comings and goings in this chapter for your students; relate the text where possible to the map. Tacitus' original narrative contains several obscurities and omissions (for example, he does not say where Nero met his mother before escorting her to Bauli), and in the interests of simplicity the version in the students' textbook has been heavily adapted; it also takes a liberty with Tacitus' account by making Agrippina arrive by land instead of sea. Nero meets his mother and escorts her to Bauli. The plan to bring her from Bauli to Baiae on the specially constructed ship is foiled, because she has got wind of Nero's intentions and decides to travel by land instead. However, when she leaves Baiae after the dinner with the great show of affection on Nero's part, the fatal ship has obviously been brought around to Baiae to wait for her, and she boards it for her return journey.

Relate the map on p. 262 of the students' textbook to the general map of the Bay of Naples area on p. 223. Slides V.35–38 show maps and views of Baiae and the Bay of Naples.

Questions 2 and 5 can be used to draw students' attention to the skillful performance which Nero puts on to win his mother over. He goes to meet her and embraces her, but this is not enough; the rumor of treachery arouses her suspicions, and she chooses a safer method of travel to Baiae. Nero eventually succeeds in reassuring her with his blandishments, sometimes putting on an act of affectionate playfulness (*familiāritāte iuvenīlī*, line 11) and sometimes pretending to treat her as a respected adviser by discussing serious matters (*graviter loquēbātur*, line 12). Discussion of question 6 should help to make it clear that Nero is either topping off his performance with a hypocritical final embrace or is genuinely moved at the sight of his mother going to her death (though if the second explanation is true, Tacitus still adds a last gibe with *saevum* in line 15 – *ferum* in the original text).

Suggestions for Consolidation: gerundive (2,3,6,14; see also the Unit 4 students' textbook, LI Section, "Review Grammar," pp. 324–25); 3rd person plural perfect in *-ēre* (10): verb + nominative word order (1,6; see also Appendix D); locative (7; see also the Unit 4 students' textbook, LI Section, "Review Grammar," p. 314).

Vocabulary Check: *occāsiō* (1); *obviam eō* (4); *excipiō* (4,10); *quasi* (5); *cēlō* (7); *vehō* (9); *metus* (10); *iuxtā* (10); *collocō* (11); *mē gerō* (11); *abeō* (13); *vel ... vel* (14); *animus* (15).

First Language Note (*Direct and Indirect Deliberative Question*)

The captioned illustration on p. 259 of the students' textbook may provide a convenient starting-point for discussion of this grammatical point.

Stage Commentaries

Further examples:

direct
1 *utrum pugnēmus an fugiāmus?*
2 *quōs deōs precēmur?*
3 *quōmodō inimīcōs meōs fallam?*

indirect
1 *senex nesciēbat quot hospitēs ad cēnam invītāret.*
2 *incertus sum quantum praemium servīs dem.*
3 *iuvenēs mercātōrem rogāvērunt unde pecūniam adipīscerentur.*

Some students may ask "How can I tell an indirect question from an indirect deliberative, since they both have verbs in the subjunctive?" The best answer may be to get them to study and discuss a particular example, such as sentence 3 in paragraph 2: which is the likelier meaning, "unsure whether to yield" or "unsure whether they were yielding"? Examples like these illustrate the point that ambiguity is normally prevented by the context. (If the context does not make the meaning plain, ambiguity can be avoided by phrasing the sentence differently, e.g. by using the gerundive of obligation instead of a deliberative.)

naufragium I (*Annals* XIV.5–6)

Notes

2 **nāvis:** not described by Tacitus; probably an open boat with a canopy or shelter towards the stern for Agrippina and her companions.
4 **gubernāculō:** If students are unsure how this fits into the clause, ask "Where was Crepereius standing?"
5 **cubitantis recumbēns:** Use comprehension questions to establish that these participles refer to Agrippina and Acerronia respectively. Acerronia was sitting on or beside the foot of the couch and leaning across Agrippina's feet.
6 **cum datō signō...:** After the long parenthesis *duōbus ... commemorābat* (lines 3–6), remind the class of the sentence's opening words *nec multum erat prōgressa nāvis*, line 2.
   ruere tēctum ... grave: The weighted canopy is intended to crush the couch's occupants and/or knock a hole in the bottom of the boat (with the help, if necessary, of those sailors who are in the plot) so that Agrippina is shot into the water as originally planned. Invite students to illustrate their own ideas about the murder mechanism on the blackboard or an overhead transparency. Encourage them throughout this passage to visualize the scene.
8 **prōtēctae sunt:** They were both lower than the sides of the couch,

Stage 48

9	which were too strongly built to give way beneath the weight of the collapsing canopy. **turbātīs omnibus:** causal. Tacitus typically varies the construction by continuing with a *quod*-clause; the question "Why did the ship not break up?" may help.
11–12	**eīs ... cōnsēnsus:** Accept such translations as "there was no agreement among them," etc.; discuss and analyze the use of the possessive dative later.
14	**dum ... clāmat:** Either ask the class "What did Acerronia shout?" or read the whole clause through to *clāmat* and ask for a translation.
16	**minus agnita:** By keeping quiet, she ensured that as few people as possible would notice or recognize her (but the fact that she was wounded suggests that she did not go completely unrecognized).
18	**vīllam:** probably Bauli.
19ff.	**animadverterat enim...:** Note how the students manage with the numerous examples of indirect statement in this paragraph.
20–21	**summā suī parte:** The "accident" originated well above the deck. Agrippina realized that if it had been a genuine accident, caused by the sea (e.g. if the sea had carried the ship onto a rock), the damage would have been more likely to originate below deck, in the ship's hull.
21	**velut terrestre māchināmentum:** A building or contraption on land might suffer damage to its upper part and collapse downwards (unlike a ship – see previous note). But Tacitus could also be referring to stage machinery (in keeping with Nero's theatrical interests) or to the device constructed in some private houses which allowed ceilings to open and shower presents or saffron water over amazed guests.
23	**sī ... vidērētur:** defines *remedium*.
25	**fortūnā eius:** *eius* refers to Nero. The emperor was believed to embody the luck of the Roman people; an individual's good fortune was bound up with, and dependent on, the emperor's *fortūna*. It was therefore plausible for Agrippina to say, albeit with heavy irony, that she had escaped disaster thanks to providence and Nero's good luck. She also implied, equally ironically, that her survival was a piece of good fortune *for* Nero.
26–27	**sibi ... quiēte opus esse:** Establish that the indirect statement is still continuing. Remind your students of the meaning of *opus est*; a simpler example (e.g. *opus est mihi pecūnia*) may help.
28	**testāmentum ... requīrātur:** evidently expecting that there was something in Acerronia's will for her. (Tacitus, *Annals* XII.7 refers to Agrippina's *cupīdō aurī immēnsa*.)

Use question 1 to establish the logic of Tacitus' first sentence: the night was bright and clear and the sea was calm, so the sudden disintegration of a ship would automatically arouse suspicion.

The second part of question 2 may help students to appreciate the ironical way in which Acerronia's joy at the fake repentance of Nero is

187

Stage Commentaries

juxtaposed with the collapse of the roof. Tacitus builds up the picture slowly and in detail, then abruptly shatters the calm scene with violent action; ask the class to compare the number of words devoted to scene-setting with the number of words describing the catastrophe. Acerronia's action (referred to in question 4) could be interpreted as a counterproductive attempt at self-preservation or as a heroic self-sacrifice, designed to distract Agrippina's enemies from their intended victim (an interpretation consistent with the facts as reported by Tacitus, though not with his authorial comment *imprūdenter*, line 14).

Question 5 involves the extraction of a lot of material from lines 19–22; it may be convenient to list the relevant points on the blackboard. Question 6 seeks to bring out the fact that Agrippina is trying as hard as she can to convince Nero that she has not realized that the "shipwreck" was a murder attempt (cf. *sī nōn intellegere vidērētur*, line 23).

After trying question 7, the class might consider whether it is appalling or admirable that someone who has just avoided death by a hair's breadth, who has had to swim for her life, and who has realized that her own son has tried to kill her and may well try again, can still take time to investigate whether her murdered friend left her a legacy. This could lead to question 8 and a discussion of Agrippina's character. *silēns* (line 16) neatly distinguishes her from the chaos around her; her quick appreciation of the situation and the bold resourcefulness of her escape from the ship contrast pointedly with her assailants' messy bungling. On reaching temporary safety, she thinks fast and effectively, formulating her plan and putting it into operation by sending her message to Nero, describing him (perhaps with a certain grim relish at the ambiguity) as *perīculō mātris perterritus*. The deceptions which Nero had practiced to lure his mother to her death (his pretended reconciliation and friendliness at the dinner, followed by the fake "shipwreck"), are matched by equally shrewd and barefaced deceitfulness on her part (cf. in particular *vidērētur*, line 23, and *simulātiōnem*, line 29). The mother takes on her son at his own game.

Encourage translations which reproduce the final epigrammatic brevity of *hoc sōlum nōn per simulātiōnem* (lines 28–29), e.g. "... her only sincere action."

For further possible questions, see Balme and Greenstock 92–93.

Suggestions for Consolidation: 3rd person plural perfect in *-ēre* (1,12; cf. "īnsidiae" II, p. 26, line 10, and see the Unit 4 students' textbook, LI Section, "Review Grammar," p. 296); deliberative question (19); possessive dative (11; see also the Unit 4 students' textbook, LI Section, "Review Grammar," p. 311, and p. 203 below); several examples of

Stage 48

indirect statement (19–27; see also the Unit 4 students' textbook, LI Section, "Review Grammar," pp. 319–21); *quī* introducing purpose clause (24).

Vocabulary Check: *sīdus* (1); *praebeō* (1); *quasi* (2); *patefaciō* (2); *comitor* (3); *haud* (4,17); *procul* (4,17); *plērīque* (9); *latus* (11); *agnōscō* (16); *excipiō* (17); *quīdam* (17); *vehō* (18); *animadvertō* (19); *lītus* (20); *velut* (21); *ēvādō* (25); *cāsus* (25); *opus est* (27); *requīrō* (28).

naufragium II (*Annals* XIV.7)

Notes

1 **Nerōnī ... exspectantī:** a difficult example of a dative noun and present participle at the front of the sentence. Ask "What was Nero doing? What happened while he was waiting? What news was brought?"

5–6 **num ... iubērentur:** Note how the students manage with the indirect deliberative.

6 **praetōriānōs:** Students may need reminding that they were, among other things, the emperor's bodyguard (see picture on p. 267).

7 **obstrictōs esse:** For the military oath, sworn by the recruit on enlistment and renewed (in abbreviated form) on 1 January each year, see Watson 49–50; the class may recall it from Stage 41, p. 122, line 5. Burrus evidently felt (or pretended to feel) that the praetorian guard's oath of loyalty extended beyond the emperor to members of the imperial family.

8 **Germānicī:** much loved by the soldiers and, according to Tacitus (*Annals* II.82–83), widely mourned when he died prematurely. Slide V.32 shows a cameo of Agrippina's family, including Germanicus.

10 **illō diē:** emphatic. Nero's original word (in *oratio recta*) was *hodiē* "Today I become emperor at last."

darī: present passive infinitive with past (historical present) verb of speaking; if it causes trouble, a simplified version may help, e.g. *Nerō dīxit imperium sibi darī*.

imperium: supreme power, the emperorship.

The questions in the students' textbook are not intended as comprehension questions for use on initial reading; they presuppose that the students have already read and translated the passage. Discussion will probably center on the behavior of the characters. Nero's consultation with his advisers reads like a parody of the *consilium prīncipis*, in which Tacitus pursues two favorite themes: the corruption of the imperial court, and Nero's unfitness to govern. Whereas Agrippina was shown in the previous passage thinking and acting with great calm and decisiveness, Nero immediately panics on learning of her escape. Equally revealing is the reaction of Burrus and Seneca – *longum utrīusque silentium* (line 4). It would be highly dangerous for them to try to dissuade Nero

Stage Commentaries

from going ahead with the murder, and equally dangerous to be his accomplices in so extreme a crime. Furthermore, if Agrippina is to be killed immediately, the problem remains: who is to do the deed? Not the army, for reasons given by Burrus in lines 6–8. With what sounds like a sudden inspiration in the last three words of his speech, Burrus thrusts the responsibility onto Anicetus, who is more than ready to arrange the murder of his old enemy (cf. "īnsidiae" I, p. 260, line 10).

Students will probably notice how the volatile Nero switches at once from panic to ecstasy. In lines 2–3, he was hysterical with terror; by lines 11–12, he is giving orders. Also noticeable is the emphatic word order in lines 10–11, culminating in *lībertum* – power at Rome is now the gift of a freedman.

Raise the question of Tacitus' reliability. How could he possibly have known what Nero and his advisers said? Most or all of them were dead long before Tacitus wrote. Does this mean that he made the episode up? If so, is his history worthless?

The photograph on p. 267 shows members of the praetorian guard, from a first-century relief in the Louvre, Paris. The guards are depicted in their distinctive dress uniform, worn for ceremonial occasions and, like that of the British royal Guards ("Beefeaters") today, old-fashioned when compared with what they wore on operational service. Note particularly the comparative lack of body armor, the decorated helmets with large plumes, and the oval shields decorated in the Republican manner (operational shields were rectangular by this date). The man second from the left is wearing a large medal (*phalera*) which was a decoration for bravery. Behind the men can be seen their eagle standard. The praetorian guard were paid more than three times as much as regular legionaries and also received peacetime bonuses, e.g. when a new emperor came to power. They were considered an élite and were definitely a power to be reckoned with in the city (see also Background Material in the students' textbook, pp. 277–79).

Suggestions for Consolidation: dative noun and participle at start of sentence (1; cf. "īnsidiae" II, p. 261, line 3; students will meet two more examples in the next passage); omission of *erat* (4; cf. "naufragium" I, p. 266, lines 28–29, students will meet a further example in the next passage); verb of speaking placed after indirect statement (7; cf. "naufragium" I, p. 264, line 14; see also Unit 4 students' textbook, LI Section, "Review Grammar," pp. 319–21, and p. 206 below); jussive subjunctive (8; see Unit 4 students' textbook, LI Section, "Review Grammar," p. 318, and p. 205 below).

Stage 48

Vocabulary Check: *pavor* (2); *ultiō* (3); *uterque* (4); *respiciō* (5); *adversus* (7); *efficiō* (8); *haudquāquam* (9); *poscō* (9); *imperium* (10); *auctor* (10); *mūnus* (11); *proficīscor* (12).

Second Language Note (*Historical Infinitive*)

Make the point that historical infinitives are normally used in pairs or groups (either within the same sentence or in successive sentences) rather than singly. The sentence from Sallust quoted in paragraph 2 is translated by Woodcock (*New Latin Syntax* 15) as "...a dreadful scene in the open plains: pursuit – flight – (men) being slaughtered and taken prisoner," which reflects very clearly the speed and compression which can be achieved by such a series of infinitives.

Several examples of the historical infinitive occur in the next reading passage.

percussōrēs (*Annals* XIV.8–9)

Quinn (*Latin Explorations* 115–17) has a very helpful and detailed discussion of this passage. Balme and Warman 59–60, and Balme and Greenstock 94–95, contain numerous ideas for questions.

Notes

2   **hī mōlēs ... cōnscendere:** If the need to supply *cōnscendere* with *mōlēs* as well as *scaphās* causes trouble, quote a simpler example, e.g. *aliī cibum, aliī vīnum laudāvērunt*.
    mōlēs: "the long dike that separated the Lucrine lake from the sea" (Woodcock).

5   **dīversa ... incerta:** Use comprehension questions to encourage such translations as "asking various things, asking various questions" and "replying with uncertainty, making uncertain answers."

15 **triērarchō ... centuriōne:** the former commanded the ship, the latter (*centuriō classiārius* in full) the marines.

21 **convīvālī lectō:** Normally a special couch (*lectus fūnebris*) would be used.

25 **astrologī:** Originally from Assyria, they established themselves in large towns throughout the empire, wherever human gullibility and superstition could earn them a living. Officially banned, they were occasionally expelled (but never for long, as Tacitus points out, *Histories* I.22). Cf. Unit 2 Manual, p. 80 and p. 86, and the Unit 3 students' textbook, p. 220.

Stage Commentaries

Some Suggested Questions

What is the mood of the crowd on the seashore? How does it change? Is it easy to visualize the scene?

Who are the *hominēs armātī et minantēs* (line 8)? (With a little help, students should be able to identify them with the *hominēs fidēlissimī* mentioned by Nero in "naufragium" II, p. 266, line 12.)

How many words in lines 8–11 indicate violent action?

How often does the scene change in lines 1–20? Students might in particular note the narrative sequence in lines 9–17, reminiscent of a familiar cinema technique. We follow the assassins to the victim's door; then go back slightly in time to accompany the victim through the moments before the assassins' arrival and (unlike the victim) we know how imminent the end is. Finally, the two sequences of events come together for the climax: "The maid makes to go away; Agrippina's gaze follows her to the door – and falls on Anicetus standing there with his thugs.... The assassins say nothing" (Quinn, *Latin Explorations* 124).

Why does Tacitus mention that the room was dimly lighted (lines 11–12)?

What is the significance of Agrippina's last words and action? Does she wish to avoid disfigurement in death (cf. Quinn, *Latin Explorations* 119) or is it a symbolic gesture?

Why was Agrippina given such a hasty funeral? (Students might consider the danger to Nero from a popular outcry provoked by a full-scale public funeral or a hostile and emotional funeral oration.)

What rumor does Tacitus report? (His use of innuendo in lines 21–23 is very characteristic: he refrains from positive assertion but makes sure that the reader is informed of the discreditable story.)

At what point (if any) do the students feel sympathy for Agrippina? If sympathy is evoked by her vulnerability in lines 13–14 and the account of her murder in lines 17–20, is it dispelled by the final anecdote in lines 23–27? What does the anecdote suggest about Agrippina's character? Is it consistent with the impression of her character created during the Stage as a whole?

The coin reproduced on p. 270 of the students' textbook is an *aureus* of Nero, minted at Rome A.D. 64–68. The obverse shows the head of Nero, wearing a laurel wreath; the reverse (not included in the students' textbook) shows a seated figure of the goddess Salus. The coin may commemorate Nero's deliverance from the great fire of Rome in A.D. 64 or his escape from the conspiracy of Piso in A.D. 65. Similar coins might have been issued at the time of Agrippina's murder as part of the general thanksgiving (described in *Annals* XIV.12–13) for Nero's alleged

Stage 48

"narrow escape." Students might compare this one with those illustrated on pp. 257 and 260, commenting on the differences between the three coins.

Suggestions for Consolidation: historical infinitive (ask students to pick out the seven historical infinitives in lines 1–8, referring back to the language note on p. 268 of their text if necessary and noting how the infinitive is used to unfold a scene of hurried activity); dative pronoun and participle at start of sentence (18,24; cf. "naufragium" II, p. 266, line 1); jussive subjunctive (26); verb + nominative word order (5–6; see also Appendix D); substantival participle (11; see Unit 4 students' textbook, LI Section, "Review Grammar," p. 315, and p. 204 below); verb of speaking, etc. following indirect statement or question (7,23,24 (analyze the effect of the second example: Tacitus gives the rumor in detail before casting doubt upon it); see also Unit 4 students' textbook, LI Section, "Review Grammar," p. 320, and p. 206 below).

Vocabulary Check: *interim* (1); *nōnnūllī* (3); *compleō* (4); *dīversus* (5); *lūmen* (6,12); *incolumis* (6); *dōnec* (7,10); *magis ac magis* (12); *abeō* (13); *comitor* (15); *īdem* (21); *vīlis* (21); *ut* + indicative (22).

Third Language Note *(Perfect Subjunctive Passive)*

The caption to the illustration on p. 269 of the students' textbook may provide a convenient starting-point for discussion; other examples of the perfect subjunctive passive met by the students are *lēctī sint* (Stage 41, p. 122, lines 4–5) and the deponent *admīrātus sit* (Stage 48, p. 270, line 23). Invite comments on the way the tense is formed. For further practice, students could convert indicative examples such as *necātī sunt*, *prohibita est*, and *secūtī sumus* into the corresponding subjunctive forms, and work out the subjunctive forms of "you (s.) have been called," "I have been sent," "they (f.) have used," etc. with the aid of the information given s.v. *vocō, mittō, ūtor*, etc. in the Unit 4 students' textbook, LI Section, "Complete Vocabulary," pp. 354–97.

Drills

Exercise 1   Type: translation from English, using restricted pool of Latin words
  Grammatical points being practiced: dative of present participle, *īdem*, vocative, gerund, comparative adverb, *nisi*, conditional sentences with indicative, 2nd person

Stage Commentaries

plural future passive, jussive subjunctive, present infinitive
of deponent verb, genitive of *hic, fīō*
Encourage students to refer to their LI Section in cases of doubt.

Exercise 2   Type: transformation
Grammatical points being practiced: present, imperfect, pluperfect, and perfect subjunctive passive, introduced in Stages 41, 43, 46, and 48; nominative and ablative cases

Discuss the reason why *ā* (*ab*) is used in sentences 1b, 4b, 5b, and 6b, but not in 2b and 3b; ask students what *servī, hostēs, barbarī,* and *prīnceps,* but not *flammae* and *inopia,* have in common. Ask them also to explain why a subjunctive is used in each example, referring if necessary to the Unit 4 students' textbook, LI Section, "Review Grammar," pp. 317–19.

If you decide that your students should work on this exercise before they have read the last Latin passage, "percussōrēs," and the last language note, they will probably need help with sentence 6b. It requires the formation of a perfect subjunctive passive, which appears only at the very end of the reading material.

The Background Material

Garnsey and Saller 1–6, 15–20, 35–39 give a very useful brief guide. Millar's vast work (if you have access to a copy) will provide a rich store of illustrative material, thoroughly analyzed; see in particular 59–131 (the emperor's assistants), 203–72 (the emperor at work), and 465–549 (the emperor's dealings with private individuals). Millar demonstrates that communication between an emperor and his subjects was normally initiated by the latter; they approached the emperor with their petitions or disputes, and he responded.

You might write up the names (and perhaps dates) of some first- and early second-century emperors on the blackboard or overhead transparency, and prompt the class to recall details or incidents in connection with each emperor, either from earlier Stages in the Course, or from elsewhere. For example:

Augustus: huge building program (mentioned in Stage 30); patron of Vergil (Stage 36); marriage laws (38); banishes Ovid (39)
Claudius: launches invasion of Britain (14); rebukes Alexandrian rioters (17); his temple at Colchester destroyed by Iceni (23); extensive use of freedmen (34); murdered by Agrippina (48)
Nero: initiates inquiry into riot at Pompeii, dismisses Pompeian *duovirī* and appoints a *praefectus* (8,11); persecutes Christians (33); murders mother (48)
Vespasian: perhaps rewards Cogidubnus with palace for loyalty (15);

building program, including start of Colosseum (30); punishes
Helvidius Priscus (35)

Titus: Pompeii destroyed during his reign (12); sacks Jerusalem (29)

Domitian: sends Salvius to Britain (13); dedicates Arch of Titus (29); has
Paris killed and Domitia exiled (34); triumphs over Germans,
punishes Vestal Virgins (35); flattered by Martial (36); recalls
Agricola (37); adopts Clemens' sons (38); kills flies with stylus (39)

Trajan: policy on Christians (33); correspondence with Pliny (41).

Start with open-ended questions such as "What can you remember about Claudius?", then prompt the students' memories with more specific questions such as "In whose reign was Pompeii destroyed? Which poet did Augustus send into exile?" etc.

Our sources' numerous anecdotes about emperor–subject relationships are often vivid and illuminating; students could track many of them down (with guidance from you) in the translations of Tacitus, Suetonius, and Pliny. They might include Suetonius, *Augustus* 53 (Augustus teases a timid petitioner); Philo, *Legatio ad Gaium* 44–5 (the Jewish embassy from Alexandria traipses in frustration around the imperial gardens after Caligula); Suetonius, *Claudius* 18 (Claudius pelted with stale crusts by a mob in the forum during a bread shortage); Tacitus, *Annals* XIII.5 (Agrippina's attempt to sit next to Nero when he receives the Armenian envoys); Tacitus, *Annals* XIV.17 (Nero's response to the riot in Pompeii); Suetonius, *Vespasian* 23 (Vespasian's mule-driver is bribed by a man who wants to petition the emperor; Vespasian demands a half-share of the bribe); Pliny, *Letters* X.2–13 (miscellaneous requests to Trajan, made by Pliny on behalf of himself or others); Historia Augusta, *Hadrian* 17, quoted by Balsdon, *Life* 30 (Hadrian treats an ex-soldier kindly during a casual visit to the baths, but refuses to repeat his generosity on a wider scale). The extraordinary range of the requests made to the emperor is well illustrated by the petition of the Balearic islanders (Pliny the Elder, *Natural History* VIII.81.218) asking Augustus for military assistance against a plague of rabbits.

The bridge at Alcantara shown on p. 275 is generally thought to be the finest example in the Roman world. It crosses the river Tagus and was built about A.D. 106, entirely without mortar. The bridge is about 655 ft. (200 meters) long, and the spans rise nearly 165 ft. (50 meters) above the river.

The Succession. Students may recall Domitian's adoption of Clemens' sons from Stage 38. It is not known whether they predeceased Domitian or were ignored or murdered after his assassination. Nerva's adoption of Trajan (students' textbook, p. 279) was a response to pressure by the army and perhaps a (successful) attempt to forestall a military coup.

Stage Commentaries

Emperor-Worship. Lewis and Reinhold II.560–68 have a useful collection of source material. See in particular Herodian's description of an emperor's apotheosis (ibid. 565–66), culminating in the release from the blazing pyre of an eagle symbolizing the emperor's soul (cf. Unit 2 students' textbook, p. 50).

The students could study the coins illustrated on pp. 257, 258, and 270 of their textbooks, and discuss the explanations for some of the emperor's titles, such as *Caesar, Augustus,* and *imperātor,* and the reason why emperors took *tribūnicia potestās.* Consider also the emperors' use of the coinage for propaganda purposes, and illustrate these either from earlier Units or from any other convenient source. Coins made it possible to familiarize the inhabitants of Italy and the provinces with the emperor's physical features, titles, achievements (e.g. the conquest of Britain, Unit 3, p. 50; the defeat of the Jews, Unit 3, pp. 157–58; and the building of the *via Trāiāna,* slide IV.39) and political slogans (e.g. from the civil war of A.D. 69, *pāx orbis terrārum* on a denarius of Otho, and *Rōma resurgēns* on a sestertius of Vespasian, both shown in the Royal Academy exhibition catalog nos. 1(n) and 1(p); further examples, on front cover and first page of Jones).

The cameo gem illustrated on p. 280 is full of details. It is 10 inches (25 cm. wide). The top row shows Augustus and Roma enthroned side by side, his birth sign of Capricorn between them. The group of three figures behind him is usually interpreted as Oikoumene, the civilized world, placing a wreath on his head, bearded Ocean, and Earth with a horn of plenty and a child on either side. Under the throne is the Eagle, bird of Jupiter. On the left, Tiberius in toga and holding a scepter steps out of a chariot (this may refer to his victory over the Germans and Pannonians in A.D. 12). Behind him is Victory, with outspread wings. The young man in armor next to Roma may be Germanicus. In the lower row four soldiers erect a trophy with a captive man and woman seated on the left, while on the right two soldiers grab another couple by their hair. The cameo must have been made either after Augustus' death or for the provinces, as Augustus did not permit in Rome the cult of himself as Jupiter with the goddess Roma.

Suggestions for Discussion

1 What are the advantages and disadvantages of giving supreme power to one man? (Cf. Tacitus' description of the principate and personal freedom as *rēs ōlim dissociābilēs* in *Agricola* 3.)
2 Why did emperors put up with such a heavy work-load instead of simply delegating the decision-making to other people? (Encourage a variety of answers: suggest, for instance, that if emperors delegated

their work, they would be delegating (and diminishing) their power; or that they enjoyed being regarded as all-powerful and paternalistic rulers, personally concerned for their subjects' welfare; or that they were impelled by a sense of duty. Quote Tiberius as an example of an emperor who did delegate the running of the empire to others when he retired to Capri; the subsequent conspiracy (real or alleged) of Sejanus illustrates the danger of such delegation, that power once delegated can easily be usurped.)
3 Compare the different methods of choosing an emperor, described on p. 279. Which way seems to you most likely to produce a good emperor? Is there anything to be said in favor of the other methods?

Vocabulary Checklist

Students might review *sī quis/quid* as well as *nē quis/quid*, and you could reinforce *velut* by reminding them of examples from their previous reading; for example, Daedalus flew ahead of Icarus *velut āles* (Stage 44, p. 186, line 4) and Catullus' love died *velut ... flōs* (Stage 45, p. 212, lines 22–23). With *metuere–metus*, compare *redīre–reditus*, *advenīre–adventus*, *currere–cursus*, *rīdēre–rīsus*, etc. Practice numbers by a "mental arithmetic" game, in which each student is allocated one of the numbers on page 281; then call out a pair of numbers (e.g. *novem* and *quīnque*) to be added together, and the student to whom the required numeral has been allocated (in this case *quattuordecim*) identifies himself or herself by raising a hand, standing up, or calling out the number. As a variation, the class can be required to subtract one number from another, or to multiply (using *bis* and *ter*).

Suggestions for Further Work

1 Read the entire Nero and Agrippina episode from *Annals* XIV in translation; follow this by a discussion of Tacitus' reliability. Competent students would enjoy Paterson's skeptical discussion in *Omnibus* 6, pp. 23–25.
2 The class could consider the problem: "If Nero was really so unsatisfactory, why was it difficult to get rid of him?" The question raises several issues: absolute power and the means by which that power was supported, notably the army and the praetorian guard; respect for the office, if not for the man; the difficulty of agreeing about a successor, caused partly by the removal, at the beginning of his reign, of any obvious rivals.
3 Ask the class to compose appeals or petitions to the emperor; their aim should be to make it as difficult as possible for him to say no.

Stage Commentaries

Each request could be an amplification of one of the examples given on pp. 276–77 of their textbook, or could be based on some other situation you may suggest or the students themselves invent. (Some students may like to work in pairs, each member of the pair presenting one side of a dispute.) Read some of the appeals and petitions to the class, so that students can judge their persuasiveness.

4 Students might look at newspaper reports and articles about speeches and activities of politicians who happen to be in the news at the time, noting the various reporting styles (serious, chatty, libelous, propagandist, etc.) and comparing them with our sources' diverse treatment of the emperors (including official pronouncements by the emperors themselves, for which see, e.g. Lewis and Reinhold II.119 and 130–31).

The Language Information Section

The Language Information Section of Unit 4 consists of four Parts: Part One: Review Grammar; Part Two: Reference Grammar; Part Three: Supplementary Reading; and Part Four: Complete Vocabulary.

Part One: Review Grammar (pp. 284–328), although students may want to consult its tables of nouns and verbs at any time, is primarily intended as a review section to be studied by students only after they have completed (or nearly completed) the Unit. Students should begin work in the Review Grammar soon after they have reached Stage 46, postponing those sections which review Stages 46–48 until they have finished these Stages. Although the Review Grammar briefly describes all the forms of words and the rules of sentence structure in Unit 4, it gives priority to numerous examples so that students can see the rules illustrated as well as described. Often, drills are appended so that students can test their ability to apply the rules.

Part Two: Reference Grammar (pp. 329–33) is designed for older or linguistically sophisticated students who may appreciate further explanation of the more complex rules of syntax studied in Unit 4, particularly of the sequence of tenses for fearing clauses; the use of the subjunctive in subordinate clauses in indirect discourse; and the tenses of the subjunctive in (a) unfulfilled, or contrary-to-fact, conditionals, and in (b) ideal, or future remote, conditionals. The students should not use Part Two as a substitute for experience in reading examples of the rules in the context of the stories in the Stages.

Part Three: Supplementary Reading (pp. 334–53) contains 255 lines of slightly adapted Latin prose, which supplements not only the readings in Latin, but also the historical and cultural content of the previous Stages. The readings are largely self-contained, i.e. they are provided with compact lexical, grammatical, and historical notes on the facing pages. Usually students will need no other resources to understand these readings, but if they find a difficult word which is not glossed on the facing page, they can look it up at the back of the textbook in the Complete Vocabulary. These supplementary readings were added specifically for the benefit of students in the province of Ontario, Canada, who need additional lines of reading in order to earn Ontario Academic Credits (OACs) in their Latin authors' course, but they will certainly also interest and benefit students elsewhere in Canada and in the United States. (See p. 210 below for contents.)

Language Information Section

Part Four: Complete Vocabulary (pp. 354–97) contains all the words in the stories, in the "Words and Phrases Checklists," and in the "Supplementary Reading" of Unit 4. Its format is explained in the notes which preface this Part (pp. 354–55). Emphasize note 2, and make certain that your students realize that special verbs and adjectives with objects other than accusative are now labeled – for the first time in the Course – with a plus mark (+), followed by the case-name of their object. Also emphasize notes 3 and 4, which contain very useful information. Note 3 explains how students can differentiate between present-tense forms of the second conjugation and future-tense forms of the third and fourth conjugations. Note 4 explains how students can determine from the principal parts of a verb whether it is regular or deponent.

The comments following are concerned with individual sub-sections of the Language Information Section. The sub-sections in the Review Grammar dealing with nouns, adjectives, and pronouns have now, with the addition of the forms of the indefinite adjective *quīdam* "one, a certain" and of the gerund, become complete. The sub-sections in the Review Grammar dealing with verbs and with various syntactic points have been expanded in Unit 4 to include various passive and subjunctive forms (perfect subjunctive active; all tenses of the subjunctive passive (including the subjunctive deponent); and all tenses of the passive forms of *ferō* and of the irregular verb *fīō*); clauses of fearing; jussive subjunctives; constructions and word order in indirect statement, including imbedded subordinate clauses; the different types of the conditional with the subjunctive; and the uses of the gerund.

Also included in the sub-sections of the Review Grammar are comments on five grammatical points which have occurred in Unit 4 without being discussed in the Stage language notes: the possessive dative (p. 311); the locative case (p. 314); indirect statement without an introductory verb of speaking (p. 321); conditional sentences with present and imperfect subjunctive (pp. 322–23; see also the Reference Grammar, p. 332); and subordinate clauses in indirect statement (p. 327; see also the Reference Grammar, p. 331).

When reviewing examples of grammatical points with your class, try whenever possible to use examples from those sentences which the students have already met in their reading (on the principle of using the known to explain the unknown) or from the examples in the Review Grammar (where many of the sentences previously met have been repeated). Sometimes, however, stretch your students' minds by using examples from the Stages or the stories in the Supplementary Reading which they have *not* read. Appendix D (pp. 238–40 below) collects some

Language Inforamtion Section

further examples of linguistic features (mainly variations on word order) which do not appear in the Review Grammar.

PART ONE: **Review Grammar** (pp. 284–328)

Nouns (pp. 284–85). Students might review these nouns by translating some simple sentences into Latin made up from them ("The king's slaves showed the city to the merchant," etc.), working either on their own or in pairs or together as a class. At first, restrict sentences to the nouns in the tables and two or three verbs such as *dedit/dedērunt*, *ostendit/ostendērunt*; add additional words as the students develop proficiency.

Pronouns (pp. 290–93). Invite comment on the relationship between *quīdam* (paragraph 10) and *quī* (paragraph 8). Elicit the general rule that *quīdam* is formed by adding *-dam* to the various cases of *quī*; then encourage the class to find and explain the exceptions to this rule, found in the accusative singular and genitive plural, e.g. *quendam* and *quōrundam*.

Examples of *is quī* (paragraph 9) from Unit 4:

... *eīs operibus quae* ...	Stage 41, p. 114, line 8
... *id quod prius accidit* ...	Stage 41, p. 120, line 13
... *culpa est penes eōs quī* ...	Stage 41, p. 122, lines 6–7
... *nōmen dederimus eīs quī* ...	Stage 41, p. 128, line 5
... *ea quae* ... *auxiliō esse possint;*	Stage 41, p. 128, line 7 (cf.
ille ... *vidētur, quī* ... in	Stage 45, p. 200, lines 1–3)
... *scelerī id assignet quod* ...	Stage 48, p. 260, lines 14–15
... *eōs impediēbant quī* ...	Stage 48, p. 264, line 10
... *eōs abripit quī obstant,*	Stage 48, p. 270, lines 9–10.

Examples where antecedent is deferred or omitted:

quās ... *mōverat aura, captābat plūmās,*	Stage 44, p. 182, lines 5–6
quī ... *possent crēdidit esse deōs.*	Stage 44, p. 187, lines 10–11
quod vidēs perīsse perditum dūcās.	Stage 45, p. 210, line 2
nec quae fugit sectāre ...	Stage 45, p. 210, line 10.

Verbs (pp. 294–310). Some students may not understand how the terms "active" and "passive" are related to "indicative" and "subjunctive." If so, write the following diagram on the blackboard or overhead transparency. First divide the blackboard or transparency into four

Language Information Section

quarters, and then label them "indicative active," "indicative passive," "subjunctive active," and "subjunctive passive." Point out to the students that the indicative active, with which they are now very familiar, is much the commonest part of the verb, and that if students know the indicative passive and subjunctive active, they will not have difficulty learning the one remaining part of the verb still to be covered, the subjunctive passive. Confirm, if a student asks, that a few verb forms, like commands, infinitives, and participles, lie outside the main system.

Indicative Passive (pp. 296–98). Drill students in the difference between present and future forms of the 2nd person singular of third-conjugation verbs, e.g. *dūceris* and *dūcēris*, *caperis* and *capiēris*, and make sure students observe the presence or absence of the long mark over the "e" in the third conjugation, of the short "e" in the present or the "i" and the long "ē" in the future of the third conjugation *-iō*.

Subjunctive Active (pp. 298–99). Note that the personal endings of the present and perfect subjunctive, e.g. *-m*, *-s*, *-t*, etc., are not new to the students. For the *-m* ending, compare the endings of e.g. *sum* and *possum*.

Subjunctive Passive (pp. 299–300). Note that the personal endings of the present and imperfect subjunctive passive, e.g. *-r*, *-ris*, *-tur*, *-mur*, *-minī*, and *-ntur* all end in "r" except for *-ris* and *-minī* (and *-ris* starts with "r").

Other Forms (pp. 300–02). For possible answers to the students' question, "What does the gerund (paragraph 10) mean, and how is it different from the gerundive?", see the Stage 41 Commentary, p. 86 above; for the students' question, "What does the gerundive (paragraph 11) mean?", see the Unit 3 Teacher's Manual, pp. 161–62.

Deponent (pp. 303–06). You can never drill some students enough on deponent verbs! Add additional examples of deponent indicative verbs to those in paragraphs 3 and 5, with an emphasis on 1st and 2nd person plural forms (e.g. *comitābimur*, *hortābāminī*, *amplectimur*, *ingrediēminī*, *moriēbāminī*, *mentīmur*, etc.), which were first introduced only in Stage 39.

Invent contrast drills for the subjunctive deponent verbs on p. 305, where there is no formal drill provided. Write on an overhead transparency a single list of jumbled deponent indicative and subjunctive verbs (correlated by number, person, and tense), and ask students to separate them into two lists on a sheet of their own paper. Then correct the list in class by putting up another overhead transparency with the verbs already separated. Examples might be (but

Language Inforamtion Section

jumbled) *suspicor/suspicer, vidēmur/videāmur, sequēbāris/sequerēris, mortuī sunt/mortuī sint, profectae erāmus/profectae essēmus*, etc.

There is a convenient list of deponent verbs in the Unit 3 students' textbook, p. 259.

Irregular (pp. 307–10). Drill the students by asking them to pick out from the table on p. 307 the indicative Latin forms for "they want," "she will be able," "you (pl.) come," "we will want," "they don't want," "you (sg.) prefer," and "I brought," etc. Invent another contrast drill like that suggested just above for deponent verbs, but this time using contrasted indicative/subjunctive pairs of irregular verbs from the tables on pp. 307–08, e.g. *poterāmus/possēmus, fuistis/fuerīmus, nōluerant/nōluissent*, etc. Invent a similar contrast drill for the indicative/subjunctive forms of *feror* and *fīō* from the tables on pp. 309–10, e.g. *ferēbāminī/ferrēminī, fīunt/fīant, factus erās/factus essēs*, etc.

Uses of the Cases (pp. 311–14). Use paragraphs 5c and 6e to review the syntax of *in*. Point out that *super* and *sub*, like *in*, are used with either the accusative or the ablative, depending on whether the subject of the verb is moving (+accusative) or stationary (+ablative). Ask the class the difference between *mūs sub pavīmentum fōdit* ("dug") and *fēlēs sub mēnsā dormiēbat; avis super urbem volāvit* and *nūbēs ingēns super monte stat; fēlēs in tabernā sedēbat* and *fēlēs in caput Eutychī īnsiluit*.

Examples of the possessive dative (paragraph 4e):

... *mihi erat tanta cupiditās aut necessitās...?*	Stage 43, p. 168, line 13
... *est mihi memoria tuī.*	Stage 43, p. 169, line 6
nōbīs ... nūllum cōnsilium abeundī erat, ...	Stage 46, p. 227, lines 21–22
dī, quibus imperium est pelagī,...	Stage 47, p. 246, line 11
nōn ... eīs erat prōmptus ... cōnsēnsus,	Stage 48, p. 264, lines 11–12

Examples of the ablative of comparison (paragraph 6f):

rīsū	Stage 42, p. 142, line 14
saxō ... undā?	Stage 42, p. 149, line 7
oculīs suīs	Stage 45, p. 205, line 5
Notō ... volucrīque sagittā	Stage 47, p. 246, line 18

Examples of the locative case (paragraph 8):

Pergamī	Stage 41, p. 112, line 4
Rōmae	Stage 41, p. 114, line 9
Nīcomēdīae	Stage 41, p. 125, line 3
Ephesī	Stage 43, p. 161, line 1
Bāiīs	Stage 48, p. 261, line 7.

Language Information Section

With the help of the explanation of the locative's formation in paragraph 8 the class might work out the Latin for "at Chester" (*Dēvae*), "at Alexandria" (*Alexandrīae*), "at Herculaneum" (*Herculāneī*), "at Athens" (*Athēnīs*), "at Carthage" (*Carthāgine*), etc.; you should supply nominative and genitive forms where needed.

Ask the students to identify the case of some of the nouns in paragraph 7 and to pick out a parallel example from paragraphs 1–6, thus making sure they know why a particular case is being used. For example, after they identify *pecūniae* (paragraph 7, example 1) as genitive, ask them to examine the three examples of the genitive in paragraph 3 and decide which of the three corresponds most closely with *pecūniae* in paragraph 7 (Answer: 3b, *parum cibī*).

Uses of the Participle (pp. 315–16). If the students have difficulty with examples 1 and 3–6 in paragraph 5, have them review the similar examples in the Unit 3 Language Information Section, "Review Grammar," pp. 286–89, paragraphs 2–4 and 9–12. If the students have difficulty with the substantival genitive participle in example 2 (*vōcēs ... laudantium*), write on the blackboard and also review some examples (in context) from their Unit 3 and Unit 4 textbooks:

grātulantium	Stage 30, p. 173, line 8
pulsantium	Stage 34, p. 248, line 18
spectantibus	Stage 41, p. 128, line 9
lūgentis ... mortuī ... lūgentem	Stage 43, p. 161, lines 18, 22, 23
sepultī	Stage 44, p. 189, line 16
amantī	Stage 45, p. 206, line 3
amantem	Stage 45, p. 207, line 7
fugientium	Stage 46, p. 226, line 4
sequentem ... euntem	Stage 47, pp. 244–46, lines 3, 17
irrumpentium	Stage 48, p. 270, line 11.

Ask the class to explain why the ablative absolute is used in sentence 6 of paragraph 5 (*sōle oriente*), but not in sentence 5 (*servō haesitantī ... obtulī*).

For further examples of the perfect passive participle used in the accusative, see Appendix D.

Uses of the Subjunctive (pp. 316–19). Practice the different tenses of the subjunctive with examples of indirect questions, in which the tense of the Latin subjunctive is generally reflected in the English translation: contrast *scīre volō quid faciās* with *scīre volō quid fēceris*, and *rēx mē rogāvit cūr redīrem* with *rēx mē rogāvit cūr rediissem*. Follow this with the study of other

Language Inforamtion Section

subjunctive usages, such as purpose clauses, in which the difference between *puer latet ut hostēs vītet* and *puer latēbat ut hostēs vītāret* can be expressed by "may" and "might" ("The boy is hiding in order that he may ..." "The boy was hiding in order that he might ..."); but be sure to point out that the idiomatic English translation of these clauses ("... in order to avoid...") does not reproduce the variation of the Latin tense.

If students express further interest in or anxiety about the tenses of the subjunctive, point out that in many subjunctive usages, only a limited number of tenses can be used. Purpose clauses, for example, can contain a subjunctive in only the present or imperfect tense. Discuss with the students the reasons why this is so, e.g. "Why would it be illogical to use a pluperfect subjunctive in a purpose clause, as (incorrectly) in 'The boy was hiding in order that he had avoided his master'?" Extend the discussion to include mention of the rule of "sequence of tenses," but bear in mind that this rule is less relevant to a course in reading Latin than to one in English-to-Latin composition.

Examples of indirect questions *preceding* the verb of asking (paragraph 2):

mātrōnae quid accidisset exposuit;	Stage 43, p. 162, lines 6–7
quārē id faciam, fortasse requīris.	Stage 45, p. 209, line 1
num īnspexerit ... et ... admīrātus sit, incertum est.	Stage 48, p. 270, lines 21–23.

Ask students to translate each of the examples in paragraph 7, say why the subjunctive is being used, and identify the tense of the subjunctive verb.

If the students inquire why *nē* is used in paragraph 8, explain that because "fear" is a negative idea, i.e. is concerned with something the speaker does *not* want to happen, it was natural for the Romans to introduce fearing clauses with the negative word *nē*.

Examples of the jussive subjunctive (paragraph 9):

vīvāmus ... amēmus ... aestimēmus ...	Stage 45, p. 202, lines 1–3
dēsinās ... dūcās.	Stage 45, p. 210, lines 1–2
vīvat valeatque ... nec ... respectet ..	Stage 45, p. 212, lines 17–21
"dēflectāmus..."	Stage 46, p. 226, line 3
"efficiat Anicōtus..."	Stage 48, p. 266, line 8
"occīdat ... dum imperet."	Stage 48, p. 270, lines 26–27.

For further examples of the jussive subjunctive, see p. 143 above.

Note how the students manage with the various examples of passive and deponent forms included in paragraph 10, and make up further examples if necessary.

205

Language Information Section

Indirect Statement (pp. 319–21). If students inquire about the future infinitive passive, confirm that it exists but is seldom met.

Encourage your students to comment on the two indirect statements in paragraph 4. If they do not see the difference for themselves, ask them why "he" is *sē* in example 1, but *eum* in example 2. Bring out the difference in meaning between the two sentences, using the accompanying direct statements as a clue if necessary, and discuss ways of conveying this difference in English, which does not normally differentiate explicitly between the two meanings but allows the intended meaning to emerge from the context. There are further sentences contrasting *sē* and *eum* in paragraph 5, sentences 1–2 and 5–6.

In paragraph 5, use sentences 7 and 8 to practice the two ways of translating *negō* given in paragraph 2.

Examples where the verb of speaking, etc. is placed after or in the middle of the indirect statement:

mātrōnam esse pulcherrimam ... animadverterat,	Stage 43, p. 162, line 28
nūllī sē dīcit mulier mea nūbere mālle...	Stage 45, p. 206, line 1
mare ... resorbērī vidēbāmus,	Stage 46, p. 223, line 3
...nusquam iam deōs ūllōs esse affirmābant.	Stage 46, p. 226, line 11
...sē Agrippīnam esse ... clāmat...	Stage 48, p. 264, line 14
...praetōriānōs ... obstrictōs esse respondit:	Stage 48, p. 266, lines 6–7
...incolumem esse Agrippīnam vulgātum est,	Stage 48, p. 269, lines 6–7
hunc fore suī fīnem ... crēdiderat Agrippīna...	Stage 48, p. 270, lines 23–24

Compare the meaning of the second half of sentence 1 in paragraph 6: *medicōs dē vītā eius dēspērāre* with that of *medicī dē vītā eius dēspērābant*; help the students to see that *medicī ... dēspērābant* would be a comment by the narrator and not part of the slave's announcement (*servus nūntiāvit*). Compose similar pairs of examples for comparison, e.g. *centuriō crēdēbat hostēs dēspērāre; ducem eōrum captum esse* (cf. *dux eōrum captus erat*).

Further examples in which an indirect statement follows either another indirect statement or an indirect command or phrase such as *cōnsilium prōposuit*:

omnibus ... mortālibus ... pereundum esse.	Stage 43, p. 162, line 24
potius sē ... neglegentiam ... pūnitūrum esse.	Stage 43, p. 162, lines 8–9

Language Inforamtion Section

tē ipsam ... quaesītūram, ac ...
   habitūram esse.   Stage 43, p. 168, lines 10–11
sē ... libenter moritūram esse,   Stage 46, p. 224, lines 17–18
nāvem posse compōnī...   Stage 48, p. 260, line 11
... ōrāre ut Nerō...; sibi ... quiēte opus
   esse.   Stage 48, pp. 265–66, lines 25–27.

Conditional Sentences (pp. 322–23). The students might use sentence 3 in paragraph 4 to practice the two ways of translating *nisi* given in paragraph 3. Which way do they think would be more appropriate for translating sentence 4?

Conditional sentences using the pluperfect subjunctive have appeared several times in the students' textbook; they have been discussed in a language note in Stage 46 and practiced in a drill in Stage 47. One example of a conditional sentence with the present subjunctive occurred in Stage 45 (p. 206, line 2) and two with the imperfect subjunctive in Stage 42 (p. 142, line 10; p. 146, III, line 2). Further examples with the present and imperfect subjunctive are included here in paragraphs 5 and 6 for those teachers who wish their class to practice the full range of tenses used in conditional sentences; but they are fairly difficult for most students, many of whom will be relatively unpracticed in the different English forms required ("If you were to say that...," "If I were sitting here...," or "If you did that..." referring to the future), and you may prefer to concentrate at first on the pluperfect subjunctive, postponing the study of "Reference Grammar," Sub-Section X, p. 332, and further discussion of present and imperfect until your students have met more examples in their reading. Emphasize, however, that if the verbs in a conditional sentence are subjunctive, the English translation of the main verb will normally contain "would" or "should."

Gerund and Gerundive (pp. 324–25). Ask students which nouns or pronouns the gerundives in paragraph 2 are agreeing with; are they singular or plural, and what is their gender? (For example, how can we tell that *nōs* in sentence 1 is masculine?) Then compare these examples with those in paragraph 1, and elicit the point that the gerunds in paragraph 1, unlike the gerundives in paragraph 2, have no noun agreeing with them.

When discussing paragraph 3, encourage the students to recall examples of gerundives of obligation which have passed into English, such as Amanda, referendum, memorandum, *(quod erat) demonstrandum*, and other examples quoted in the Unit 3 Manual, pp. 129 and 161–62. If students ask anxiously, "How can we tell whether a gerundive means 'ought' or not?", compare pairs of examples of the different types of

Language Information Section

gerundive, e.g. *latrō interficiendus est* and *centuriō gladium dēstrīnxit ad latrōnem interficiendum*, and invite students to say what differences they notice between the two sentences. Confirm that the gerundive of obligation is usually used in the nominative and accompanied by a form of *esse*, whereas other gerundives are normally used in the accusative, genitive, dative, or ablative, and are unaccompanied by any part of *esse*. (At this point, discussion of exceptions to these generalizations is unlikely to be very profitable. If students ask, the only examples they have met of gerundives of obligation in a case other than nominative are *repetenda*, Stage 44, p. 186, line 3, and some examples in indirect statement.)

Hitherto, the vast majority of the gerundives met by the students (except those of obligation) have been in the accusative with *ad*, but quote some simple examples in other cases, such as *servus artem cibī coquendī didicit* or *Nerō amīcōs dē mātre interficiendā cōnsuluit* to demonstrate that the context normally makes the significance of the gerundive clear.

Sentences with *dum* (meaning "while") (p. 326). Students may be worried or upset about the use of the seemingly illogical present tense in these *dum* "while"-sentences. If so, point out that they have already met the present tense being used to refer to past events, in Stage 39, "versūs Ovidiānī" (the "historical" present), and that the Romans normally used a historical present with *dum* to indicate that something happened *at a moment when* something else was going on. If students are curious, point out that this use of the present tense enabled the Romans to make a distinction:

dum custōdēs dormiunt, captīvus effūgit. (*dum* + present)
(While (i.e. at a moment when) the guards were asleep, the prisoner escaped.)

dum custōdēs dormiēbant, ego vigilābam. (*dum* + imperfect)
(While (i.e. throughout the time when) the guards were asleep, I was awake.)

Longer Sentences (pp. 326–28). Encourage comment on the examples in paragraph 1. For example, students may notice, with or without a little prompting, that main clauses and subordinate clauses each contain a verb. Demonstrate the final point in the paragraph by getting students to write down subordinate clauses in English ("because I was tired," "which I saw yesterday," etc.) for other students to turn into complete sentences by adding main clauses.

After students have read paragraphs 1–3, write the first examples from paragraphs 1 and 4 on the blackboard or overhead transparency, and invite the class to compare them, eliciting that one is a direct

Language Information Section

statement, the other indirect, and that in the latter, the verb in the subordinate clause is subjunctive. Have the students then turn to pp. 327–28 of their textbook for further study of paragraphs 4 and 5.

The main point to emphasize is the use of the subjunctive. (Help the class to see that in sentence 1 of paragraph 5, the relative clause is part of what the slave said, whereas *quās ille senex vēndit* would be an incidental comment by the narrator.) Some observant students, on comparing the second examples in paragraphs 1 and 4, may note that the verb in the indirect statement has not only become subjunctive, but also changed its tense. Confirm that this happens regularly after a past verb of speaking, etc., and point out that the same change of tense occurs in the English translation.

Further examples:

affirmāvērunt nūllum perīculum īnstāre quod Salvius vir magnae auctōritātis esset.	Stage 40, p. 95, lines 6–7
dīxit ... imāginem ... quae aulam rēgis Cogidubnī ōrnāvisset ā Salviō ... vēnditam esse;	Stage 40, p. 98, lines 10–12
affirmāvit mē, quod iuvenis essem, ... posse;	Stage 46, p. 224, line 17
sē, quae ... gravārētur, ... moritūram esse,	Stage 46, p. 224, lines 17–18

PART TWO: **Reference Grammar** (pp. 329–33)

The Reference Grammar comprises twelve sub-sections. Sub-sections I–VI are simple references to the tables of nouns, adjectives, pronouns, regular verbs, deponent verbs, and irregular verbs in the Review Grammar. Although students often use these tables for reference as well as review, they are printed only once, in the Review Grammar. Sub-sections VII–XI are more formal descriptions of the major grammatical rules taught in Unit 4: (VII) fearing clauses, (VIII) jussive subjunctives, (IX) indirect statement, (X) conditional sentences with the subjunctive, and (XI) gerunds and gerundives. Sub-section XII is a list of major sentence patterns introduced in Unit 4, with examples. Usually, the students who want or need to study these formal explanations of syntax should do so only after they have successfully completed the grammatical work in the Stages and the Review Grammar. Memorizing rules is no substitute for experience in reading them.

Language Inforamtion Section

PART THREE: **Supplementary Reading** (pp. 334–53)

Because many of the passages in the Supplementary Reading often complement in topic and background some of the stories in this and previous Units, use them in Latin or, if time is short, in translation to help students recall those stories and thus review the narrative, historical, and cultural content of the Course. Use passages 3 and 4b as amplifications on diagnostic tests 8 and 13; for example, assign these passages as extra credit homework some time after the students have taken the diagnostic tests.

Following is a list of the passages and the previous stories which they amplify:

SUPPLEMENTARY READING	COMPLEMENTARY, PRIOR MATERIAL
1 The Werewolf Soldier (Petronius, *Satyrica* LXII)	Unit 1, Stage 7, "fābula mīrābilis," pp. 102–103
2(a) The Lifestyle of Pliny's Uncle (Pliny the Younger, *Letters*, III.5.10–17)	
2(b) Marvelous Animals (Pliny the Elder, *Natural History*, VIII.21.57–60; 38.92–93; 40.96)	
2(c) The Death of Pliny's Uncle (Pliny the Younger, *Letters*, VI.16.12–20)	Unit 4, Stage 46, "tremōrēs" I and II, pp. 222–24; "tenebrae," pp. 226–27
3 The Romans Win at Mount Graupius (Tacitus, *Agricola* 37.2–39.1)	Unit 4, Stage 37, "epistula," pp. 35–36; Diagnostic Test 8, Unit 3 Teacher's Manual, pp. 170–72
4(a) The Lifestyle of the Emperor Domitian (Suetonius, *Domitianus* 18–21)	Unit 4, Stage 39, "hērēdēs prīncipis" I and II, pp. 74–78
4(b) The Death of the Emperor Domitian (Suetonius, *Domitianus* 14–17)	Diagnostic Test 13, Unit 4 Teacher's Manual, pp. 213–15 below

Introductory material in English about the author and passage, new grammatical points, and particularly difficult new vocabulary are explained on the pages facing the Latin passages (and sometimes on the same page as the Latin). An English summary of each passage prefaces

Language Inforamtion Section

the Latin. All vocabulary in the passages is included in the Complete Vocabulary, pp. 354–97.

PART FOUR: Complete Vocabulary (pp. 354–97)

Note 3 (p. 354) explains how students may use verb listings in the Complete Vocabulary to distinguish present tense endings of second-conjugation verbs (e.g. *vidēs*) from future tense endings of third- and fourth-conjugation verbs (e.g. *mittēs, dormiēs*). Demonstrate, if necessary, to students that they will not need to consult the Complete Vocabulary in this way every time they meet an *-ēs, -et*, etc. ending in their reading, because the tense of a verb is often established by the context.

Remind the students that although the kind of checking described and practiced in Notes 4 and 5 is sometimes advisable, it is often clear from the whole sentence whether a particular verb form is part of a deponent verb-system or not. For example, *hortābātur* in sentence 1 of Note 5 must be from a deponent verb and have an active meaning; for if it were a passive form of an ordinary verb, it would mean "he was being urged on," and this meaning would not have allowed the writer to fit the accusative *mīlitēs* into the sentence.

Demonstrate to the students how to use the Complete Vocabulary to check the conjugation of a verb by asking them to identify the following forms:

- *-ēs ... -ent, -ēris ... -entur*, which may be present tense of a 2nd conjugation verb, or future of a 3rd or 4th conjugation, or present subjunctive of a 1st conjugation
  (Examples: *habēmus, mittēmus, laudēmus; salūtentur, dūcentur, monentur*)

- *-ās ... -ant, -āris ... -antur*, which may be present indicative of a 1st conjugation verb, or present subjunctive of a 2nd, 3rd, or 4th conjugation
  (Examples: *audiās, necās; vocāminī, regāminī; precātur, sequātur*)

- *-am, -ar*, which may be present subjunctive of a 2nd conjugation verb, or present subjunctive/future indicative (indistinguishable) of a 3rd or 4th conjugation
  (Examples: *iubeam, faciam, docear, iubear*)

Do not overdo work of this kind, and give generous help if the students are confused. Emphasize again that the context of a sentence will often provide numerous clues to the meaning of a verb form.

Diagnostic Tests

For a discussion on the purpose of the diagnostic tests, and suggestions for their use, see the Unit 1 Teacher's Manual, p. 110. The words in boldface have not occurred in the Stage Checklists. A few words not in the Checklists are not in boldface, if their meaning is obvious or if they have occurred frequently or prominently in recent Stages.

Test 12

To be given at the end of Stage 37.

epistula

C. Helvidius Lupus Aciliō Glabriōnī amīcō salūtem dīcit.
amphorās vīnī, quās mihi mīsistī, libenter accēpī et grātiās agō.
mox **vērō** grātiās tibi praesentī agam; nam brevī tempore Rōmam
reveniam. ad hanc vīllam ideō vēnī ut ex morbō, quō afflīgēbar,
convalēscerem; nunc, ex morbō **recreātus**, ad urbem revenīre   5
cupiō ut tē cēterōsque amīcōs meōs iterum videam, domum
familiamque īnspiciam, rēs clientium administrem.

    ā **colōnīs** meīs cotīdiē vexor. dīcunt sē tōtam **aestātem**
dīligentissimē labōrāvisse; addunt tamen sē **annōnam** pessimam
exspectāre, et mē ōrant ut auxilium sibi praebeam.   10

    Helvidius, fīlius meus, quī nūper hūc ex urbe advēnit, nūntiat
tōtum populum dē victōriā Agricolae nunc gaudēre, et in omnibus
templīs sacerdōtēs victimās dīs immortālibus sacrificāre. crās
Helvidius Rōmam redībit; eī igitur hanc epistulam mandābō,
quam tibi trādat. suspicor eum ideō ad urbem quam celerrimē   15
regredī velle, ut puellam aliquam vīsitet.

    dē tē ipsō, mī Glabriō, multōs variōsque **rūmōrēs** audiō, quibus
tamen vīx crēdere possum. aliī dīcunt tē Imperātōrem valdē
offendisse; aliī **affirmant** tē in carcerem coniectum et **maiestātis**
accūsātum esse. nōnne tē dē īrā Imperātōris saepe monuī, mī   20
amīce? nisi cāveris, in **iūdicium** sine dubiō vocāberis, damnāberis,
pūniēris. longum colloquium quam celerrimē tēcum habēre volō;
nam dē tē valdē perturbor. valē.

Diagnostic Tests

Points

1 What present has Glabrio sent to Lupus?   1
2 Quote the Latin word in line 3 which suggests that Lupus will be meeting Glabrio. Where will their meeting take place?   2
3 What was Lupus' original reason for coming to his country villa?   2
4 For what three purposes does he now wish to return to Rome?   3
5 Translate the second paragraph (lines 8–10, "ā colōnīs ... praebeam").   6
6 What two items of news are reported to Lupus by his son?   5
7 What task is Lupus going to ask his son to perform for him?   2
8 What suspicions does Lupus have about his son's wish to hurry back to Rome?   1
9 Translate the last paragraph (lines 17–23, "dē tē ipsō ... valē").   13

                                                     35

Notice how students are coping with the following features in particular:

1st person passive: *vexor* (line 8); *perturbor* (23). *afflīgēbar* occurs (4), but is not tested directly by a question.

2nd person passive: *vocāberis* (21); *damnāberis* (21); *pūniēris* (22).

present subjunctive: *videam* (6); *īnspiciam* (7); *administrem* (7); *praebeam* (10); *trādat* (15); *vīsitet* (16).

indirect statement with present active infinitive: *exspectāre* (10); *gaudēre* (12); *sacrificāre* (13). *velle* occurs (16), but is not tested directly by a question.

indirect statement with perfect active infinitive: *labōrāvisse* (9); *offendisse* (19).

indirect statement with perfect passive infinitive: *coniectum et ... accūsātum esse* (19–20).

purpose clause introduced by a relative pronoun: *quam tibi trādat* (15).

vocabulary: *praesēns* (3); *vexāre* (8); *ōrāre* (10); *praebēre* (10); *mandāre* (14); *conicere* (19); *monēre* (20); *nisi* (21); *cavēre* (21); *damnāre* (21).

Test 13

To be given at the end of Stage 40, preferably in two successive lessons.

Part I: Written Translation
coniūrātiō

Imperātor Domitiānus, vir saevus et suspīciōsus, crēdēbat inimīcos ubīque adesse, quī sē interficere vellent. multōs innocentēs **capitis**

Diagnostic Texts

damnāvit; etiam nōnnūllōs lībertōs suōs, quamquam nūllum scelus commīserant, necārī iussit.
  tandem paucī virī coniūrātiōnem ad Domitiānum occīdendum fēcērunt. inter eōs erat lībertus quīdam, Stephanus nōmine, cuius patrōnus, Flāvius Clēmēns, ā Domitiānō **iniūstē** interfectus erat. Stephanus, quī **iūrāverat** sē mortem patrōnī **vindicātūrum esse**, diū rem cōgitāvit. "difficile erit nōbīs" sibi inquit, "Domitiānum in aulā **aggredī**; nēmō enim ad eum admittitur nisi lībertī fidēlissimī. sī autem īnsidiās contrā eum in viā vel in forō parāverimus, ā mīlitibus **praetōriānīs** comprehendēmur et interficiēmur."
  Stephanō cōgitantī quō modō Domitiānum occīderet, subvēnit Apicāta uxor. "mī Stephane" inquit, "cōnsilium habeō. tū amīcīque tuī, sī cōnsiliō meō ūtēminī, rem efficere poteritis; neque prohibēbiminī neque comprehendēminī."

Part II: Comprehension Test

Stephanus uxōrī imperāvit ut cōnsilium sibi patefaceret. quō audītō, **calliditātem** eius admīrātus, ea quae prōposuit efficere cōnstituit.
  prīmum, **fasciīs** comparātīs, bracchium **sinistrum obvolvit**. complūrēs diēs simulāvit bracchium vulnere laesum esse. deinde, cum omnēs bracchium obvolūtum vidēre solitī essent, **ōstiārium** ōrāvit ut ad Domitiānum sē admitteret. dīxit sē coniūrātiōnem perīculōsam **dēprehendisse**; addidit sē **libellum** quendam habēre, in quō nōmina **coniūrātōrum** scrīpta essent; nēminem nisi Imperātōrem dēbēre hunc libellum vidēre.
  Domitiānus, quod cōnfīdēbat hominem vulnerātum haudquāquam timendum esse, ōstiāriō imperāvit ut Stephanum admitteret. quī ingressus, omnibus custōdibus **remōtīs** ut Imperātor sōlus verba eius audīret, libellum trādidit; tum pugiōne, quem in fasciīs cēlāverat, extractō, Domitiānum intentē legentem **trānsfīxit**. quī, graviter vulnerātus, fortiter tamen Stephanō restitit et magnōs clāmōrēs sustulit. coniūrātī cēterī, quī in aulam ab Apicātā arcessītī erant, audītīs clāmōribus, intellēxērunt quid accidisset; statim irrūpērunt Domitiānumque multīs vulneribus interfēcērunt.

Diagnostic Texts

	Points
1 What did Stephanus order his wife to do? What did he then decide?	2
2 What did he do with the bandages?	1
3 What did he say had happened to him?	1
4 What reasons did he give for wanting to see Domitian?	3
5 Why was the emperor not suspicious?	2
6 Why were the guards removed?	2
7 Where had Stephanus put the dagger?	1
8 Why did Domitian not see what Stephanus was doing?	1
9 How successful was Stephanus? What did Domitian do?	3
10 How did the other conspirators come to be in the palace?	1
11 How did they learn what had happened?	1
12 What did they then do?	2
	20

Notice how students are coping with the following features in particular:

1st person plural passive: *comprehendēmur* (line 12); *interficiēmur* (13).
2nd person plural passive and deponent; *ūtēminī* (16); *prohibēbiminī* (17); *comprehendēminī* (17).
indirect statement after past verb of speaking, etc.:
  with present active infinitive: *adesse* (2); *habēre* (26); *dēbēre* (27); *esse* (29).
  with perfect active infinitive: *dēprehendisse* (25).
  with perfect passive infinitive: *laesum esse* (22).
  with future active infinitive: *vindicātūrum esse* (8–9).
ad + gerundive: *ad Domitiānum occīdendum* (5).
extended sentence with no expressed subject: *nōnnūllōs ... iussit* (3–4).
noun + present participle in dative at start of sentence: *Stephanō cōgitantī* (14).
ūtor + ablative: *cōnsiliō meō ūtēminī* (16).
vocabulary: *ubīque* (2); *quīdam* (6 and 25); *comprehendere* (12 and 17); *subvenīre* (14); *prohibēre* (17); *bracchium* (21 and 22); *cēlāre* (32); *legere* (32).

The test contains two examples of the pluperfect subjunctive passive (or deponent): *solitī essent* (line 23) and *scrīpta essent* (26). These forms are not introduced into the students' reading material until Stage 46, but *solitī essent* is not tested directly by a question, and the context of *scrīpta essent* is straightforward and undemanding.

Diagnostic Texts

Test 14

Give this test after the students have finished Stage 48. Give Part I and Part II either in a single period or in two consecutive ones, leaving another period for Part III.

Part I: Introduction for Oral Translation
Translate this orally and informally with the class.

incendium

Nerōne imperātōre, incendium maximum Rōmae accidit. initium in 1
eā parte Circī maximī ortum est quae Palātīnō Caeliōque
montibus **adiacet**; deinde flammae per tabernās proximās, in
quibus multum inerat **mercimōnium**, celerrimē sunt sparsae.

Part II: Comprehension Test

cīvēs, quī in illā regiōne urbis habitābant, prīmō flammās 5
exstinguere cōnātī sunt; amīcīs et familiīs **hamās** trādidērunt
quibus aquam ferrent. tandem, dē domibus dēspērantēs, salūtem
fugiendō petere cōnstituērunt. sed tanta erat multitūdō ut paucī ad
loca tūta per viās angustās pervenīre possent. multī, quia vel fessī
vel ignārī viārum erant, flammīs circumventī periērunt. praetereā, 10
turba fugientium eōs impediēbat quī aquam ferēbant. nōnnūllī
quidem, omnī spē effugiendī **omissā**, in domibus suīs mortem
exspectāre māluērunt.

illō tempore, Nerō ab urbe aberat; nam Antium ierat ad diem
fēstum celebrandum. nūntiātō tamen incendiō, Rōmam profectus 15
est. celerrimē equitandō, iter duābus hōrīs cōnfēcit. simulatque
advēnit, illīs cīvibus, quōrum domūs dēlētae erant, hortōs suōs
patefēcit, ubi aedificia **subitāria** exstruī iussit. hīs tamen beneficiīs
favōrum populī sibi haudquāquam **conciliāvit**; rūmor enim
vagābātur Nerōnem, cum flammae urbem cōnsūmerent, montem 20
proximum ascendisse unde Rōmam ardentem spectāret, atque
versūs aliquōs dē **excidiō** Trōiae compositōs cantāvisse.
reminīscēbantur quoque cīvēs Nerōnem mātrem suam occīdisse,
deōsque contempsisse. "sī imperātor noster homō minus **impius**
fuisset," sibi inquiunt, "deī hanc clādem nōbīs nōn mīsissent." 25

Points

1 What was the citizens' first reaction to the outbreak of fire? 1
2 How did they get their friends and households to help them? 2
3 What decision did they eventually take (lines 7–8)? 1

Diagnostic Texts

4 "sed tanta ... perierunt" (lines 8–10). Find three reasons why
   many people failed to escape.   3
5 What further difficulty was caused by those who were running
   away?   2
6 What did some people prefer to do? Why did they not behave
   like the others?   3
7 Why was Nero away from Rome when the fire broke out?   2
8 How long did his journey back to Rome take, and why?   2
9 What action did he then take, and for whose benefit (lines
   17–18)?   3
10 What order did he give?   2
11 How grateful were the citizens for these kind actions (lines
   18–19)?   1
12 According to the rumor, where had Nero gone when the fire
   was at its height, and for what purpose? What else was he
   believed to have done?   4
13 Read lines 23–25 (*reminīscēbantur ... mīsissent*). What
   explanation occurred to the citizens for the disaster they had
   suffered?   2
14 What previous actions of Nero made this explanation seem
   likely to them?   2

                                                                   ——
                                                                   30

Part III: Written Translation

per quīnque diēs incendium saeviēbat. flammīs sextō diē exstīnctīs,
damnum aestimārī poterat. cognōvērunt magistrātūs ex
quattuordecim urbis regiōnibus quattuor tantum **integrās**
manēre; trēs omnīnō dēlētās esse; in cēterīs superesse aedificia
pauca. nisi cīvēs mīlitēsque strēnuissimē labōrāvissent ad   30
incendium exstinguendum, tōta urbs flammīs cōnsūmpta esset.
   deinde novī rūmōrēs per urbem **serpēbant**; multī iam
crēdēbant Nerōnem ipsum Rōmam incendī iussisse, ut urbs
secunda, priōre splendidior, exstruerētur. quibus rūmōribus audītīs,
Nerō in hominēs quōsdam, quī Chrīstiānī appellābantur, culpam   35
trānsferre cōnātus est. quī, ā mīlitibus Nerōnis comprehēnsī,
crūdēliter interfectī sunt. Nerō enim imperāvit ut aliī in
amphitheātrō contrā leōnēs pugnāre cōgerentur, aliī, vestīmenta
picea gerentēs et **pālīs affīxī**, nocte ad lūcem praebendam in
hortīs pūblicīs incenderentur. quō spectāculō vīsō, multī cīvēs,   40
quamquam Chrīstiānī eīs erant odiō, **misericordiā** movēbantur.

Diagnostic Texts

Notice how your students are managing with the following features in particular:

is quī, etc.: *eōs ... quī* (line 11); *illīs cīvibus quōrum* ... (17)
gerund: *fugiendō* (8); *effugiendī* (12); *equitandō* (16)
gerundive with *ad*: *ad diem fēstum celebrandum* (14–15); *ad incendium exstinguendum* (30–31); *ad lūcem praebendam* (39)
indirect statement: *Nerōnem ... cantāvisse* (20–22); *Nerōnem ... contempsisse* (23–24); *ex ... pauca* (27–30); *Nerōnem iussisse* (33)
conditional clauses with pluperfect subjunctive: *sī ... mīsissent* (24–25); *nisi ... cōnsūmpta esset* (30–31)
present passive infinitive: *aestimārī* (27); *incendī* (33)
pluperfect subjunctive passive: *cōnsūmpta esset* (31)
substantive participle: *fugientium* (11)
ablative of comparison: *priōre* (34)
connecting relative: *quibus* (34); *quī* (35); *quō* (40)
imperfect subjunctive passive: *cōgerentur* (38); *incenderentur* (40)
vocabulary: *haudquāquam* (19); *tantum* (28); *quōsdam* (35)

The later reading passages in Dunlop (see Bibliography, p. 255 below), and the earlier ones in Dale (see Bibliography, p. 255 below), may also be useful during the reading of Unit 4 when you wish to measure your students' progress and give them practice in working unaided. Several passages in both Dunlop and Dale systematically practice particular syntactical points.

Appendix A: Cumulated List of Checklist Words (Stages 1–48)

Words and phrases in the Unit 4 (Stages 35–48) Checklists are printed in boldface.

a
ā, ab (= "by") (21)
ā, ab (= "from") (17)
abesse (6)
abīre (10)
ac (28)
accidere (25)
accipere (10)
accūsāre (26)
ācriter (33)
ad (3)
addere (32)
adeō (27)
adeptus (22)
adesse (5)
adhūc (30)
adipīscī (34)
adīre (20)
aditus (27)
adiuvāre (21)
adloquī (42)
administrāre (23)
adstāre (24)
advenīre (13)
adventus (27)
adversus (adj.) (32)
adversus (prep.) (40)
aedificāre (16)
aedificium (13)
aeger (13)
aequō animō (32)
aequor (47)
aequus (32)
aestās (45)
afficere (30)

affirmāre (40)
ager (35)
agere (4)
aggredī (43)
agitāre (8)
agmen (15)
agnōscere (9)
agricola (5)
aliī ... aliī (29)
aliquandō (29)
aliquid (18)
aliquis (25)
alius (15)
alter (13)
altus (31)
amāre (19)
ambō (30)
ambulāre (5)
amīcitia (40)
amīcus (2)
āmittere (12)
amor (22)
amplectī (34)
amplexus (29)
amplissimus (37)
amplius (37)
an (35)
ancilla (2)
angustus (31)
animadvertere (36)
animus (17)
annus (21)
ante (31)
antea (27)
antīquus (14)

219

Cumulated List of Checklist Words

ānulus (4)
aperīre (25)
appārēre (27)
appellāre (32)
appropinquāre (17)
aptus (38)
apud (14)
aqua (15)
āra (17)
arbor (39)
arcessere (20)
ardēre (27)
argenteus (14)
arma (36)
arrogantia (28)
ars (20)
ascendere (21)
aspicere (44)
at (33)
atque (28)
ātrium (1)
attonitus (14)
auctor (34)
auctōritās (24)
audācia (29)
audāx (24)
audēre (18)
audīre (5)
auferre (26)
augēre (40)
aula (14)
aureus (22)
auris (20)
aurum (37)
aut (39)
autem (25)
auxiliō esse (40)
auxilium (16)
avārus (6)
avidē (22)
avis (32)

b
barbarus (21)
bellum (26)
bellum gerere (26)
bene (17)
beneficium (28)
benignus (17)
bibere (3)
bona (43)
bonus (16)
bracchium (38)
brevis (33)

c
cadere (39)
caecus (42)
caedere (19)
caedēs (48)
caelum (22)
callidus (10)
campus (39)
candidus (45)
canis (1)
cantāre (13)
capere (10)
capillī (39)
captīvus (25)
caput (18)
carcer (24)
carēre (47)
carmen (29)
cārus (19)
castīgāre (19)
castra (25)
cāsus (32)
catēna (31)
causa (36)
cautē (19)
cavēre (35)
cēdere (23)
cēlāre (21)
celebrāre (9)
celeriter (9)

Cumulatede List of Checklist Words

cēna (2)
cēnāre (7)
centum (28, 33, 39 & 48)
centuriō (7)
cēra (4)
certāmen (27)
certāre (33)
certus (38)
cēterī (13)
cibus (2)
cinis (12)
circum (21)
circumspectāre (3)
circumvenīre (29)
cīvis (9)
clādēs (46)
clam (38)
clāmāre (3)
clāmor (5)
clārus (23)
claudere (15)
cliēns (31)
coepisse (18)
cōgere (25)
cōgitāre (19)
cognōscere (18)
cohors (26)
colligere (26)
collocāre (20)
colloquium (24)
comes (27)
comitārī (34)
commemorāre (23)
commendāre (38)
commodus (15)
commōtus (26)
comparāre (19)
complēre (12)
complūrēs (37)
compōnere (32)
comprehendere (24)
cōnārī (34)
cōnātus (32)

condūcere (32)
cōnfectus (38)
cōnficere (19)
cōnfīdere (21)
conicere (33)
coniungere (44)
coniūnx (37)
coniūrāre (44)
coniūrātiō (13)
cōnscendere (24)
cōnsentīre (16)
cōnsilium (16)
cōnsistere (18)
cōnspicārī (34)
cōnspicātus (23)
cōnspicere (7)
cōnstat (37)
cōnstituere (28)
cōnsul (40)
cōnsulātus (34)
cōnsulere (30)
cōnsūmere (8)
contemnere (43)
contendere (5)
contentus (10)
contrā (33)
convenīre (11)
convertere (32)
cōpiae (38)
coquere (4)
coquus (1)
corōna (29)
corpus (28)
cotīdiē (14)
crās (33)
creāre (30)
crēdere (11)
crēscere (44)
crīmen (40)
crūdēlis (20)
cubiculum (6)
culpa (45)
culpāre (37)

Cumulated List of Checklist Words

cum (= "when") (24)
cum (= "with") (7)
cupere (9)
cupīdō (44)
cūr (4)
cūra (23)
cūrae esse (35)
cūrāre (19)
cūria (40)
currere (5)
cursus (29)
custōdīre (12)
custōs (13)

d
damnāre (34)
dare (9)
dē (= "about") (11)
dē (= "down from") (19)
dea (18)
dēbēre (15)
decem (20, 28, 33, 39 & 48)
decēre (27)
dēcidere (13)
decimus (33, 39 & 48)
dēcipere (22)
decōrus (14)
dēfendere (19)
dēfessus (29)
dēicere (21)
deinde (16)
dēlectāre (16)
dēlēre (14)
dēmittere (30)
dēmōnstrāre (18)
dēmum (40)
dēnique (20)
dēnsus (12)
dēpōnere (25)
dērīdēre (16)
dēscendere (24)
dēserere (24)
dēsilīre (17)

dēsinere (25)
dēspērāre (17)
deus (14)
dextra (38)
dī immortālēs! (25)
dīcere (13)
dictāre (14)
diēs (9)
diēs nātālis (9)
difficilis (14)
dignitās (25)
dignus (37)
dīligenter (14)
dīligentia (25)
dīligere (28)
dīmittere (16)
dīrus (22)
discēdere (18)
discere (37)
discipulus (36)
discrīmen (39)
dissentīre (22)
diū (17)
dīversus (41)
dīves (30)
dīvitiae (30)
dīvus (37)
docēre (26)
doctus (20)
dolēre (28)
dolor (29)
domina (14)
dominus (2)
domus (20)
dōnāre (26)
dōnec (48)
dōnum (14)
dormīre (2)
dubitāre (37)
dubium (30)
ducentī (28, 33, 39 & 48)
dūcere (8)
dulcis (19)

dum (34)
duo (12, 20, 28, 33, 39 & 48)
duo mīlia (48)
duodecim (39 & 48)
duodēvīgintī (39 & 48)
dūrus (21)
dux (31)

e
ē, ex (4)
ecce! (3)
efferre (43)
efficere (21)
effigiēs (15)
effugere (16)
effundere (32)
ego (4)
ēgredī (34)
ēgressus (24)
ēheu! (4)
ēicere (33)
ēlātus (37, 43)
ēligere (22)
emere (6)
ēmittere (9)
enim (23)
epistula (12)
eques (24)
equitāre (20)
equus (15)
ergō (39)
ēripere (38)
errāre (23)
esse (1)
et (3)
et ... et (33)
etiam (15)
euge! (5)
eum (8)
ēvādere (48)
exanimātus (17)
excipere (33)
excitāre (13)

exclāmāre (10)
exemplum (37)
exercēre (9)
exercitus (37)
exilium (40)
exīre (3)
exīstimāre (40)
exitium (22)
explicāre (25)
exspectāre (3)
exstinguere (34)
exstruere (30)
extrā (25)
extrahere (21)
extrēmus (36)

f
faber (16)
fābula (5)
fābulam agere (5)
facere (7)
facile (8)
facilis (17)
facinus (26)
factum (41)
fallere (39)
falsus (26)
fāma (40)
familia (38)
familiāris (14)
favēre (11)
favor (31)
fax (27)
fēlīx (44)
fēmina (5)
ferōciter (6)
ferōx (8)
ferre (9)
ferrum (29)
fessus (13)
festīnāre (6)
fēstus (30)
fidēlis (14)

223

Cumulated List of Checklist Words

fidēs (26)
fīdus (43)
fierī (37)
fīlia (19)
fīlius (1)
fingere (40)
fīnis (36)
flamma (12)
flēre (45)
flōrēre (40)
flōs (16)
flūctus (47)
fluere (19)
flūmen (24)
fōns (21)
fortasse (18)
forte (19)
fortis (6)
fortiter (12)
fortūna (18)
forum (3)
fossa (15)
frāctus (15)
fragor (39)
frangere (18)
frāter (10)
fraus (31)
frūmentum (16)
frūstrā (12)
fuga (33)
fugere (12)
fulgēre (17)
fundere (22)
fundus (12)
fūr (6)
furēns (25)

g
gaudēre (27)
gaudium (34)
geminī (13)
gemitus (28)
gemma (17)

gēns (11)
genū (42)
genus (39)
gerere (23)
gladius (8)
glōria (41)
grātiās agere (19)
grātus (38)
gravis (21)
graviter (17)
gustāre (2)

h
habēre (4)
habitāre (8)
haerēre (17)
haesitāre (25)
haruspex (21)
hasta (17)
haud (34)
haudquāquam (31)
haurīre (13)
hercle! (10)
hērēs (28)
heri (7)
hic (8)
hīc (33)
hiems (20)
hinc (39)
hodīe (5)
homō (9)
honor (23)
honōrāre (15)
hōra (21)
horreum (13)
hortārī (34)
hortus (1)
hospes (9)
hostis (22)
hūc (17)
humī (24)

i

iacere (23)
iacēre (12)
iactāre (22)
iam (12)
iānua (3)
ibi (18)
īdem (31)
identidem (32)
ideō (35)
ideō ... quod (35)
igitur (12)
ignārus (27)
ignāvus (8)
ignis (36)
ignōrāre (38)
ignōscere (32)
ille (9)
illūc (19)
immemor (25)
imminēre (34)
immortālis (25)
immōtus (23)
impedīre (15)
imperāre (27)
imperātor (16)
imperium (10)
impetus (17)
impōnere (34)
in (1)
in animō volvere (31)
inānis (37)
incēdere (27)
incendere (27)
incendium (41)
incēnsus (37)
incidere (12)
incipere (22)
incitāre (8)
incolumis (48)
inde (35)
indicium (34)
induere (23)

inesse (35)
īnfāns (6)
īnfēlīx (21)
īnferre (20)
īnfestus (24)
ingenium (23)
ingēns (7)
ingredī (34)
ingressus (22)
inicere (22)
inimīcus (10)
initium (37)
iniūria (10)
inopia (43)
inquit (4)
īnsānus (26)
īnsidiae (27)
īnspicere (9)
īnstruere (26)
īnsula (17)
intellegere (7)
intentē (6)
inter (16)
intereā (24)
interficere (13)
interim (40)
intrā (38)
intrāre (2)
invenīre (10)
invidēre (37)
invidia (40)
invītāre (11)
invītus (18)
iocus (27)
ipse (14)
īra (28)
īrātus (3)
īre (10)
irrumpere (20)
iste (14)
ita (16)
ita vērō (13)
itaque (17)

Cumulated List of Checklist Words

iter (19)
iterum (9)
iubēre (21)
iūdex (4)
iūdicāre (46)
iungere (38)
iussum (27)
iuvāre (39)
iuvenis (5)
iuxtā (43)

l
lābī (47)
labor (32)
labōrāre (1)
lacrima (22)
lacrimāre (7)
laedere (25)
laetus (2)
lapis (46)
latēre (25)
latrō (17)
latus (48)
lātus (20)
laudāre (2)
laus (47)
lavāre (14)
lectīca (34)
lectus (15)
lēgātus (26)
legere (11)
legiō (25)
lēniter (33)
lentē (15)
leō (3)
levis (40)
lēx (38)
libenter (18)
liber (10)
līberālis (11)
līberāre (20)
līberī (29)
lībertās (32)
lībertus (6)
licet (44)
līmen (38)
lingua (28)
littera (39)
litterae (39)
lītus (15)
locus (19)
locūtus (23)
longē (42)
longus (18)
loquī (34)
lūdere (41)
lūdus (30)
lūgēre (42)
lūmen (46)
lūna (20)
lūx (29)

m
magis (35)
magister (30)
magistrātus (43)
magnopere (24)
magnus (3)
male (35)
mālle (29)
malus (28)
mandāre (28)
mandātum (23)
māne (19)
manēre (9)
manus (="band") (27)
manus (="hand") (18)
mare (17)
marītus (14)
māter (1)
maximē (24)
maximus (17)
medicus (20)
meditārī (40)
medius (9)
melior (16)

meminisse (42)
mendāx (4)
mēns (38)
mēnsa (2)
mēnsis (39)
mentīrī (35)
mercātor (2)
merēre (41)
meritus (35)
metuere (48)
metus (28)
meus (5)
mīles (18)
mīlia (28)
mīlle (28 & 48)
minārī (40)
minimē! (11)
minimus (22)
minus (46)
mīrābilis (12)
mīrārī (36)
miser (15)
mittere (12)
modo (34)
modo ... modo (45)
modus (23)
molestus (22)
mollis (42)
monēre (22)
mōns (12)
mora (47)
morārī (35)
morbus (21)
morī (34)
mors (20)
mortuus (7)
mōs (31)
movēre (33)
mox (9)
mulier (45)
multī (5)
multitūdō (17)
multō (28)

multus (5)
mūnus (48)
mūrus (11)
mūtāre (40)

n
nam (18)
nārrāre (7)
nāscī (34)
nātus (30)
nauta (15)
nāvigāre (16)
nāvis (3)
nē (36)
nē quid (48)
nē ... quidem (32)
nē quis (48)
nec (42)
nec ... nec (42)
necāre (7)
necesse (14)
negāre (43)
neglegēns (19)
neglegere (31)
negōtium (17)
negōtium agere (4)
nēmō (18)
neque (42)
neque ... neque (24)
nescīre (25)
niger (36)
nihil (7)
nihilōminus (32)
nimis (30)
nimium (23)
nisi (33)
nōbilis (14)
nocēre (27)
nōlle (13)
nōmen (25)
nōn (3)
nōnāgintā (28, 33, 39 & 48)
nōndum (41)

nōngentī (48)
nōnne? (16)
nōnnūllī (21)
nōnus (33, 39 & 48)
nōs (10)
noster (11)
nōtus (9)
novem (20, 28, 33, 39 & 48)
nōvisse (19)
novus (13)
nox (18)
nūbere (38)
nūbēs (12)
nūllus (13)
num (26)
num? (14)
numerāre (13)
numerus (23)
numquam (17)
nunc (11)
nūntiāre (10)
nūntius (8)
nūper (21)
nusquam (24)

o
obicere (40)
oblivīscī (37)
obscūrus (29)
obstāre (18)
obstupefacere (33)
obviam īre (34)
occāsiō (37)
occīdere (28)
occupāre (26)
occupātus (21)
occurrere (27)
octāvus (33, 39 & 48)
octingentī (48)
octō (20, 28, 33, 39 & 48)
octōgintā (28, 33, 39 & 48)
oculus (20)
odiō esse (33)

ōdisse (29)
odium (37)
offendere (36)
offerre (9)
officium (35)
ōlim (6)
omnīnō (30)
omnis (7)
opēs (28)
oportet (26)
oppidum (21)
opprimere (32)
oppugnāre (24)
optāre (47)
optimē (12)
optimus (5)
opus (30)
opus est (41)
ōrāre (31)
ōrātiō (39)
orbis (45)
orbis terrārum (45)
ōrdō (13)
orīrī (38)
ōrnāre (23)
ōs (= "face") (25)
ōsculum (27)
ostendere (9)
ōtiōsus (32)
ōtium (45)

p
paene (12)
pallēscere (30)
pallidus (28)
pār (36)
parāre (7)
parātus (16)
parcere (22)
parēns (20)
pārēre (23)
pars (18)
parum (47)

Cumulated List of Checklist Words

parvus (6)
passus (24)
patefacere (24)
pater (1)
patī (34)
patria (37)
patrōnus (31)
paucī (17)
paulātim (44)
paulīsper (9)
paulō (37)
paulum (46)
pauper (32)
pavor (30)
pāx (10)
pectus (48)
pecūnia (4)
peditēs (41)
pendēre (34)
per (6)
perdere (= "destroy") (39)
perdere (= "lose") (41)
perficere (29)
perfidia (26)
perfidus (24)
perīculōsus (18)
perīculum (19)
perīre (16)
perītus (21)
permōtus (32)
persuādēre (20)
perterritus (4)
perturbāre (37)
pervenīre (17)
pēs (8)
pessimus (20)
pestis (7)
petere (= "attack") (5)
petere (= "beg for") (18)
pietās (48)
placēre (11)
plaudere (5)
plaustrum (15)

plēnus (21)
plērīque (36)
plūrimī (19)
plūrimus (19)
plūs (21)
pōculum (7)
poena (25)
poenās dare (25)
poēta (4)
pollicērī (38)
pompa (19)
pondus (47)
pōnere (16)
pōns (24)
pontifex (38)
populus (29)
porta (8)
portāre (3)
portus (10)
poscere (19)
posse (13)
possidēre (43)
post (9)
posteā (18)
postquam (6)
postrēmō (18)
postrīdiē (16)
postulāre (8)
potēns (23)
potestās (33)
praebēre (26)
praeceps (27)
praecō (31)
praeesse (15)
praefectus (37)
praeficere (28)
praemium (27)
praesēns (36)
praesertim (36)
praesidium (18)
praestāre (30)
praeter (36)
praetereā (30)

229

Cumulatede List of Checklist Words

praeterīre (31)
prāvus (23)
precārī (34)
precātus (22)
precēs (20)
premere (48)
pretiōsus (14)
pretium (21)
prīmus (11, 33, 39 & 48)
prīnceps (15)
prīncipia (26)
prior (15)
prius (29)
priusquam (34)
prō (18)
prō certō habēre (38)
probāre (40)
prōcēdere (7)
procul (34)
prōcumbere (18)
prōdere (40)
proelium (37)
profectus (32)
proficīscī (34)
prōgredī (34)
prōgressus (31)
prohibēre (38)
prōmittere (11)
prope (7)
propter (43)
prōvincia (26)
proximus (27)
prūdentia (22)
pūblicus (31)
puella (5)
puer (8)
pugna (11)
pugnāre (8)
pulcher (7)
pulsāre (6)
pūnīre (16)
putāre (35)

q
quadrāgintā (20, 28, 33, 39 & 48)
quadringentī (48)
quaerere (4)
quālis (27)
quam (= "how") (14)
quam (= "than") (10)
quamquam (14)
quandō? (35)
quantus (22)
quārē? (30)
quartus (33, 39 & 48)
quasi (34)
quattuor (20, 28, 33, 39 & 48)
quattuordecim (39 & 48)
-que (14)
querī (38)
quī (15)
quia (32)
quicquam (28)
quīcumque (42)
quīdam (32)
quidem (35)
quiēs (29)
quīndecim (39 & 48)
quīngentī (48)
quīnquāgintā (20, 28, 33 & 48)
quīnque (20, 28, 33, 39 & 48)
quīntus (33, 39 & 48)
quis? (4)
quisquam (45)
quisque (48)
quisquid (46)
quisquis (46)
quō? (18)
quō modō? (22)
quod (6)
quodcumque (42)
quondam (17)
quoniam (47)
quoque (2)
quot (26)
quotiēns (35)

r

rapere (11)
ratiōnēs (31)
rē vērā (32)
recipere (17)
recitāre (36)
rēctē (36)
recumbere (8)
recūsāre (18)
reddere (4)
redīre (15)
redūcere (29)
referre (26)
reficere (31)
regere (38)
rēgīna (33)
regiō (36)
rēgnum (26)
regredī (34)
regressus (23)
relēgāre (35)
relinquere (20)
reliquus (46)
remedium (20)
repente (43)
reperīre (42)
requīrere (46)
rēs (6)
rēs adversae (32)
resistere (18)
respicere (39)
respondēre (3)
retinēre (13)
revenīre (9)
revertī (34)
revocāre (37)
rex (14)
rīdēre (3)
rīpa (24)
rogāre (7)
ruere (13)
rumpere (45)
rūrsus (25)
rūs (35)

s

sacer (18)
sacerdōs (15)
saepe (8)
saevīre (18)
saevus (26)
sagitta (47)
saltāre (16)
salūs (29)
salūtāre (2)
salvē! (3)
sānē (26)
sanguis (8)
sapiēns (21)
satis (4)
saxum (15)
scelestus (25)
scelus (29)
scindere (32)
scīre (23)
scrībere (6)
sē (13)
secāre (31)
secundus (11, 33, 39 & 48)
sēcūrus (37)
secūtus (32)
sed (4)
sēdecim (39 & 48)
sedēre (1)
sēdēs (30)
sella (14)
semper (10)
senātor (11)
senex (5)
sententia (10)
sentīre (12)
sepelīre (42)
septem (20, 28, 33, 39 & 48)
septendecim (39 & 48)
septimus (33, 39 & 48)
septingentī (48)
septuāgintā (28, 33, 39 & 48)
sepulcrum (30)
sequī (34)

Cumulatede List of Checklist Words

serēnus (31)
sermō (20)
servāre (10)
servīre (29)
servus (1)
sescentī (48)
sevērus (33)
sex (20, 28, 33, 39 & 48)
sexāgintā (28, 33, 39 & 48)
sextus (33, 39 & 48)
sī (26)
sī quid (41)
sī quis (41)
sīc (28)
sīcut (20)
sīdus (42)
signum (4)
silentium (27)
silva (8)
similis (40)
simul (35)
simulac (16)
simulāre (39)
sine (17)
socius (40)
sōl (30)
solēre (17)
sollicitus (11)
sōlus (10)
solvere (28)
somnus (46)
sonitus (19)
sordidus (17)
soror (30)
sors (29)
spargere (39)
spatium (47)
speciēs (45)
spectāculum (8)
spectāre (5)
spērāre (31)
spernere (29)
spēs (28)

stāre (5)
statim (8)
statiō (25)
sternere (46)
stilus (39)
stola (19)
strēnuē (32)
strepitus (30)
studēre (44)
studium (39)
stultus (11)
suādēre (40)
suāvis (25)
suāviter (13)
sub (27)
subitō (6)
subvenīre (32)
summus (16)
sūmptuōsus (32)
superāre (6)
superbus (31)
superesse (16)
supplicium (35)
suprā (39)
surgere (3)
suscipere (21)
suspicārī (34)
suspicātus (28)
suus (9)

t
taberna (3)
tacēre (10)
tacitē (7)
tacitus (27)
taedēre (27)
tālis (23)
tam (20)
tamen (7)
tamquam (23)
tandem (12)
tangere (36)
tantum (24)

Cumulatede List of Checklist Words

tantus (27)
tardus (22)
tēctum (= "building") (46)
tēctum (= "roof") (33)
tegere (45)
tellūs (44)
tempestās (30)
templum (12)
temptāre (20)
tempus (31)
tenebrae (34)
tenēre (15)
tenuis (45)
tergum (17)
terra (12)
terrēre (7)
tertius (11, 33, 39 & 48)
testāmentum (28)
testis (25)
timēre (12)
timor (30)
tollere (16)
tot (19)
tōtus (8)
trādere (9)
trahere (13)
trāns (38)
trānsīre (24)
trēcentī (48)
trēdecim (39 & 48)
trēs (12, 20, 28, 33, 39 & 48)
tribūnus (26)
trīgintā (20, 28, 33, 39 & 48)
trīstis (24)
tū (4)
tuba (8)
tum (6)
tum dēmum (40)
tumultus (40)
turba (5)
tūtus (22)
tuus (6)

u
ubi (= "when") (14)
ubi (= "where") (5)
ubīque (31)
ulcīscī (43)
ūllus (39)
ultimus (26)
ultiō (34)
ultrā (46)
umbra (7)
umerus (19)
umquam (23)
ūnā cum (44)
unda (15)
unde (21)
ūndecim (39 & 48)
ūndēvīgintī (39 & 48)
undique (29)
unguere (38)
ūnus (12, 20, 28, 33, 39 & 48)
urbs (5)
ut (= "as") (28)
ut (= "that") (26)
uterque (44)
ūtī (40)
ūtilis (11)
utrum (33)
utrum ... an (35)
uxor (10)

v
vacuus (36)
valdē (7)
valē! (11)
validus (37)
vehementer (10)
vehere (31)
vel (34)
vel ... vel (48)
velle (13)
velut (48)
vēnatiō (8)
vēndere (4)

233

Cumulated List of Checklist Words

venēnum (23)
venia (23)
venīre (5)
ventus (28)
verberāre (11)
verbum (22)
verērī (38)
vērō (38)
vertere (16)
vērum (24)
vērus (32)
vester (29)
vestīmenta (34)
vestis (38)
vetus (36)
vexāre (19)
via (1)
vīcīnus (35)
victor (15)
vidēre (3)
vidērī (40)
vīgintī (20, 28, 33, 39 & 48)
vīlis (41)
vīlla (3)

vincere (15)
vincīre (31)
vinculum (44)
vīnum (3)
vir (11)
vīrēs (47)
virgō (22)
virtūs (22)
vīs (48)
vīta (17)
vītāre (22)
vitium (41)
vituperāre (6)
vīvere (19)
vīvus (29)
vix (19)
vocāre (4)
volvere (31)
vōs (10)
vōx (19)
vulnerāre (13)
vulnus (20)
vultus (31)

Appendix B: Cumulated List of Word-Search Words (Stages 1–40)

As the students approach the end, in Stage 40, of the long historical novel about Quintus, Salvius, and others which began in Stage 1, review with them some of the basic vocabulary in Stages 1–40, i.e. the words in the Checklists, by asking them for the Latin parent word (or a close relative of it) of each of the following English words, which they have studied in the Word-Search sections.

The following list contains all the Word-Search vocabulary (Stages 1–40). The number(s) in the parentheses refer to the Stage Checklist(s) in which the parent word(s) is found, and the word(s) after the colon is (a) the parent Latin word(s) or (b) a word(s) from the parent's close family.

a
aberrant (17: ab (="from"); 23: errāre)
acrimony (33: ācriter)
advent (3: ad; 5: venīre)
adversary (32: adversus (adj.))
advocate (3: ad; 4: vocāre)
affection (30: afficere)
affiliate (3: ad; 1: fīlius)
agent (4: agere)
agitation (8: agitāre)
alien (15: alius)
allocate (3: ad; 19: locus)
altitude (31: altus)
ameliorate (16: melior)
amicable (2: amīcus)
ancillary (2: ancilla)
annually (21: annus)
aperture (25: aperīre)
apparition (27: appārēre)
appellation (32: appellāre)
approximate (3: ad; 27: proximus)
aptitude (38: aptus)
arboreal (39: arbor)
ardent (27: ardēre)
audacious (24: audāx)
audience (5: audīre)
augment (40: augēre)
aural (20: auris)
auxiliary (16: auxilium)
avarice (6: avārus)
aviation (32: avis)

b
barbaric (21: barbarus)
belligerent (26: bellum gerere)
beneficial (28: beneficium)
brevity (33: brevis)

c
cadence (39: cadere)
canine (1: canis)
captivate (25: captīvus)
casualty (32: cāsus)
centrifugal (centrum+33: fuga)

235

Cumulated List of Word-Search Words

civilization	(9: cīvis)	culpability	(45: culpa)
cogitation	(19: cōgitāre)	curator	(19: cūrāre)
colloquy	(24: colloquium)	custodian	(12: custōdīre)
commerce	(7: cum (= "with") + 2: mercātor)	**d**	
		debt	(15: dēbēre)
commotion	(26: commōtus)	decapitate	(19: dē (= "down from"); 18: caput)
compassion	(7: cum (= "with"); 34: patī)		
complete	(12: complēre)	deciduous	(13: dēcidere)
concatenate	(7: cum (= "with"); 31: catēna)	delectable	(16: dēlectāre)
		delegate	(19: dē (= "down from"); 26: lēgātus)
concede	(7: cum (= "with"); 23: cēdere)		
		delete	(14: dēlēre)
concerted	(7: cum (= "with"); 33: certāre)	demonstrable	(18: dēmōnstrāre)
		density	(12: dēnsus)
concomitant	(7: cum (= "with"); 27: comes)	depose	(25: dēpōnere)
		depravity	(19: dē (= "down from"); 23: prāvus)
confidence	(21: cōnfīdere)		
conjugal	(37: coniūnx)		
conjure	(13: coniūrātiō)	deride	(16: dērīdēre)
consecutive	(7: cum (= "with"); 34: sequī)	diligence	(25: dīligentia)
		dire	(22: dīrus)
		disciple	(36: discipulus)
consensus	(16: cōnsentīre)	discriminate	(39: discrīmen)
conservation	(7: cum (= "with"); 10: servāre)	disgust	(dis- (= "not") + 2: gustāre)
conspicuous	(7: cōnspicere)	dissolve	(dis- (= "not") + 28: solvere)
contented	(10: contentus)		
contravene	(33: contrā; 5: venīre)	doctor	(26: docēre)
convene	(7: cum (= "with"); 5: venīre)	doleful	(28: dolēre)
		domesticate	(20: domus)
		domination	(2: dominus)
conversely	(32: convertere)	dormitory	(2: dormīre)
coronation	(29: corōna)	dulcet	(19: dulcis)
cubicle	(6: cubiculum)		

Cumulated List of Word-Search Words

e

edifice	(13: aedificium)
effect	(21: efficere)
effulgence	(4: ex + 17: fulgēre)
effusive	(32: effundere)
elocution	(4: ē + 23: locūtus)
emit	(9: ēmittere)
endure	(in- (intensive) + 21: dūrus)
enumerate	(4: ē + 13: numerāre)
equine	(15: equus)
evacuate	(4: ē + 36: vacuus)
exercise	(9: exercēre)
exhort	(4: ex + 34: hortārī)
extemporaneous	(4: ex + 31: tempus)
extinct	(34: exstinguere)

f

fabulous	(5: fābula)
facilitate	(17: facilis)
feminine	(5: fēmina)
ferocity	(8: ferōx)
fiction	(40: fingere)
fidelity	(14: fidēlis)
finite	(36: finis)
flume	(24: flūmen)
fortuitous	(19: forte)
fracture	(15: frāctus)
fraternal	(10: frāter)
fraudulent	(31: fraus)
frustrate	(12: frūstrā)
fugitive	(12: fugere)

h

homicide	(9: homō + 19: caedere)
horticulturalist	(1: hortus + cultūra)
hospital	(9: hospes)
hostile	(22: hostis)

i

ignite	(36: ignis)
illiterate	(in- (= "not") + 39: littera)
imbibe	(1: in + 3: bibere)
imminent	(34: imminēre)
immutable	(in- (= "not") + 40: mūtāre)
impassive	(in- (= "not") + 24: passus)
impecunious	(in- (= "not") + 4: pecūnia)
impede	(15: impedīre)
imperial	(10: imperium)
imperious	(27: imperāre)
impetuous	(17: impetus)
imprecation	(1: in + 34: precārī)
impunity	(in- (= "not") + 16: pūnīre)
incarcerate	(1: in + 24: carcer)
inception	(22: incipere)
incident	(12: incidere)
incinerate	(1: in + 12: cinis)
incite	(8: incitāre)
incorporeal	(in- (= "not") + 28: corpus)

Cumulated List of Word-Search Words

incredible	(in-(="not")+11: crēdere)	**l**	
		laboratory	(1: labōrāre)
		latent	(25: latēre)
incriminate	(1: in+40: crīmen)	latitude	(20: lātus)
		laudable	(2: laudāre)
indecorous	(in-(="not")+14: decōrus)	lavatory	(14: lavāre)
		legislation	(38: lēx)
		levity	(40: levis)
indignity	(in-(="not")+25: dignitās)	liberal	(11: līberālis)
		library	(10: liber)
		loquacious	(34: loquī)
indubitably	(in-(="not")+30: dubium)	ludicrous	(30: lūdus)
infamy	(in-(="not")+40: fāma)	**m**	
		magisterial	(30: magister)
		magnitude	(3: magnus)
		malice	(28: malus)
infant	(6: īnfāns)	manually	(18: manus (="hand"))
infidel	(in-(="not")+26: fidēs)		
		marine	(17: mare)
		marital	(14: marītus)
inhabit	(1: in+8: habitāre)	maternity	(1: māter)
		merit	(35: meritus)
inscribe	(1: in+6: scrībere)	militant	(18: mīles)
		molest	(22: molestus)
insidious	(27: īnsidiae)	monitor	(22: monēre)
insuperable	(in-(="not")+6: superāre)	moratorium	(35: morārī)
		morbid	(21: morbus)
		mural	(11: mūrus)
intelligible	(7: intellegere)		
interrogation	(16: inter+7: rogāre)	**n**	
		nascent	(34: nāscī)
invent	(10: invenīre)	naval	(3: nāvis)
inveterate	(1: in+36: vetus)	nocturnal	(18: nox)
invidious	(37: invidēre)	nullify	(13: nūllus)
irate	(3: īrātus)		
irrevocable	(in-(="not")+37: revocāre)	**o**	
		oblivion	(37: oblivīscī)
		obscurity	(29: obscūrus)
		odious	(37: odium)
j		officious	(35: officium)
judicial	(4: iūdex)	omnipotent	(7: omnis; 23: potēns)

238

Cumulated List of Word-Search Words

operate	(30: opus)	relinquish	(20: relinquere)
opulent	(28: opēs)	repugnant	(re- (= "against") + 8: pugnāre)
ostensible	(9: ostendere)		
		retard	(re- (= "back") + 22: tardus)
p			
patronize	(31: patrōnus)	revere	(re- (intensive) + 38: verērī)
paucity	(17: paucī)		
pendulous	(34: pendēre)		
perdition	(39: perdere (= "destroy"))	revive	(re- (= "again") + 19: vīvere)
perfidy	(24: perfidus)	ridicule	(3: rīdēre)
pessimist	(20: pessimus)	rural	(35: rūs)
pestilence	(7: pestis)		
petition	(18: petere (= "beg for"))	**s**	
		sacrilege	(18: sacer + 11: legere ("gather up"))
placate	(11: placet)		
pontificate	(38: pontifex)		
populous	(29: populus)	salutary	(29: salūs)
portable	(3: portāre)	sanguinary	(8: sanguis)
potentate	(23: potēns)	sapient	(21: sapiēns)
principal	(15: prīnceps)	satisfy	(4: satis + 7: facere)
procedure	(7: prōcēdere)		
procrastinate	(18: prō (= "forwards"); 33: crās)	sedentary	(1: sedēre)
		sentence	(10: sententia)
		service	(1: servus)
progressive	(31: prōgressus)	servile	(29: servīre)
provincial	(26: prōvincia)	simulate	(39: simulāre)
pulse	(6: pulsāre)	solicitude	(11: sollicitus)
putative	(35: putāre)	sororal	(30: soror)
		sparse	(39: spargere)
		spectacular	(8: spectāculum)
q		spectator	(5: spectāre)
querulous	(38: querī)	state	(5: stāre)
		stultify	(11: stultus + 7: facere)
r			
recipient	(17: recipere)		
recital	(36: recitāre)	stupefaction	(33: obstupefacere)
regal	(14: rēx)		
regress	(33: regressus)	suave	(25: suāvis)
reiterate	(re- (= "again") + 9: iterum)	subliminal	(27: sub + 38: līmen)
relegate	(35: relēgāre)		

Cumulated List of Word-Search Words

suffuse	(27: sub + 22: fundere)
summit	(16: summus)
surge	(3: surgere)

t

tacit	(7: tacitē)
tactile	(36: tangere)
tedious	(27: taedet)
tempestuous	(30: tempestās)
terrify	(4: (per)territus; 7: facere)
testify	(25: testis + 7: facere)
total	(8: tōtus)
transition	(24: trānsīre)
turbulent	(5: turba)

u

ubiquitous	(31: ubīque)
ultimate	(26: ultimus)
undulate	(15: unda)
unguent	(38: unguere)
utilitarian	(11: ūtilis)

v

validate	(37: validus)
vendor	(4: vēndere)
venial	(23: venia)
ventilate	(28: ventus)
veritable	(24: vērum)
vex	(19: vexāre)
vicinity	(35: vīcīnus)
vitality	(17: vīta)
vulnerable	(13: vulnerāre)

Appendix C: Cumulated List of Synonym-Search Words (Stages 41–48)

Following is a list of words in the Synonym-Search sub-sections (Stages 41–48). The number in parentheses is the number of the Stage Checklist where *the synonym will be found*; the word after the colon is the synonym found there.

Note: No two synonyms are exact equivalents in *every* nuance of meaning or context. If all synonyms were exactly the same, they would not be needed in a language.

a
aedificium (46: tēctum)
aliquis (45: quisquam)
āmittere (41: perdere)
apud (43: iuxtā)
ardor (41: incendium)
augērī (44: crēscere)

c
catēna (44: vinculum)
clārus (45: candidus)
cupere (47: optāre)

d
dēicere (46: sternere)
dōnum (48: mūnus)
dum (+*subj*.) (48: dōnec)

e
effugere (48: ēvādere)
error (41: vitium)

f
fēmina (45: mulier)
fidēlis (43: fīdus)
fortūnātus (44: fēlīx)
frangere (45: rumpere)

g
glōria (47: laus)

i
inūtilis (41: vīlis)
invenīre (42: reperīre)

l
lacrimāre (45: flēre)
longius (46: ultrā)
lūx (46: lūmen)

m
mare (47: aequor)

o
obscūrus (42: caecus)
officium (48: pietās)
oppugnāre (43: aggredī)
ōrāre (47: precārī)

p
paucitās (43: inopia)
paulum (47: parum)
poscere (46: requīrere)
precārī (47: ōrāre)
procul (42: longē)

q
quia (47: quoniam)
quodcumque (46: quidquid/quicquid)

r
rēs (pl.) (43: bona)

s
saxum (46: lapis)
spectāre (44: aspicere)
spernere (43: contemnere)
subitō (43: repente)

t
tellūs (45: orbis terrārum)
tenēre (43: possidēre)
terra (44: tellūs)
timēre (48: metuere)
tūtus (48: incolumis)

u
unda (47: flūctus)

v
vitium (45: culpa)

Appendix D: Classified Examples of Some Grammatical Points

For suggestions on the use of these examples, see the introduction to the Language Information Section, pp. 200–01 above. Most of the examples below are taken from the text of Stages 41–48; a few have been made up.

1 Perfect Passive Participle in Accusative

repertōs	Stage 41, p. 122, line 3
corruptum	Stage 42, p. 141, line 13
dētractum	Stage 43, p. 162, line 3
dētracta	Stage 43, p. 167, line 8
cēlātum	Stage 43, p. 167, line 14
compositās	Stage 44, p. 182, line 2
victam	Stage 47, p. 238, line 16
convocātōs	Stage 48, p. 259, line 3.

Encourage the students not only to analyze the participial phrase and identify the noun to which the participle refers, but also to produce natural and idiomatic translations.

2 Predicative and Appositional Use of Noun or Adjective

voluntāriī	Stage 41, p. 122, line 4
vicāriī	Stage 41, p. 122, line 5
superior	Stage 42, p. 140, line 2
īnferior	Stage 42, p. 140, line 3
morbum	Stage 42, p. 142, line 7
candidī	Stage 45, p. 210, line 3
attonitī	Stage 46, p. 226, line 18
signum	Stage 47, p. 237, line 6
rēctor ...	
magister	Stage 47, p. 240, line 4
interior	Stage 47, p. 242, line 3.

242

3 Variations of Word Order

(a) verb + accusative + nominative
īnstrūxit mīlitēs centuriō.
īnspiciēbant victimam haruspicēs.
involvēre diem nimbī. — Stage 42, p. 150, line 7
irrūpit cubiculum meum māter. — Stage 46, p. 222, lines 5–6.

(b) accusative + verb + nominative
hastās coniēcērunt barbarī.
eōs spectābat dominus.
altum tenuēre ratēs. — Stage 42, p. 150, line 1
eum ... audiit ... omnis Nēreidum ... chorus — Stage 47, p. 246, lines 15–16.

(c) accusative + nominative + verb
culpam mīlitēs in servōs ... trānsferre poterunt. — Stage 41, p. 116, lines 8–9
quīntum ... diem mātrōna sine cibō agēbat. — Stage 43, p. 161, line 11
amantem iniūria tālis cōgit amāre magis. — Stage 45, p. 207, lines 7–8
illum ... Teucrī ... rīsēre. — Stage 47, p. 240, line 9
hōs successus alit. — Stage 47, p. 246, line 7.

(d) dative + nominative + verb
āctōribus spectātōrēs plausērunt.
captīvō rēx pepercit.
sī precibus nostrīs fortūna fāvisset ... — Stage 43, p. 168, line 3.

(e) verb + nominative (very common; the following are a few of the examples to be found in Stages 41–48)

inveniuntur mēnsōrēs.	Stage 41, p. 114, lines 9–10
manent ... paucissimī arcūs.	Stage 41, p. 119, line 9
dēcurrit ... liquor.	Stage 42, p. 140, line 8
... docentur equī.	Stage 42, p. 149, line 4
ingeminant ... ignēs.	Stage 42, p. 150, line 8
tābuerant cērae;	Stage 44, p. 189, line 8
fulsēre ... sōlēs,	Stage 45, p. 210, line 3
iam dēcidēbat cinis,	Stage 46, p. 226, line 1
effugit ... Gyās;	Stage 47, p. 238, lines 11–12
exarsit ... dolor	Stage 47, p. 240, line 1
cōnsurgunt nautae	Stage 47, p. 242, line 5
metuēbat Nerō ...	Stage 48, p. 260, line 8
placuit Nerōnī calliditās	Stage 48, p. 261, line 1
stābat prope vīllam nāvis.	Stage 48, p. 261, line 5.

Classified Examples

(f) separation of noun and adjective (very common, especially in poetry; many examples are highlighted in the students' textbook by underlining, and some of the remainder are listed below)

mollī ... aquā	Stage 42, p. 149, line 8
flāvam ... cēram	Stage 44, p. 182, line 6
ignōtās ... ālās	Stage 44, p. 184, line 7
audācī ... volātū	Stage 44, p. 188, line 4
nūdōs ... lacertōs	Stage 44, p. 189, line 8
tenuis ... flamma	Stage 45, p. 200, lines 9–10
rapidā ... aquā	Stage 45, p. 206, line 4
meum ... amōrem	Stage 45, p. 212, line 21
viridem ... mētam	Stage 47, p. 237, line 5
longā ... carīnā	Stage 47, p. 238, line 18
salsōs ... flūctūs	Stage 47, p. 240, line 10
spatiō ... inīquō	Stage 47, p. 242, line 3
frāctōs ... rēmōs	Stage 47, p. 242, line 7
scopulō ... altō	Stage 47, p. 244, line 3
candentem ... taurum	Stage 47, p. 246, line 12
portū ... altō	Stage 47, p. 246, line 19.

Appendix E: Time Chart of Events in the *C.L.C.*, Stages 1–48

Listed below are some of the historical events between 57 B.C. and Pliny's departure for Bithynia *c.* A.D.110. They are correlated with the dates we have imagined or deduced for the stories in Units 1–4, Stages 1–40. These are shown in italics.

Date	Event	Unit	Stage
B.C.			
?57/56	Catullus visits his brother's tomb in Asia	4	42
56	Charges by Clodia ("Lesbia") against M. Caelius rebutted by Cicero's "Pro Caelio"	4	mentioned in 45
49–45	Civil War between Julius Caesar and Pompey (and his allies)	4	mentioned in 43
44–31	Civil War between Octavian (Augustus) and Antony	4	mentioned in 43
43	Vespillo declared public enemy ("proscribed")	4	mentioned in 43
*c.*40	Maecenas becomes literary patron of Vergil	4	mentioned in 39
27	**Augustus becomes first Emperor**	4	mentioned in 43
A.D.			
8	Ovid exiled by Augustus	4	mentioned in 38
14	**Tiberius becomes Emperor**		
37	**Caligula becomes Emperor**	4	mentioned in 48
41	**Claudius becomes Emperor**		
43	Vespasian, at that time Commander of Second Legion, defeats the Durotriges (helped by Cogidubnus?)	2	mentioned in 16
	Emperor Claudius goes to Britain	2	mentioned in 16
?43	Cogidubnus made King of Regnenses (tribespeople previously called the Atrebates)	2	mentioned in 15
54	Emperor Claudius poisoned by his wife Agrippina	4	mentioned in 48
	Nero becomes Emperor		
55	Claudius' son Britannicus poisoned on Nero's orders	4	mentioned in 48

245

59	Riot at Pompeii	1	8
	March: Agrippina murdered on Nero's orders	4	48
69	**Vespasian becomes Emperor**	2	mentioned in 16
c.73	Elder Pliny becomes Governor of Spain	4	mentioned in Supplementary Reading 2a
78	Agricola becomes Governor of Britain	3	mentioned in 24
		4	mentioned in 37
79	*Events in the life of Caecilius and his family at Pompeii*	1	1–7, 9–12
	March elections in Pompeii	1	11
	Titus becomes Emperor on June 23		
	Eruption of Mt. Vesuvius on August 24	1	12
		4	46 & Supplementary Reading 2c
	Elder Pliny dies on August 25		
	Winter: Quintus liquidates his father Caecilius' estates	2	mentioned in 16
80	*Spring: Quintus and Clemens travel to Athens*	2	mentioned in 16
	Autumn: Quintus and Clemens travel to Alexandria	2	mentioned in 16
	Winter: Quintus and Clemens settle in Alexandria	2	17–18
81	*March 5: festival of Isis watched by Quintus*	2	19
	Spring: Barbillus' injury during hunt, and death	2	19–20
Domitian becomes Emperor on September 13			
	September: Dedication of arch of Titus in Rome; *dedication attended by Salvius; confrontation of Salvius and Haterius*	3	29–30
?81	Winter: Salvius is sent to Britain by Domitian	3	mentioned in 23
82	*Winter: Quintus comes to Britain, searches for Rufus*	3	mentioned in 26
	Spring (?): Salvius buys farming estate on site at modern Angmering	2	mention in 14
	Summer: Rufilla meets Quintus in Londinium	2	mentioned in 14
	Autumn: Harvest, and arrival of Quintus at Salvius' estate	2	13–14
	Arrival of Euphrosyne in Rome; Haterius' birthday party	3	31–32
	October 13: Ceremony and funeral games at Noviomagus for Claudius Divus	2	15
	Winter: Escape of bear at Cogidubnus' banquet; friendship of Cogidubnus and Quintus	2	16

83	*Early spring: Cogidubnus becomes ill, goes to Aquae Sulis*	3	21
	Spring: Salvius' plot to poison Cogidubnus; escape of Quintus and Dumnorix; confrontation of Salvius and Agricola; death of chieftain Belimicus	3	21–28
	Salvius and Quintus separately return to Italy	(not mentioned)	
	Performance by Paris; death of Paris and divorce by Emperor of Domitia, orchestrated by Epaphroditus and Salvius	3	33–4
	German triumph of Domitian; execution of three Vestals; *recitation by Martial*	4	35–36, Supplementary Reading 3
84	Battle at mons Graupius; recall of Agricola	4	37, Supplementary Reading 3
?86	Consulship of Salvius	4	mentioned in 40
?87	Trial of Salvius in Rome; *witness by Quintus against Salvius*	4	40
90	Clemens' sons named as heirs of Domitian	4	38
	Wedding of Polla, Clemens' daughter	4	38
	Lesson by Quintilian	4	39
92	Domitian's Palace completed: praised by Martial	4	3
96	Domitian is assassinated on September 18	(4	Diagnostic test 13, Supplementary Reading 4b)
	Nerva becomes Emperor		
98	**Trajan becomes Emperor**		
c110	Pliny becomes Governor of Bithynia et Pontus	4	41

Appendix F: Summary of Changes from the North American Second Edition

General

The principles on which the North American Second Edition was designed remain the same for this Edition (see "Objectives of the Course," in the Unit 1 Teacher's Manual, pp. 5–6). The North American Third Edition is compatible with the North American Second Edition. In the Third Edition, however, the students' textbook has been written in American English throughout, with punctuation, spelling, and analogies in the American style. Many new photographs, mainly color ones, have been added.

Changes from the North American Second Edition of Units IVA and IVB include the following:

1 Units IVA and IVB, with the Language Information sections bound in, have been combined into one Unit, now called Unit 4, with an Arabic numeral to avoid confusion between the name of the textbook and "Latin, Level IV," the traditional name for fourth-year high-school Latin. In most high schools, Unit 4 will be used throughout the third year (= Latin III); in colleges and universities, towards the end of the second, intensive semester of Latin.

2 The students' material in Units IVA and IVB has been bound, along with the two former Language Information sections, into a single hardbound volume. There have been added a selection (255 lines) of additional, slightly adapted Latin prose passages (by Petronius, Pliny the Younger, Pliny the Elder, Tacitus, and Suetonius), called Supplementary Reading; a Reference Grammar, containing formal explanations of the major syntactical points introduced in Unit 4; an Index of Authors, Characters, Cultural and Political Topics, and Works; an Index of Grammatical Topics; a Time Chart giving key dates for literary and historical events relating to Rome, and the world.

3 The contents of the two former Language Information sections have been collated into a single Language Information Section. Part One of the Language Information Section has had its name changed from former Part One, "Morphology," and former Part Two, "Syntax," to

new combined Part One, "Review Grammar"; the former Part Three, "Vocabulary," has been renamed the "Complete Vocabulary" and transferred to Part Four, thus making room for the completely new "Reference Grammar" and completely new "Supplementary Reading," which now become Part Two and Part Three respectively. The "Guide to characters and places in Unit IVA" in Unit IVA, the "Index to authors, major works, characters and places" in Unit IVB, and the "Index to cultural topics" in the Unit IVA Teacher's Manual have been combined into a single "Index of Authors, Characters, Cultural and Political Topics, and Works" at the back of the Unit 4 students' textbook (just before the Index of Grammatical Topics and the Time Chart). The Index of Grammatical Topics is completely new.

4   Latin Names and Proper Adjectives are now glossed in sections separate from the other Latin words in the running vocabularies.

5   Two new drills have been appended to the Stage Checklists: a Word Search at the end of the Checklists for Stages 35–40, and a Synonym Search at the end of the Checklists for Stages 41–48. The answers to all the Word Searches for Stages 1–40 and all the Synonym Searches for Stages 41–48 are contained in Appendix B and Appendix C respectively of this Teacher's Manual, pp. 235–40 and pp. 241–42 above. Both drills refer students to Latin words in the preceding Checklists so that they can match the given definitions with their correct English words or the Latin words with their correct synonyms.

6   The Teacher's Manual has been streamlined to make it more accessible. New charts outlining Narrative Points in the stories of Stages 35–40, Digests of the literary selections in Stages 41–48, Grammatical Points, and Sentence Patterns have been introduced into the beginning of each of the Stage Commentaries. The Bibliography has been updated. As there is now a Word Search drill in Stages 35–40 of the students' textbook, the lists of derivatives formerly in Appendix A of the Unit IVA Teacher's Manual have been omitted. As a Teacher's Manual for Unit IVB was never published (because the publication of the Units in the Third Edition was well advanced, the shelf life of a Second Edition Unit IVB Teacher's Manual would have been excessively short), the early chapter on "Teaching Methods," the Stage Commentaries for Stages 41–48, and the "Classified Examples of Some Grammatical Points" in Appendix D are new to North American teachers.

Bibliography

Books marked with an asterisk are suitable for use by junior high or high school students; other books, by college or university students (or high school students under your guidance). Included are some recommended books which, though out of print (O.P.), may sometimes be found in libraries or second-hand bookstores.

Unless stated otherwise, publishers cited are British. But if a book originally printed in Great Britain is available from a North American distributor, the name of the latter – should it differ from that of the British publisher – is listed. If in print, British books without North American distributors may be ordered from Heffers Bookstore, 10 Trinity Street, Cambridge CB2 3NG, England. To establish a personal account (and obtain instructions for ordering), request an application blank from Heffers, c/o Customers' Accounts Department, P.O. Box 33, Cambridge CB2 1TX, England.

For an up-to-date listing of audio-visual materials and the addresses of their suppliers, consult the annual listings in *Classical World* (journal of the Classical Association of the Atlantic States (C.A.A.S.)). The most recent listing is J. C. Traupman, "1989 Survey of Audio-Visual Materials in the Classics," *Classical World* Vol. 82 (1989), pp. 237–305.

For a current list of supplementary materials and examinations available specifically for users of the *Cambridge Latin Course*, write to William D. Gleason, Director, Resource Center, North American Cambridge Classics Project (N.A.C.C.P.), Box 932, Amherst, M.A. 01004-0932 U.S.A.

For a current list of the J.A.C.T. publications available for purchase in North America (including subscriptions to *Omnibus*, and purchase of *Omnibus Omnibus*, the books by Garnsey and Saller and by Sharwood Smith (see pp. 255–57 below)) and/or an application form for membership in the J.A.C.T., write to Professor Ed Phinney, J.A.C.T., American Representative, Department of Classics, University of Massachusetts, Amherst, MA 01003 U.S.A.

Stages 35–40

Allen, W. S. *Vox Latina* (Cambridge U.P. 1965)
Balme, M. G. and Greenstock, M. C. *Scrutanda* (Oxford U.P. (pbd) 1973)

Balsdon, J. P. V. D. *Life and Leisure in Ancient Rome* (Bodley Head 1969 O.P.)
 Roman Women (Bodley Head, 2nd edn 1974; Totowa, NJ: Barnes & Noble Books (pbd) 1983)
Bieber, M. *History of the Greek and Roman Theater* (Princeton U.P., 2nd edn (pbd) 1980 O.P.)
Bonner, S. F. *Education in Ancient Rome* (Methuen 1977)
Cambridge School Classics Project *The Roman World, Units I and II* and *Teacher's Handbook* (Cambridge U.P. 1978, 1979, 1980)
 Pompey and Caesar and *Teacher's Handbook* (Cambridge U.P. 1986)
Carcopino, J. *Daily Life in Ancient Rome* (Yale U.P. (pbd) 1940)
Corbett, P. E. *The Roman Law of Marriage* (Oxford U.P. 1930 O.P.)
Cowell, F. R. *Everyday Life in Ancient Rome* (Batsford 1961)
Crook, J. A. *Consilium Principis* (Cambridge U.P. 1955; rprt Salem, NH: Ayer Company Publishers, Inc. 1975)
 Law and Life of Rome (Cornell U.P., new edn (pbd) 1984)
Dilke, O. A. W. *The Ancient Romans: How They Lived and Worked* (David and Charles 1975 O.P.)
Hammond, N. G. L. and Scullard, H. H. (eds.) *Oxford Classical Dictionary* (Oxford U.P., 2nd edn 1970)
Hopkins, K. M. "The Age of Roman Girls at Marriage" in *Population Studies* 18, 1965
 Death and Renewal (Cambridge U.P. (pbd) 1983)
Juvenal *Satires* ed. J. D. Duff (Cambridge U.P., 2nd edn 1970 O.P.)
Kenney, E. J. and Clausen, W. V. (eds) *The Cambridge History of Classical Literature: Volume II, Latin Literature* (Cambridge U.P. 1982)
Levens, R. G. C. "Martial VIII.69 (Vacerra): Versions," *Greece and Rome* 2nd series Vol. XVIII, April 1971, pp. 30–31
Lewis, N. and Reinhold, M. *Roman Civilization: A Sourcebook. Volume I: The Republic. Volume II: The Empire* (Harper Torchbooks (pbd), Harper and Row 1966)
McKay, A. G. *Houses, Villas and Palaces in the Roman World* (Thames and Hudson 1975)
Massey, M. *Society in Imperial Rome* (Cambridge U.P. (pbd) 1982)
Masson, G. *Italian Gardens* (Thames and Hudson 1961 O.P.)
Millar, F. *The Emperor in the Roman World* (Cornell U.P. 1977)
Ogilvie, R. M. *Roman Literature and Society* (Totowa, NJ: Barnes & Noble Imports 1980)
Omnibus (available with membership in Joint Association of Classical Teachers (J.A.C.T.) from Professor Ed Phinney, Department of Classics, University of Massachusetts, Amherst, MA 01003)
Ovid, *Metamorphoses I* ed. A. G. Lee (Cambridge U.P. 1953 O.P.; Bristol Classical Press 1984)

Bibliography

Paoli, U. E. *Rome, Its People, Life and Customs (Longmans 1963)
Pliny *The Letters of the Younger Pliny* trans. B. Radice (Penguin 1963)
Reynolds, L. D. and Wilson, N. G. *Scribes and Scholars* (Oxford U.P., 2nd rev edn (pbd) 1974)
Sherwin-White, A. N. *The Letters of Pliny: a Historical and Social Commentary* (Oxford U.P. 1966)
Tacitus *Agricola* ed. R. M. Ogilvie and I. Richmond (Oxford U.P. 1967)
Tingay, G. I. F. and Badcock, J. **These Were the Romans* (Chester Springs, PA: Dufour Editions (pbd) 1979)
White, K. D. *Country Life in Classical Times* (Cornell U.P. 1977)
Widdess, D. S. (ed.) **Britain in Roman Times* (Countryside Publications (pbd) 1981)

Abbreviations
C.I.L. *Corpus Inscriptionum Latinarum* (Berlin, 1863–   )
R.I.B. Collingwood, R. G. and Wright, R. P. *The Roman Inscriptions of Britain. Volume I: Inscriptions on Stone* (Oxford U.P. 1965)

Stages 41–48

Any list for the range of authors and topics appearing in Stages 41–48 must necessarily be highly selective. The following list is restricted to the books and articles referred to in the main body of this Manual.

Arias, P. E. *History of Greek Vase Painting* (Thames and Hudson 1962)
Austin, R. G. (ed.) *M. Tulli Ciceronis pro M. Caelio oratio* (Oxford U.P., 3rd edn 1960)
Balme, M. G. *Intellegenda* (Oxford U.P. (pbd) 1973)
   The Millionaire's Dinner Party (Oxford U.P. (pbd) 1973)
Balme, M. G. and Greenstock, M. C. *Scrutanda* (Oxford U.P. (pbd) 1973)
Balme, M. G. and Warman, M. S. *Aestimanda* (Oxford U.P. (pbd) 1965)
Balsdon, J. P. V. D. **Life and Leisure in Ancient Rome* (Bodley Head 1969 O.P.)
   *Roman Women (Bodley Head, 2nd edn 1974; Totowa, NJ: Barnes and Noble Books (pbd) 1983)
Brett, S. (ed.) *The Faber Book of Useful Verse* (Faber and Faber 1981; pbd 1987)
Bruun, B. and Singer, A. *The Hamlyn Guide to Birds of Britain and Europe* (Hamlyn (pbd) 1970)
Bulfinch, T. and Holme, B. *Myths of Greece and Rome* (Penguin (pbd) 1981)
Cambridge School Classics Project *Greek Foundation Course Folder V* (Cambridge U.P. 1975)
   The Roman World, Units I and II and *Teacher's Handbook* (Cambridge U.P. 1978, 1979, 1980)

Camps, W. A. *An Introduction to Virgil's Aeneid* (Oxford U.P. (pbd) 1969)
Carcopino, J. *Daily Life in Ancient Rome* (Penguin 1970)
Casson, L. *Travel in the Ancient World* (Allen and Unwin 1974)
Coleman, R. G. G. "The Study of Language and the Study of Literature" in *Didaskalos* Vol. 2, no. 2 (1967)
Corbett, P. E. *The Roman Law of Marriage* (Oxford U.P. 1930 O.P.)
Crook, J. A. *Law and Life of Rome* (Cornell U.P., new edn (pbd) 1984)
Dale, C. M. *Latin Passages for Translation and Comprehension* (Cambridge Latin Texts, Cambridge U.P. (pbd) 1981)
Didaskalos (back issues available from J.A.C.T., 31–34 Gordon Square, London WC1H 0PY, England)
Dilke, O. A. W. *The Ancient Romans: How They Lived and Worked* (David and Charles 1975 O.P.)
  Greek and Roman Maps (Cornell U.P. 1985)
  The Roman Land Surveyors: An Introduction to the Agrimensores (David and Charles 1971)
Drees, L. *Olympia: Gods, Artists and Athletes* (Pall Mall Press 1968)
Dunlop, P. *Short Latin Stories* (Cambridge U.P. (pbd) 1987)
Durry, M. *Éloge Funèbre d'une Matrone Romaine* (Budé 1950)
Feder, T. H. *Great Treasures of Pompeii and Herculaneum* (Abbeville Press (pbd) 1978)
Fitzgerald, R. (tr.) *The Aeneid, Virgil* (NY: Vintage Books 1983)
Fordyce, C. J. (ed.) *Catullus: A Commentary* (Oxford U.P. 1961)
Frenkel, E. *Aeneas: Virgil's Epic Retold for Young Readers* (Cambridge, MA: Focus Information Group 1986)
Furneaux, H. (ed.) *Tacitus: Annals* (2nd edn revised by H. F. Pelham and C. D. Fisher (Clarendon Press 1896–1907, rprt 1951–56))
Garnsey, P. and Saller, R. *The Early Principate: Augustus to Trajan* (New Surveys in the Classics no. 15), published by *Greece and Rome* in collaboration with the J.A.C.T. (Oxford U.P. (pbd) 1982)
Gordon, A. E. *Illustrated Introduction to Latin Epigraphy* (U. of California P. 1983)
Grant, M. (tr.) *Tacitus: The Annals of Imperial Rome* (Penguin (pbd) 1956, rev edn 1971)
Greece and Rome (Oxford U.P. for the Classical Association)
Gregory, H. (tr.) *Ovid: The Metamorphoses* (NY: New American Library 1960)
Greig, C. (ed.) *Experiments: Nine Essays on Catullus for Teachers* (C.S.C.P. 1970)
Griffin, M. T. *Nero: The End of a Dynasty* (Batsford 1984)
Hamey, L. A. and Hamey, J. A. *Roman Engineers* (Introduction to the History of Mankind Series, Cambridge U.P. 1981)
Hammond, N. G. L. and Scullard, H. H. (eds) *Oxford Classical Dictionary* (Oxford U.P., 2nd edn 1970)

Bibliography

Hardy, E. G. (ed.) *Pliny's Correspondence with Trajan* (Macmillan 1889)
Harmon, W. *The Oxford Book of American Light Verse* (Oxford U.P. 1979)
Harris, H. A. *Sport in Greece and Rome* (Cornell U.P. 1972)
   "The Games in *Aeneid V*" in *Meminisse Iuvabit*, ed. F. Robertson (Cambridge, MA: Focus Information Group 1988)
Hollis, A. S. (ed.) *Ovid: Ars Amatoria Book I* (Oxford U.P. 1977)
   Ovid: Metamorphoses Book VIII (Oxford U.P. (pbd) 1970)
Horsfall, N. "Some Problems in the 'Laudatio Turiae'" in *Bulletin of the Institute of Classical Studies*, Vol. 30 (1983)
James, M. R. *More Ghost Stories* (Edward Arnold 1911; Penguin (pbd) 1959; rprt 1911 Salem, NH: Ayer Company Publishers)
Jones, P. V. *Selections from Tacitus: Histories I–III* (Cambridge Latin Texts, Cambridge U.P. (pbd) 1974)
Lefkowitz, M. R. "Wives and Husbands" in *Greece and Rome* Vol. 30, no. 1 (1983)
Lefkowitz, M. R. and Fant, M. B. *Women's Life in Greece and Rome* (Duckworth 1982; Johns Hopkins U.P. 1982)
Levens, R. G. C. (ed.) *A Book of Latin Letters* (Methuen 1930, 2nd edn 1938; rprt 1930 Darby, PA: Arden Library)
Lewis, N. and Reinhold, M. *Roman Civilization: A Sourcebook. Volume I: The Republic. Volume II: The Empire* (Harper Torchbooks (pbd), Harper and Row 1966)
Lyne, R. O. A. M. *The Latin Love Poets* (Oxford U.P. 1980)
   Selections from Catullus: Handbook (Cambridge Latin Texts, Cambridge U.P. (pbd) 1975)
Mandelbaum, A. (tr.) *The Aeneid of Virgil* (U. of California P. 1982)
Massey, M. *Society in Imperial Rome* (Cambridge U.P. (pbd) 1982)
Matthiessen, F. O. (ed.) *The Oxford Book of American Verse* (Oxford U.P. 1950)
Millar, F. *The Emperor in the Roman World* (Cornell U.P. 1977)
Morford, M. P. O. "Bruegel and the First *Georgic*" in *Greece and Rome* Vol. 13, no. 1 (1966)
Muir, J. V. "The Study of Ancient Literature" in *Didaskalos* Vol. 4, no. 3 (1974)
Omnibus (available with membership in Joint Association of Classical Teachers (J.A.C.T.) from Professor Ed Phinney, Department of Classics, University of Massachusetts, Amherst, MA 01003; the anthology, *Omnibus Omnibus*, is available for purchase from the same address)
Page, T. E. (ed.) *The Aeneid of Virgil Books I–VI* (Macmillan 1894)
Paoli, U. E. **Rome, Its People, Life and Customs* (Longmans 1963)
Quinn, K. *Latin Explorations: Critical Studies in Roman Literature* (Routledge and Kegan Paul 1963)

Richardson, J. *Roman Provincial Administration* (Inside the Ancient World, Macmillan Education (pbd) 1976; Cambridge, MA: Focus Information Group (pbd) 1984)

Royal Academy Exhibition Catalogue *Pompeii A.D. 79* (Imperial Tobacco Ltd. 1976 O.P.)

Rudd, N. *Lines of Enquiry* (Cambridge U.P. 1976)

Sedgwick, W. M. (ed.) *The Cena Trimalchionis of Petronius* (Oxford U.P. 1925, 2nd edn 1950)

Sharwood Smith, J. E. *On Teaching Classics* (Students Library of Education, Routledge and Kegan Paul 1977)

Sherwin-White, A. N. *The Letters of Pliny: A Historical and Social Commentary* (Oxford U.P. 1966)

"Pliny, the Man and his Letters" in *Greece and Rome* Vol. 16, no. 1 (1969)

Stace, C. and Jones, P. V. *Stilus Artifex* (Cambridge U.P. (pbd) 1972)

Swaddling, J. *The Ancient Olympic Games* (British Museum Publications 1980; U. of Texas P. 1984)

Tennick, M. *Libellus: Selections from Horace, Martial, Ovid and Catullus: Handbook* (Cambridge Latin Texts, Cambridge U.P. (pbd) 1978)

Tingay, G. I. F. (ed.) *Comprehendite* (Longmans (pbd) 1973)

(tr.) *Empire and Emperors: Selections from Tacitus' Annals* (Cambridge U.P. (pbd) 1983)

Tingay, G. I. F. and Badcock, J. *These Were the Romans* (Chester Springs, PA: Dufour Editions (pbd) 1979)

Toynbee, J. M. C. *Death and Burial in the Roman World* (Thames and Hudson 1971)

Verity, A. C. F. *Latin as Literature* (Macmillan (pbd) 1971)

Warde Fowler, W. *Social Life at Rome in the Age of Cicero* (Macmillan 1908)

Warmington, B. H. *Nero: Reality and Legend* (Chatto and Windus 1969)

Watson, G. R. *The Roman Soldier* (Cornell U.P. (pbd) 1985)

Wilkinson, L. P. *Golden Latin Artistry* (Cambridge U.P. 1963; U. of Oklahoma P. (pbd) 1986)

Williams, G. *Tradition and Originality in Roman Poetry* (Oxford U.P. 1968): abridged version *The Nature of Roman Poetry* (Oxford U.P. (pbd) 1970)

Williams, R. D. (ed.) *The Aeneid of Virgil Books 1–6* (Macmillan 1972)

P. Vergili Maronis Aeneidos Liber Quintus (Oxford U.P. 1960)

P. Vergili Maronis Aeneidos Liber Tertius (Oxford U.P. 1962)

Wiseman, T. P. *Catullus and his World* (Cambridge U.P. 1985)

Woodcock, E. C. *A New Latin Syntax* (Methuen 1959; rprt Oak Park, IL: Bolchazy-Carducci)

Woodcock, E. C. (ed.) *Tacitus: Annals Book XIV* (Methuen 1939)

Bibliography

Woodman, A.J. and West, D. (eds) *Creative Imitation and Latin Literature* (Cambridge U.P. 1979)

Abbreviations
C.I.L. Corpus Inscriptionum Latinarum (Berlin, 1863–)
I.L.S. Dessau, H. *Inscriptiones Latinae Selectae* (Berlin, 1892–1916)